Born in Melbourne in April 1942, Peter Alexander Thompson was raised in Queensland, educated at Brisbane Grammar School and began in journalism as a cadet reporter on the *Courier-Mail* in 1960. He moved to London in 1966 and was a Fleet Street journalist for 20 years, deputy editor of the *Daily Mirror*, editor of the *Sunday Mirror* and a director of Mirror Group Newspapers.

Since turning to writing in 1988, he was written biographies of the Princess of Wales, the Duchess of York, Robert Maxwell, Elvis Presley, Aristotle Onassis and Jack Nicholson.

Robert Macklin is the author of the novels *The Queenslander*, *The Paper Castle* and *Juryman* (adapted to the screen as *Storyville*, starring James Spader and Jason Robards), *The Journalist*, *Newsfront*, *Glass Babies*, and the non-fiction works, *100 Great Australians* and *The Secret Life of Jesus*.

As a journalist he has worked on the *Courier-Mail*, the *Age*, the *Bulletin*, and is currently Associate Editor of the *Canberra Times*.

The Battle of Brisbane

Australians and the Yanks at War

PETER A. THOMPSON
and
ROBERT MACKLIN

ABC
BOOKS

Published by ABC Books for the
AUSTRALIAN BROADCASTING CORPORATION
GPO Box 9994 Sydney NSW 2001

First published November 2000
Reprinted February 2001

National Library of Australia
Cataloguing-in-Publication entry
Thompson, Peter Alexander.
  The battle of Brisbane : Australia and America at war.

  ISBN 0 7333 0896 1

  1. Americans—Queensland—History—20th century. 2.
  Americans—Queensland—Public opinion. 3. Public opinion
  —Queensland—Brisbane. 4. World War, 1939–1945—Social
  aspects—Queensland—Brisbane. 5. United States—Armed
  Forces—Queensland—Brisbane. I. Macklin, Robert, 1941- .
  II. Australian Broadcasting Corporation. III. Title.

940.53943

Designed by Jim Shepherd
Set in 11/13 pt Bembo by
Midland Typesetters, Maryborough, Victoria
Colour separations by Finsbury, Adelaide
Printed and bound in Australia by
Griffin Press, Adelaide

5 4 3 2

Contents

[Australian history] is full of surprises, and adventures and incongruities, and incredibilities; but they are all true, they all happened.

Mark Twain (1835–1910)

Authors' Notes

ONE rainy Saturday afternoon in the early sixties I was working in the sports department at the old *Courier-Mail* building in Queen Street, Brisbane, when all hell broke loose in a Rugby League Test match between Australia and Great Britain at the Exhibition Ground.

Players from both teams slugged it out in the downpour until the blood flowed, and if I remember correctly, one English forward played most of the second half with a broken arm. The fighting on the pitch was so violent that a headline writer on the *Sunday Mail* labelled the match 'The Battle of Brisbane'.

Some of the old-timers on the staff nodded appreciatively at the headline and I vaguely knew that it also referred to an incident during World War II when Australian and American troops had been involved in some sort of altercation. Apart from that, I was as ignorant of the facts as many of my contemporaries—our minds were on current events. Kennedy had just been elected President of the United States and the international scene was far more exciting than anything that had preceded it.

I grew up on Brisbane's south side, where there were relics of the war, such as shabby old Nissen huts and rusty army trucks, and we were always finding odd bits of military equipment at the dump and playing war games with them. Every 25 April I donned my cub scout's uniform and took a tram to the Anzac Day parade at Yeronga Park for the memorial service in honour of the war dead.

I was an avid consumer of the American and British war movies screened at the Odeon and the Boomerang on Ipswich Road, but these celluloid epics were primarily concerned with Allied victories in Europe or other parts of the Pacific; none of them made any reference to the Battle of Brisbane.

In hindsight, I can understand the reluctance of my parents' generation to talk about such matters because of the loved ones they had lost during the war, or the hardship they had endured themselves, some as prisoners of war.

It wasn't until I visited Brisbane in 1997 that I decided to find out what had really happened in the original Battle of Brisbane in 1942 during the American 'occupation' of Queensland.

From research at the Oxley Library, a picture rapidly emerged of a frightened city invaded by a friendly, though foreign, army. Inevitably, there was friction and occasionally, violence.

I looked up the heavily censored report of the Battle of Brisbane in the *Courier-Mail* on 27 November 1942, and learned that a soldier had been killed in the fighting. From other sources, I identified him as Gunner Edward Webster, a former member of the 2/2nd Anti-Tank Regiment, 7th Division, AIF.

At the Anzac Day parade in the city centre a few weeks later I introduced myself to some of the survivors of that regiment and I am very grateful to them for helping me to compile this account of their wartime adventures, and to Colonel Ronald Shea for sharing his memories of Edward Webster with me.

I also met Major Williams A. Bentson, who had served on the staff at General Douglas MacArthur's headquarters in Brisbane and had personally witnessed the anti-American riots on the nights of 26 and 27 November 1942. Bill Bentson settled in Brisbane after his retirement from the United States Army and he allowed me full access to the World War II archive he has painstakingly compiled in the basement of his home. He also provided me with contact numbers for former US servicemen who had served in Brisbane at the relevant time.

When the first draft of the manuscript of *The Battle of Brisbane* was completed, I sent a copy to Robert Macklin, a former classmate and newspaper colleague, who is now Associate Editor of the *Canberra Times*. Rob immediately saw that there was an opportunity to take the story further and, using his contacts at the National Archives of Australia in Canberra, uncovered vital unpublished documents which allowed me to greatly broaden the perspective of the book and made it considerably more authoritative.

My thanks go to him for his professional expertise. I also thank the many soldiers and civilians—Australians and Americans—who agreed to be interviewed about their wartime experiences.

In a war disfigured by treachery and betrayal, the sacrifice of the common soldier glows through their stories like a beacon of enduring hope.

Peter Thompson
London 2000

WHEN THE DISK containing Peter's first draft arrived I was immediately intrigued. There was the natural curiosity of a man who had been born in Brisbane himself a year and a month before the Battle of Brisbane took place. I had grown up surrounded by stories of it, and of both World Wars. My Uncle Vic was one of the Rats of Tobruk, my father a serving aircraftsman in the RAAF. Both of their fathers had fought— each in ignorance of the other—at Gallipoli. Uncle Vic's wife, Jess had come to Brisbane for long periods to stay with my mother and myself during the war. I was, in so many senses, a war baby.

In other circumstances I would have been hesitant about reading an unsolicited manuscript. As an author of eight books I had been through that unhappy experience many times. All too often it led to awkwardness, hypocrisy or the end of a friendship.

Happily, I knew that would not be the case with Peter. We had been too close for too long. And he was a fine writer. I was not prepared, however, for the utterly engrossing experience as I roved through his wonderful re-creation of that time and place, that mighty drama of war in the Pacific and the forces that led to an explosion of hatred and violence between allies in our home town.

I was also aware as I read that my close journalistic association with the wonderfully helpful team at the National Archives of Australia might well be put to use to add that extra layer of official confirmation to Peter's research. And so it proved.

I would also like thank Brian Johns at the ABC, whom I approached first for possible publication and the publisher of ABC Books, Matthew Kelly, who immediately shared in the enthusiasm for the project and brought his special skills to it.

Robert Macklin
Canberra 2000

Chapter One

◄○►

Men Came Running

TWO men's lives crossed on America's Thanksgiving Day 1942, and then only for as long as it took one to kill the other. The victim was a decorated Australian soldier, Gunner Edward Webster; his killer, a United States military policeman, Private Norbert J. Grant.

To the outside world, Webster and Grant were allies fighting against a common enemy, the Japanese. But in fact Webster's death during the Battle of Brisbane on 26 November 1942 was symbolic of an ambivalence in the relationship between the fledgling superpower and the former convict colony struggling towards its own identity.

It is an ambivalence that echoes down the years and is still audible today when America is the world's undisputed imperial power and Australia continues its quest for identiy on the fringe of Asia.

That explosion of anger and resentment in 1942 epitomised a deep and dangerous divide between the fighting men of both countries which seriously threatened Allied unity in the Battle of the Pacific. A 'most secret' report compiled by Australian Military Intelligence at the time declared: 'It is of utmost importance that every step should be taken to combat the spread of ill-feeling between the men of the two armies and to prevent a recurrence of incidents which, if unchecked, may have serious effect upon our combined war effort.'

The story behind the Battle of Brisbane has never been told in full. While the vague outlines have been known from a single eight-paragraph report in the *Courier-Mail* of 27 November 1942, the extent and intensity of the conflict have remained secret. Civil and military authorities on

1

both sides of the Pacific have been content to keep it so, for it reflects little credit on either side. For more than half a century those with access to the truth about what really happened that day were the ones least likely to tell.

The American MP who fired the fatal shots has never been correctly identified in print before and only the barest details have ever been released about his Australian victim.

In fact, eight Australian servicemen received gunshot wounds in one climactic day and 11 Americans were injured—one with a factured skull.

An official inquiry was held in secret. Its findings have never previously been released. The Americans demanded that their men be exonerated. In this, they were successful. And while there can be no doubt that the Australians started the physical clash, the Americans were also at fault. The testimony at the inquiry reveals that an American legal team kept the terms of reference focused totally on the 'riotous behaviour' of the Australians. Norbert J. Grant, the man with the gun, was not even called as a witness, much less questioned about his actions by the Court of Inquiry. An American lawyer simply provided the briefest of statements in his name.

By contrast, three Australian soldiers—Private Roy Michael Cocciardi, Private Richard John Scott and Private Alfred James Osborne—were jailed for up to six months. It is difficult to escape the conclusion that they were scapegoats. The Australian authorities clearly felt that they had to be seen to be cracking down on their own men and the three privates were in the wrong place at the right time.

They were picked up the following day by Queensland police. Private Cocciardi was dubbed a 'ringleader' because at the height of the battle, when by varying estimates between 2000 and 4000 troops were involved, he said the unsayable: 'Come and fight, you bastards. You bastards, you're not game, you are yellow, you ran away at Milne Bay.' A little later he shouted, 'Why don't you go and fight the Japs instead of our men?'

That earned him imprisonment with hard labour for five months. Civilian police records show Scott and Osborne made the same mistake. On the evidence of a single policeman, Constable Benjamin Frank Neuendorf, Private Scott also accused the Americans of cowardice. 'They ran away at Milne Bay and they will run away again,' he allegedly shouted as Neuendorf tried to pull him away from the fighting. He served 120 days' detention.

Osborne accused Neuendorf of being 'a cobber to these American bastards'. He was 'known to the police' because his brother in Cloncurry had been accused of murdering Go Lum, a Chinese fruitseller. He received six months' hard labour.

Brisbane at the time was ablaze with rumour; stories of the clash between American and Australian troops took many forms. A favourite told of two trains, one packed with Americans preparing to travel north, the other filled with Australians coming back from the front-lines and slowing to a halt beside it at Roma Street station. On the platform were scores of Aussie girls saying affectionate goodbyes to the Yanks.

As the storytellers would have it, the Australians, some walking wounded, others shattered by the horrors of war on the Kokoda Track, simply boiled over. Angry shouts were followed by threats and taunts; someone fired a shot; carriage doors flew open and hundreds of men fought each other with bare fists and anything else that came to hand.

This story was not true—at least, we have been unable to substantiate it—but because the authorities were so afraid of just such an outbreak they censored the reality, which was no less dramatic.

An eyewitness to the actual event, a young Australian woman married to an American, wrote to her mother in Sydney:

> Dear Mum,
>   I've got a rather terrible story to tell you . . .
>   On Thursday night two Australians caused a fight in the American canteen and there was a frightful riot and one of our men was shot and killed and about 20 of each army wounded. So last night all the Australians came to town to kill Americans . . .
>   I got knocked over twice and hit in the stomach and back and jaw . . . honestly Mum I can't explain the terror [of] all these hundreds yelling, 'Kill him—kick him—kick his brains out' . . .
>   Have you ever seen a mob gone mad? Well it's the most dreadful thing I've ever come up against.

The official inquiry held at Victoria Barracks, Brisbane the following month under Lieutenant-Colonel G. R. Hammer found that a 'spark exploded an accumulation of pent up ill-feeling by certain types of poorly disciplined Australians, inflamed by excess of alcohol, against the methods of United States Military Police.

'This ill-feeling degenerated into open hostility on the night of 26 November and, fanned by distorted rumours of events of that night, developed into semi-organised attacks on US MPs on the night of 27 November.'

Hammer's findings were never publicly released and this only fed the rumour machine.

Gossip was the currency of the day. This was hardly surprising given the lack of official news and the nature of a city with most of the characteristics of a biggish country town. In 1941 Brisbane had boasted a population of only 300,000. A tramway connected its older suburbs, and its citizens dressed up—usually in the outdated fashions of Britain— for the trip to the city. Men sweltered in worsted suits and ties in the sub-tropical heat and humidity. Provincialism reigned. Housewives nattered with neighbours over cups of tea in their 'best rooms'; men mowed their lawns with hand mowers and yarned with the bloke next door over the back fence. Catholics rarely married Protestants; divorce was a scandal akin to 'living in sin'. It simply wasn't done. A convict ancestor was a 'skeleton in the cupboard'; Aboriginal blood—'a touch of the tar'—was quite beyond the pale.

Frangipani scented the suburban air; mauve jacarandas and scarlet hibiscus bushes lined the grassy footpaths by the neat weatherboard homes on stilts; lantana burst into tiny blooms by the roadsides and in the gullies; creeks with native crayfish meandered around the cool bush places and into the Brisbane River. Nothing of note ever seemed to happen.

The war was a massive shock. Suddenly all the certainty and security was gone. Suddenly air-raid shelters were dug beneath the backyard vegetable patch and the boys were enlisting and the women tuned their wirelesses to the war news. Air-raid sirens struck panic day and night as women and children filled the bath as instructed in case the 'Japs' bombed the reservoir—then bolted for the shadowy cool of the shelter until the All Clear sounded.

When the Americans came they seemed to have arrived from a different planet. That they looked alike only confused the issue. When you looked closely, they weren't really that similar at all.

Very soon after their arrival it became clear that a gulf separated the two fighting forces. In Britain a similar realisation produced the complaint that the Yanks were 'overpaid, over-sexed and over here'. The Brisbane experience was exacerbated by the city's provincialism. Where the Londoners were fortified by their centuries of history and a status as having the Mother of Parliaments, the Brisbanites had no such internal defences. And the same applied to the soldiers like Gunner Webster, who would be shot to death because of the gulf.

Major Bill Thomas, who in 1943 investigated the cause of anti-American disturbances told the authors: 'The Australians had grievances, and they had very solid reasons to be aggrieved. The Yanks had everything—the girls, the canteens and all the rest of it—and our blokes were completely ostracised in their own city.'

The Americans' higher pay was part of the problem. Their smart outfits contrasted with the ill-cut, poorly fitting woollen uniforms of the Australians. In the shops, the hotels, the cafes and the taxicabs, the big-tipping Americans always took precedence. In the American Postal Exchange (PX) they seemed to have an almost unlimited range of goodies, including ice-cream and chocolate, hams and turkeys, cigarettes and booze; and the almost magical nylon stockings which seemed to have the power to turn a good Brisbane girl into a tart, at least in the eyes of her Methodist neighbours and the dislocated, love-starved Australian soldiers.

More than anything, it was the girls. Many Australians down the line certainly held their Allies' fighting methods in contempt; they hated the way they boasted about their deeds of derring-do on the battlefield. The Australians who had fought in New Guinea reckoned they knew the truth about that.

They hated the way some of the Americans picked on Australian men who had not joined up without knowing some of the tragic reasons behind their decisions—or their rejections.

Australians hated the way they treated the black Americans, even thought their own race record with the Aborigines was no less reprehensible.

They hated the way the Americans carried knives and were quick to produce them in any bar-room brawl. They hated American MPs with a special passion—they were the swaggering, gun-toting epitome of everything different and contemptible about the Yankee persona.

But it was the way the Americans grabbed the girls that really stuck in the Aussie craw. And grab them they did, quite literally, in the buses and trams of the provincial capital, and in the dark corners of the city streets and the shadowed doorways, the Botanic Gardens, the little parks, by the fountains in King George Square, in the picture theatres, the cafes, and on the dance floors. And the rotten thing, the insupportable thing, was that the girls—so many of them—responded.

A bloke simply didn't rate. In the vernacular of the time, he just couldn't take a trick. So he turned back to an old Australian strategy drawn from the earliest days of the colonly when men outnumbered women 10 to one—he got drunk with his mates; he buried the great need for sexual release and womanly comfort beneath an ocean of beer and rum and the camouflaged homoeroticism of maudlin mateship.

Such a state of mind practically demands an enemy close at hand. And for men whose most recent training and experience centred on violence, the result was virtually inevitable.

The American leadership should have known it and done something about it. The Australian authorities, civil and military, should also have been alive to the dangers. They were not, at least until it was too late.

The rivalry, anger and hatred that threatened to disrupt the Alliance in Brisbane went to the heart of the Allied High Command and, at the most crucial stage of the Battle of Papua, caused the Commander-in-Chief of the Australian Military Forces, Sir Thomas Blamey, to signal Prime Minister John Curtin: 'American troops cannot be classified as attack troops. They are definitely not equal to the Australian Militia and from the moment they met opposition they sat down and have hardly gone forward a yard . . . My faith in the Americans has sunk to zero.'

The American Supreme Commander, General Douglas MacArthur was even more contemptuous of the Australian fighting man.

Not surprisingly, these attitudes filtered down through the ranks.

The outbreak of hostilities between the Allies in Brisbane caused great alarm. Prime Minister Curtin cabled General Blamey: 'I am in receipt of a report by the Intelligence Branch on the subject. I should be glad if you would furnish a further report as to the outcome of the corrective action suggested by the Intelligence Branch.'

The 'corrective action' included a total ban on all news reports of the clashes, reinforcement of the military police and an end to 'brown-outs' in Brisbane. Henceforth, despite fears of Japanese air attacks, the city would be fully lit throughout the night.

The report to the Prime Minister, released to us by the National Archives, reveals that the affray on 26 November involved up to 4000 troops. It centred on the American PX near the corner of Adelaide and Creek Streets in the city centre.

An altercation began when an American MP in the early evening— between 6.45 pm and 7.15 pm—demanded to see one of his own soldier's leave passes. An Australian soldier intervened; shouts erupted; an Australian soldier threw a punch at the MP; men came running.

According to the report, 'The crowd of Australians, estimated at 7.30 pm at about 50, had grown by 7.45 to between 2000 and 4000.

'A detective of the CIB estimated 4000 of whom he estimated about one third to be Americans . . .'

At 8 pm the first shot rang out. When the smoke cleared, Edward Sidney Webster was lying fatally wounded. Among the Australians, Private Richard Ledson was shot in the left foot, left thigh and left hand, condition serious; Private Walter George Maidment, shot in the upper right thigh, condition serious; Private Ian Kerr Tieman, shot in the right shoulder; Private Edward Henry French, gunshot wounds to the head, fractured skull; Private John Tavasso, shot in the upper thigh; Private Frank Muscatt Corrie, shot in the upper left thigh; Private Kenneth Christopher Henkel, shot in the left forearm; Driver John Raymond Campbell, injury to back; Private Joseph Blake, scalp wound.

Among the Americans Private J. J. Hoffmann suffered a fractured skull and contusions; Private E. E. Evans received an incised wound on the scalp; and Norbert J. Grant (the man with the gun) received scalp lacerations. Others injured were Sergeants B. J. McGrath and J. J. Jones and Privates J. J. Celiberti, A. O'Sullivan, J. Kapinus, A. Nicholson, W. Perilie and H. Burtis.

All recovered.

While many of the participants themselves were shocked by what had happened, reactions from colleagues who gave testimony to the secret inquiry were mixed. For example, an American Chaplain, Samuel Kerr volunteered that 'the riot was planned and premeditated'.

He said he watched as civilian Queensland police stood by and did nothing while Australians took parking signs and smashed the windows of the American PX.

'I went to the PX when [the riot] got to very serious proportions,' he said. 'Several Australian military police came in and took off their MP armbands. I said, "In heaven's name, go out there and take care of your own mob"; they replied that if they went out there with their armbands on that the Australians would kill them.

'When I went among the crowd several Australian soldiers told me that the men of their camp had planned to wreck the Post Exchange for the last two or three weeks, that they did not like the Americans and the reason for it was because the Americans had more money, better dress, and got more privileges than they did.

'Since then I have enquired as a chaplain to find the reason for the attitude of the Australian soldiers. Up to the present I can find nothing other than the fact of jealousy and a resentment that the American is taking out the Australian girls.

'I spent last night with an Australian chaplain and he told me that the Australians causing the trouble were similar to some who had been with him in the Middle East. They had riots until such time as they were able to weed out the troublemakers and put them behind bars.

'In my judgement the riot was planned and premeditated. I want to submit my criticism of the PX officials and the officials of the American Red Cross. For the last month or six weeks there have been periodic fights around the Post Exchange. It was daylight clear to anyone that the situation that climaxed on Thursday and Friday nights had been gathering for some time.'

It had indeed.

Nor was it the only example of deteriorating relations between the Allies.

An Australian intelligence report of 4 December 1942 notes that,

'When Australia was in immediate danger of invasion some nine months ago, US air corps and army troops began to arrive here in large numbers. Since then the friendly relations based on comradeship and common service against the enemy have been marred by a long series of street brawls, stabbings, and actual fights between small groups.

'The incidents have been widespread, but have occurred principally in Townsville, Brisbane and Melbourne. It is plain that feelings on both sides are running high and that only a spark is needed to "touch off" the explosive material which undoubtedly still remains.'

Japanese propagandists were quick to seize on the conflict. A broadcast from Batavia (now Jakarta) taunted the Australians and claimed America only intervened for their own strategic interests.

The brigadier-general in charge of Allied Intelligence penned a memo to all staff warning of 'enemy fifth column elements' provoking dissension between the Allies.

'It must be impressed upon all ranks that this kind of thing is exactly what the enemy wants, and is what his fifth columnists are always trying to foster.'

Evidence of such pro-Japanese activity, however, was not forthcoming from the brigadier-general. Nor has an extensive search of the records uncovered any.

However, the censors immediately issued an order: 'All references to disturbances or riots involving members of the Forces must be submitted to censorship. Publication is prohibited of anything likely to prejudice training, discipline or administration of Australian or Allied Forces, or inter-Allied relations. In reports of disturbances, references to Service personnel should not distinguish the Services of Nationalities concerned.'

The single report in the *Courier-Mail*, which provoked outrage from both civil and military authorities, was in fact positively anodyne, speaking only of a 'city riot' with no suggestion of conflict between Australian and American troops.

From then on, the cover-up was in place. And so it remained for more than 50 years.

The situation on the ground was not all anger and hatred, however. On the contrary, the broad mass of Australians welcomed the Americans as saviours and, in the early days at least, the Americans responded warmly. The bonds forged then have provided a firm foundation for an international friendship made of mutual affection, curiosity and exasperation.

Perhaps only now, with the hindsight of half a century, can the significance of the 12 tumultuous months preceding the events of Thanksgiving Day 1942 be accurately assessed. In doing so, one thing becomes crystal clear: overshadowing the backbiting at the top of the Allied command is the heroism of the young American and Australian soldiers, many of them still teenagers, who fought back valiantly after the disasters of Pearl Harbor, the Philippines, Malaya, Singapore, Sumatra and Java had brought the Japanese swarming, implacably it seemed, towards Australia. Without them it would have taken a great deal longer for the Rising Sun to set.

The first American writer of note to cross the Pacific and make contact with the great southern landmass that formed the Australian colonies was Samuel L. Clemens, the legendary Mark Twain.

Deeply in debt after the failure of a business venture to invent an automatic typesetting machine, Clemens was induced to make a lecture tour of Australia in 1895. He later professed to have enjoyed his encounter with the 'incongruities and incredibilities' of Australiana, even though the trip was purely a way of cashing in on his not inconsiderable fame among the English, Scottish, Irish and native-born Australians who formed the bulk of the colonies' population.

What Clemens saw during his travels, however, not only delighted his curiosity as a writer but also appalled him as a humanitarian. Writing about his experiences in *Following the Equator*, Clemens said the average Australian was 'as vain about his unpretty country as if it were the final masterpiece of God'. However: 'Australians did not seem to me to differ noticeably from Americans, either in dress, carriage, ways, pronunciation, inflexions, or general appearance. There were fleeting and subtle suggestions of their English origin, but these were not pronounced enough, as a rule, to catch one's attention. The people have easy, cordial manners from the beginning—from the moment that the introduction is completed. This is American. To put it another way, it is English friendliness with the English shyness and self-consciousness left out.'

Clemens visited Sydney, Melbourne and Adelaide, as well as a number of provincial towns. Wherever he went he was lionised as a great sage, wit and writer and showered with the very best in colonial hospitality. An enthusiastic crowd met his train at Spencer Street station in Melbourne and he stayed with his wife at Menzies Hotel on Collins Street.

In one of his lectures in that most Victorian of British cities, Clemens addressed the theme of racial solidarity: 'When all is said and done, the Americans and the English and the great overflow in Canada and Australia are all one. On yes! blood is thicker than water, and we are all related. We do belong together and we are parts of a greater whole— the greatest whole this world has ever seen—a whole that some day will spread over this world.'

Clemens was keenly aware of Australia's morbid fear of 'the Yellow Peril', a xenophobic term that captured the anxiety about the territorial aspirations of the people of Asia. In 1894, the year before the writer reached Sydney, Japan had sent an expeditionary force to Korea after China intervened to quell a rebellion against the Korean king. The Japanese defeated the Chinese forces on land and sea and drove them back into China. In the Treaty of Shimonoseki of April 1895, Japan seized the Chinese island of Formosa (now Taiwan) and the Chinese Liaotung peninsula on Korea's western flank.

This clear evidence that Japan had arrived as an expansionist military power in the Pacific caused great consternation in the Australian colonies, and nowhere was that concern more strongly felt than in Queensland, Asia's closest Australian neighbour. Illness, however, prevented Clemens from travelling further north in Australia, and the Brisbane leg of his journey had to be cancelled. But it did not prevent him from telling several critical stories about the place.

Exposing the genocide that was widely practised on the Aboriginal population by European settlers, Clemens recounted the story of how a Queensland farmer had wiped out troublesome members of one tribe by feeding them with poisoned fruit cake. He also decried the practice of 'blackbirding' under which South Sea Islanders were brought to Queensland to work on the sugar plantations as indentured 'kanaka' labour, a legalised form of slavery.

It would have come as no surprise to Clemens that, fewer than 50 years after his visit to Australia, Japan, posing as the liberator of Asia's oppressed millions, launched massive military offensives throughout the Pacific. As well as ultimately destroying Europe's grasp on 'the Far East', the Japanese onslaught had the immediate effect of propelling Australia and the United States into an armed alliance that was to prove as explosive as it was beneficial.

It was ironic that in March 1942 another famous American, renowned for his egotism and his oratory, was greeted at Melbourne's Spencer Street station, stayed with his wife at Menzies Hotel and made a speech about the racial bonds that linked Australians and Americans. That man was Douglas MacArthur and he was the prime mover behind America's wartime invasion of Australia after it had been chosen as the most suitable place from which to launch a counter-attack against the Japanese.

From 1942 onwards, Brisbane was one of the final staging posts to the frontline. One night, in an unforeseen and unforeseeable way, it became the frontline itself. Yet, just 12 months earlier, the first American troops following in Mark Twain's wake across the Pacific had arrived to rousing cheers.

Chapter Two

-<o>-

Pepsi-Cola Convoy

November 1941

ARK Twain Muller, as his given names suggest, was destined
to travel a long way from his native New York City, with
rivers, oceans and ships well starred. 'My dad was a great
admirer of Samuel Clemens,' he wrote in his diary, 'and I've read
everything he's ever written from *Tom Sawyer* and *Huck Finn* to *Following
the Equator.*'

In the autumn of 1941, Mark Muller, a graduate of Cornell University
and 2nd lieutenant in the Signal Corps of the United States Army, was
ordered to pack his bags and proceed to a secret overseas destination
which the Pentagon had codenamed PLUM.

Muller was 26 years old and ready to go. 'I was in the best physical
shape of my life, and there were no romantic attachments or worries on
my mind.'

At Fort Bragg, North Carolina, Muller was issued with a first-class
Pullman railroad ticket to California and told to report to Fort Mason
on San Francisco Bay on 20 November. He was also given a couple of
weeks' leave, more than ample time to put his affairs in order and say
goodbye to his family. He sold his old Ford to a guy at the base and
sent his foot locker ahead to Fort Mason for shipment to his destination.
His unit turned out for a farewell parade and presented him with a
fountain pen to write up a journal of his travels.

Shortly before he left Fort Bragg, Muller was astonished to discover
that PLUM was army code for the Philippines—*P* for Philippines, *LU*
for Luzon and *M* for Manila—and that his new posting was assistant
signal officer, Manila, at the headquarters of the Supreme Commander

11

of the United States Army Forces in the Far East, General Douglas
MacArthur.

But the way things worked out, Mark Muller never made it to Manila
and he never saw his foot locker again, but he did see more than he
might have wished of Douglas MacArthur.

Operation PLUM had been approved by President Franklin D.
Roosevelt a few months earlier after MacArthur had repeatedly
bombarded Washington with demands for men, guns and planes when
Japan moved troops into French Indochina and was poised to strike at
Thailand, Malaya, Singapore, the Philippines and the prized oilfields of
Borneo.

Roosevelt's first response, however, was economic: he imposed a total
embargo on the sale of American oil to Japan, thus cutting off her main
source of petroleum. When Britain and Holland joined the embargo,
Borneo became an even more attractive prospect for membership of the
Greater East Asia Co-Prosperity Sphere, as Japan's armed expansion was
misleadingly named, and, from that point on, war in the Pacific was only
a matter of time.

The first leg of Muller's odyssey took him from Fort Bragg to New York
City. He was born in Queens on 22 August 1915, and his parents then
moved to a new home at No. 900 Bronx Park South, just across the
street from the Bronx zoo. At his old school, James Monroe High, one
of his teachers, Mrs Marion Sweet, kissed him in front of the class and
told him he was a hero. Muller wasn't the slightest bit embarrassed about
the show of adulation; he was a patriotic American and it felt good to
be serving his country in these uncertain times.

He said farewell to his relatives and friends and, dressed in civvies,
departed Penn Station on 10 November. His first stop was New
Orleans, where he had just eight hours to check out the French
Quarter, sample the gumbo at Tujacs and listen to a trumpet wail over
Bourbon Street before hopping aboard the Southern Pacific for the
journey across Louisiana and Texas. After a stopover in El Paso, the
train headed north-west through Phoenix, Arizona, and across to Los
Angeles, where Muller checked into the Rosemont Hotel, hoping for
a good night's sleep.

'At 2 am I awoke and thought I was dreaming,' he said. 'The
chandelier above my head was swaying to and fro and I felt the entire
building shake. The next morning I learned that a minor earthquake had
hit Los Angeles.'

Donning his army uniform, Muller visited the NBC studios in
Hollywood, where the motion picture actor Andy Devine was

performing in a radio show. After the broadcast, Devine asked the young soldier where he was going.

'I'm on my way to Manila,' replied Muller, somehow forgetting the need for secrecy.

The portly cowboy shook his famous jowls.

'Well, that's jes' too bad, young fella,' he rasped. 'We're gonna be at war pretty soon and I'm afraid you might be in the middle of it.'

In San Francisco, Muller met up with Julius Wild, a gambling man from Louisville, Kentucky. Wild, a Runyonesque character on the risk-taking side of life, took him to the Top of the Mark for drinks and thence to Tanforan racetrack and a casino to lay down some bets.

'He was like the last of the riverboat gamblers—loudly dressed, raucous and loud,' said Muller. 'I've never seen so many hundred dollar bills change hands so fast. Julius didn't blink; he bet a hundred here and there, almost a month's pay to me. I didn't bet a cent.'

Muller didn't really care about the money; he was going overseas and he wanted some vivid memories of the United States to take with him: jazz in the Carré; tumbleweed bowling along the railroad tracks; the chandelier shaking at the Rosemont; Julius Wild working the craps table. This was the way America was at the end of 1941, and this was what he wanted to remember.

In case the images started to blur, he had colour photographs that he'd shot with his new Kodak camera. He took pictures wherever he went; you could tell a pal about a place you'd been to or someone you'd met, but show him a picture and he was there himself. Muller always shared his experiences with his buddies.

At Fort Mason he was inoculated against cholera, yellow fever and plague, then used his new pen to write home to tell his folks about it. On his last evening in America he had dinner at Fisherman's Wharf with Major Leo Dupre, who was also being posted to the Philippines. 'We had abalone steak, oysters, shrimp and lots of beer,' Muller said. 'That night I thought, "Well, at least fate cannot harm me for I've dined well tonight."'

Mark Twain Muller's send-off might have been more picturesque than most, but throughout that November in Idaho, South Dakota, Texas and all points east and west soldiers, sailors and airmen involved in Operation PLUM, around 5000 in all, kissed girlfriends goodbye, provided backs to be slapped and enjoyed a few days' leave in the company of old friends. They arrived in San Franciso in ones and twos, or sometimes a whole battalion at a time, tumbling noisily off the trains while their artillery pieces and ammunition followed behind in dusty army trucks.

Private Willard A. 'Bill' Heath of Portland, Oregon, a member of the 148th, discovered he would be travelling to his new destination in the

Willard A. Holbrook and took that as an omen. 'With the same first name and middle initial, I figured we would go far,' he said (in view of the misfortunes that lay ahead, a remark he later regretted having made).

Private Kenneth R. Scurr from South Dakota, who was also on the *Holbrook*, thought he was going to Alaska when Arctic equipment was assigned to his battalion, but two weeks prior to departure he had discovered that the real destination was the Philippines.

Frank 'Foo' Fujita, a 21-year-old Japanese–American from Abilene, Texas, who was a sergeant in the 2nd Battalion, 131st Field Artillery Regiment, had a berth in the other transport ship, the *Republic*. His comrades included Clyde Fillmore, Hollis G. Allen, Houston 'Slug' Wright, Corky Woodall and 530 other young Texans. All but one of these young gunners would soon be prisoners of the Japanese and many would not survive the ordeal.

The two troopships that formed the nucleus of what would become famous as the *Pensacola* Convoy, carrying a total of 4600 National Guardsmen and officers under the command of Brigadier General Julian F. Barnes, left San Francisco at 11 am on 21 November. They cut through a heavy curtain of sea fog in the bay, passed under the Golden Gate bridge and headed out into the Pacific Ocean.

Captain Howard L. Steffy wrote in his diary on the *Republic* that night: 'The news just prior to embarking indicated that diplomatic relations between the United States and Japan have reached their crisis. The Japanese envoys Saburo Kurusu and Kickisaburo [sic] Namura have expressed Japan's reluctance to continue diplomatic conversations along the lines of our ultimatum. The White House Secretary, Stephen T. Early, disclosed that the result may be a Japanese attack on Thailand within the next few days.'

On board the *Holbrook* were the 1st Battalion, 148th Idaho Field Artillery, and the 1st and 2nd battalions, 147th South Dakota Field Artillery. The ship was pure Conrad, an old rustbucket ideally suited to a trip to the heart of darkness. Originally the 27,000-ton liner SS *President Taft*, the United States Army had renamed her *Willard A. Holbrook* in honour of a former chief of cavalry. The general would not have been flattered to know that the ship was not only rusty, but also stank like a horse's rear end. Young men from Boise, Idaho, and Sioux Falls, South Dakota, sniffed the farmyard air emanating from the holds and turned up their noses in disgust.

Bill Heath noted: 'The ship obviously hadn't carried passengers for quite a while. It had been stripped for cargo and, in fact, had been carrying jute and copra from the Philippines. This terrible odour would permeate our lives.'

Added to the smell was the claustrophobia of the cabins, with bunks slung four high against both walls to sleep eight and the portholes blacked out and screwed tightly shut. With the stench of rotting copra in their nostrils and the ship rolling beneath their feet, the men lined up for their first meal. Cliff Causton of B Battery, 148th Artillery said: 'The first day out we had mutton stew. The nauseating smell of several cauldrons of meat bubbling away in the galley made me thankful we had stairs leading up to the main deck. If I had been forced to climb a ladder, I never would have made it topside to the rail . . .'

Although the *Holbrook* was technically a dry ship in accordance with United States naval regulations, some of the troops had smuggled bottles of hard liquor on board. One of the worst offenders was the most senior officer in the ship, Colonel John A. Robenson. Ken Scurr related: 'The commander of troops on the *Holbrook* was an old passed-over colonel, John Robenson, who had an alcoholic problem and was abusive to troops and even the ship's crew until the captain warned him that he was subject to his command on the sea. In fact, one of the Filipino stewards tried to knife him and thereafter he required one of the troops to sleep in front of his cabin door at night.'

The *Republic* was an altogether more civilised proposition than the *Holbrook*; almost streamlined by comparison. She had undergone several transformations since beginning life as a German passenger ship before World War I. The US Navy had captured her during the war, renamed her USS *Grant* and, after an extensive refit, put her back to sea as the Army transport *Republic*. The officers shared spacious cabins which opened onto the boat deck and there were movies and card games for all ranks in saloons on the next two decks.

Lower down towards the waterline, three rows of portholes indicated the presence of less luxurious quarters. It was only the four 3-inch anti-aircraft guns in each quadrant and, at the stern, a 5-inch naval rifle and a line of depth-charges that marked the *Republic* as a troopship; that— and the food, which was fish and cabbage on that first night. Thereafter, the *Republic* smelled of fish and cabbage.

In addition to the four national guard battalions, the ships were home to 48 pilots, 18 air cadets and a couple of navigators, the ground crew of the 7th Bomber Group, the 34th Pursuit Squadron and the 8th *Matériel* Squadron. There were also some chemical warfare technicians from the 3rd Chemical Field Laboratory Company, Mark Muller's signal platoon, a variety of auxiliary personnel and even a few civilians, among them a lone war correspondent who was forbidden by military censorship regulations to report a word about anything he saw or heard.

Lieutenant Milton Kaslow was typical of the force's 'odds and sods' blend, an Army officer serving with the 8th *Matériel* Squadron attached to the bombardment group. He had led his men out of Fort Douglas, Salt Lake City, to join the *Republic* at San Francisco without a clear destination in mind. Lieutenant Bob Firehock, a fellow army officer attached to the 34th Pursuit Squadron, said: 'We didn't know where we were going. The subterfuge was such that the army had been teaching us Spanish because they told us we were going to South America. The next thing we knew we were in Hawaii.'

After spending Thanksgiving at sea, the two ships had steamed into Honolulu at 11 am on 28 November 1941. The *Republic* tied up at the Dole Company docks to refuel and take on supplies, while the *Holbrook* went into dry-dock for repairs to a rudder that had been damaged during the journey. She also took on as deckload two wooden-hulled prototype boats that the army wanted to test in the waters of Manila Bay.

The men from both ships were given eight hours' liberty and allowed to wear civilian clothes ashore. Mark Muller sampled the tempting alcoholic products at Trader Vic's, which included a 'stinger' of alcohol and tropical fruits served in a huge bowl and drunk through straws. Some of the Texans, figuring it might be some time before they had female company again, dived into the girlie bars along Hotel Street.

Around the docks, the soldiers noted machine-gun emplacements, barbed wire entanglements and a general air of military activity. When some war planes loomed overhead, one of the troops asked a sentry how he could tell they were friendly. 'If they weren't ours,' the sentry replied, 'somebody would tell us.' Kenneth Scurr met a young lieutenant from the 147th who had been posted to Hawaii the previous month. This man told him the islands were not really prepared for an attack and 'some Sunday morning the Japs are going to blow this place off the face of the earth'.

At sunrise the following day, the *Republic* made smoke and departed, leaving the *Holbrook* to catch up at sea. Byron Wilhite, an army pilot with a poetic turn of phrase, recorded the departure scene in his diary that night: 'There's something about leaving that gets you. When that ship begins to slip from the land and the narrow ribbon of water between boat and pier becomes wider and wider, there's a feeling that creeps over you and, try as you may to down it, it remains to remind you that you may never see this place again.

'It's sort of like the feeling you get at New Year when, for a short moment amid all the gaiety and laughter of the party, you pause to reflect and realise that here is something slipping from you that can never be returned as it is. The tugboats tugged, coughed, chugged and strained steadily with their exhausts puffing with a metallic staccato. But at last we were free of the tugs and, after an exchange of salutes, we were ready to slide silently from Honolulu while the sun was still low over Diamond Head. Army planes buzzed us *aloha*.'

Around noon on the first day out from Hawaii, the *Republic* rendezvoused with the heavy cruiser USS *Pensacola*, the submarine chaser USS *Niagara* and five other ships—the *Meigs*, *Coast Farmer*, *Admiral Halstead*, *Chaumont* and the Dutchman *Bloemfontein*. The *Republic*, flagship of the convoy, had to slow down to 15 knots to stay in touch because two of the ships were sluggish cargo vessels accustomed only to coastal waters. On the third day, the *Holbrook* caught up with them and the task force that would go down in history as the *Pensacola* Convoy was complete.

Byron Wilhite speculated about the imminence of war: 'We have taken up a course of around 200 degrees and, if followed, this would take us somewhere in the vicinity of the Fiji Group. There must be some secrecy attached to this trip. From the rumour that has spread we are avoiding the Japanese mandated islands around Micronesia. Just why is hard to say unless our relations with that nation are more strained than would seem at present.'

For the time being, however, the men had nothing more serious to worry about than the normal discomforts of shipboard life: greasy food, seasickness, cramped living quarters and, to conserve supplies of fresh water for drinking and cooking, the discomfort of having to take baths in salt water. Boat drill was called at all hours, sometimes in the middle of the night, and the troops donned their lifejackets and cursed as they shambled bleary eyed to their stations.

Although this was his first voyage, Milton Kaslow was accustomed to military ways and quickly adapted to the new conditions. At 22, he was one of the Army's rising stars, an officer who had gained the respect of the airmen under his command during their weeks of preparation at Fort Douglas. He was 5 foot 9 inches tall, dark-haired with a slim, well-groomed figure. While some of those on board the *Republic* lounged around in non-regulation shirts and shorts, Kaslow was particular about his appearance and stuck to army khaki.

'We were having a wonderful time on board wearing our civilian clothes,' said Byron Wilhite. 'Then the order came out from this Lieutenant Colonel Galwey stating that the uniform would be khaki and the uniform would be worn at all times. I had sent my uniform shirts to the laundry for cleaning and every time I asked the laundry to hurry them up they told me the same story: that the laundry was working overtime as it was. At present, I have managed to borrow a shirt and will wear it until the thing begins to walk.'

On starlit nights, the men could just make out the shapes of the other vessels in the convoy churning rhythmically through the swell, but at daybreak they seemed all too visible and not particularly well protected at that, with just the *Pensacola* in the vanguard or scouting the flanks and the *Niagara*, a converted tender, bringing up the rear.

One of the pilots on the *Republic*, Bob McMahon, took out his sketch pad and drew the *Pensacola* as she went by off the port side. The cruiser had 10 8-inch .55-calibre guns, four 5-inch .25-calibre anti-aircraft guns and two three-pounders. She also had four aircraft for surveillance purposes. The *Pensacola*, named after a seaport on the Gulf of Mexico, had been in service for 12 years, but had never been called upon to fire a shot in combat.

Except for the *Republic*, the *Holbrook* and the *Bloemfontein*, the convoy was loaded with supplies and *matériel*. The deck of the 12,568-ton transport *Meigs* was crammed with wooden crates containing 18 Kittyhawk fighters and 52 Dauntless dive-bombers, while the other ships were heavily laden with 340 vehicles, 20 75-millimetre artillery pieces, half a million rounds of ammunition, 9600 anti-aircraft shells, 5000 bombs and 9000 drums of aviation fuel—all destined to bolster MacArthur's armed forces in defending the Philippines against a Japanese attack.

Bob Firehock said: 'As a reserve officer, I'd been called to duty and I'd been in the army for five or six months before we sailed. I was the adjutant, the administrative officer, of the 34th Pursuit Squadron based at Hamilton Field, just outside San Francisco. All the senior pilots and ground crew had left in October and gone ahead to Clark Field in the Philippines. I was in the convoy with the Kittyhawks and 12 of the younger pilots. The plan was for us to rejoin the rest of the unit in the Philippines. They were in quite a hurry to get us out there; they knew something was going to happen and we were the reinforcements.'

Like the *Republic*, the Dutch freighter *Bloemfontein* was also a converted liner and one of its passengers was the convoy's lone war correspondent, Lee Van Atta of the International News Service. Van Atta was described by one of the army officers as 'a friendly, talented, extrovert sort of person . . . one of those types who could get by on quick wits and fast talk'. But no amount of fast talk could break the embargo on transmitting news stories about shipboard life and Van Atta had to restrict himself to writing reports in his notebook.

The tedium was hard on him and everyone else; the heat, too. The tropical wetness soaked their clothes, dampened the spirits and made the body itch with tropical rash.

'There is very little excitement for anyone; nothing ever happens,' Byron Wilhite noted. 'I have breakfast, read and sun on the top deck until noon, have lunch, take a nap, read and write, dine and shoot the bull until bedtime. The routine is killing. In order to break the monotony more than anything else, the *Pensacola* sent up the four planes from her catapult today. It was interesting to watch them being shot into the air and was something new for an army flier. I wonder how it feels to be shot out into space; all the innards of a man would take a tough beating.'

Things livened up as the convoy approached the Equator on 5 December and the men prepared for the ritual ceremony in honour of King Neptune. Wilhite explained: 'The shellbacks, men who had made previous crossings, made elaborate plans for an initiation of the pollywogs, those who had never crossed the Equator. For several days prior to the occasion, they met in the social hall aft on D deck to cook up their sinister plans. On the morning of 6 December, breakfast was served early in order to have more time for the initiation before noon. At exactly seven o'clock the whistle and siren blew and the blood began to flow.'

Shellbacks subjected pollywogs to as much brutal indignity as naval regulations would permit and several old scores were settled during the initiations. The most vicious treatment was handed out to a group of soldiers who had locked some shellbacks in the dog cages on the sun deck of the *Republic* and drenched them with firehoses.

Pollywogs were forced to crawl through a 40-foot long canvas tube during which they were pummelled by shellbacks with socks filled with hardened kapok. After this softening-up process, they were held down in a barber's chair, their faces smeared with a mixture of oil and paint and shaved with an open razor connected to a low voltage electricity supply. Thus shaven and stunned, they were then tipped backwards into a pool of saltwater, where the shellbacks gave them a good ducking.

When these shenanigans were over, the pollywogs were handed certificates identifying them as 'subjects of the Kingdom of Neptunus Rex' and they went to bed that night cheerfully nursing bruised bodies and aching limbs.

It was the last night of peace in the Pacific.

The shooting started at Pearl Harbor at 7.55 am Hawaiian time the following morning while the *Republic*, the *Holbrook* and the rest of the *Pensacola* Convoy were in mid-Pacific heading for Manila on a south-westerly course. Some of the troops had assembled in the *Republic*'s main saloon for a church service conducted by Chaplain John Kenny when wireless silence was abruptly broken by a communique from Honolulu: *Japan started hostilities . . . govern yourself accordingly.*

Colonel Alexander Johnson and Lieutenant-Colonel Jeff Galwey appeared in the saloon to break the news to the men. Howard Steffy wrote: 'We were informed that Japanese planes had bombed Pearl Harbor and that although war had not been officially declared, it could be considered that a state of war exists between the United States and Japan.'

The crews of all ships jumped into action to carry out a well-rehearsed drill. Gangs of seamen ripped up deck timbers, threw them overboard and got busy with pots of battleship-grey paint. Mark Muller said: 'The *Republic* had been white, but all the hands went over the side on ropes and painted on camouflage colours.'

Lee Van Atta suddenly had a big story to send, but had to content himself with scribbling in his notebook: 'The gaily painted ships, flourishing red, white and blue flags, were hastily converted in the space of a few hours to dingy grey troopships bent on a war errand of utmost importance . . .'

Bill Heath described the transformation of the *Holbrook*: 'Hundreds of men scrambled over the ship, repainting her from stem to stern and waterline to top mast. Any slowpokes who didn't move fast enough were also painted battleship grey.'

Machine guns were broken out from the hold and mounted on bow, bridge and stern. One ordnance company on the *Republic* opened some ammo boxes to discover that two cases of bourbon had been stashed inside for safekeeping. Mark Muller said: 'The whisky was quickly opened, passed around and the entire machine-gun crew received a spiritual uplifting they hadn't expected.'

All personnel were ordered to wear lifejackets and carry a full canteen of water. In the excitement, one of the soldiers confided to the chaplain: 'I feel like a kid who's just seen a Boris Karloff picture and is scared, but doesn't know of what.' Howard Steffy knew precisely what the emergency was about. He wrote: 'Later in the day the ship's wireless reported that simultaneous with the bombing of Pearl Harbor the Japanese attacked Malaya, Thailand, Hong Kong, Guam, Midway and Wake Island.'

For Japan and the United States, *Dainiji Sekai Taisen*—World War II—had started in a blaze of treachery and bloodshed and, simultaneously, the Allied battle against the Axis powers had turned into a global conflict. When the first anniversary of Pearl Harbor rolled around on 7 December 1942, the map of Asia had been redrawn, and names like Bataan and Corregidor, Kokoda, Buna, Gona and Guadalcanal had been written into history.

On the Hawaiian island of Oahu, 354 aircraft from six Japanese carriers— *Akagi* (Red Castle), *Kaga* (Increased Joy), *Soryu* (Green Dragon), *Hiryu* (Flying Dragon), *Zuikaku* (Happy Crane) and *Shokaku* (Soaring Crane) under the command of Vice-Admiral Chuichi Nagumo—had attacked the naval base, harbour and airfields.

Within three hours they had sunk the battleships *Arizona*, *Oklahoma*, *West Virginia* and *California*, and crippled the battleships *Maryland*, *Pennsylvania* and *Tennessee*. Nineteen ships had been hit, 2403 people killed and 1178 wounded. Japanese intelligence sources had informed the striking force that four American aircraft carriers—*Lexington*, *Yorktown*, *Enterprise* and *Hornet*—were based at Pearl Harbor. However, *Lexington* and *Enterprise* were at sea at the time of the attack, delivering fighters and pilots to marine units at Midway and Wake islands, while *Yorktown* and *Hornet* were far away from Hawaii on duty in the Atlantic. The *Saratoga* was not due at Pearl Harbor until the following week and was safely out of harm's way at the big US naval base at San Diego.

The Japanese commanders had known from early-morning aerial reconnaissance that none of the carriers was in harbour, but Commander Minoru Genda, who had drawn up the battle plan, had not made the carriers a prerequisite for his attack; battleships, the great leviathans of the ocean, were still big game as far as the Japanese hunters were concerned and there were several of them sitting unawares at Pearl Harbor. The carriers would have to wait.

Back at Imperial Headquarters in Tokyo, however, the Commander-in-Chief of the Combined Fleet, Admiral Isoruko Yamamoto, knew that without the US carriers at the bottom of the ocean, Japan was entering the war with only a short-term advantage. Unless he could lure the carriers into a trap and destroy them, the United States, the most powerful industrial nation on earth, would regain naval supremacy within two years.

Across the Pacific in Manila, General MacArthur heard about Pearl Harbor in a phone call from his chief of staff, Brigadier-General Richard K. Sutherland. Manila was 19 hours ahead of Hawaii on the western side of the International Date Line and MacArthur was asleep when the phone rang around 4 am on 8 December in the penthouse suite of the Manila Hotel. MacArthur, a devoutly religious man, immediately reached for his mother's Bible and read a few passages of scripture, then headed for the American military headquarters in the old moss-covered Spanish fortress at No. 1 Calle Victoria in the Walled City.

MacArthur was then 61 and, despite his formidable reputation as a military strategist, his term as pre-war military supremo in the Philippines could hardly be described as successful. His biggest mistake was that he had incorrectly anticipated Japanese intentions in the Pacific. With the bulk of the Japanese forces committed to a long war of attrition in many provinces of China, MacArthur had not believed that Japan possessed the military capability to launch a successful invasion of the Philippines.

MacArthur had in fact retired from the US Army and had been on the payroll of the Philippines President, Manuel Quezon, a former guerrilla leader turned playboy/statesman. Quezon elevated the distinguished American warrior to the rank of field marshal, but despite that lofty title MacArthur had lost the clout he had previously enjoyed as US Chief of Staff in Washington, where a powerful isolationist bloc now ruled Congress. President Roosevelt personally backed the British Prime Minister, Winston Churchill, in a 'Europe First' policy that placed Britain's resistance to Nazi Germany ahead of all other requirements and these factors had kept the Philippines low on the priority list of US defence expenditure.

When MacArthur was recalled to active service as US Commander-in-Chief on 26 July 1941, he persuaded Washington that the Philippines could be held against a Japanese attack for up to six months, provided he was supplied with more men, more ships and more planes. The troops in the *Pensacola* Convoy were part of that build-up, although most of the men were replacements for soldiers already serving in the Philippines and not additional to overall strength.

On America's first day of war, MacArthur inexplicably dithered after receiving the news from Pearl Harbor, apparently waiting for the Japanese to make the first move. It was a fatal mistake. At 12.35 pm that day, his command virtually collapsed when the US bombing force at Clark Field, north of Manila, was caught on the ground owing to his own indecision and the incompetence of Major-General Lewis Brereton, commander of the Far Eastern Air Force. Eighteen out of 35 B-17 Flying Fortresses were lost in the Japanese attack, as well as 53 fighters and 25 other aircraft, at a cost of only seven enemy aircraft destroyed.

Many of the B-17s had flown to Clark Field via northern Australia in advance of the *Pensacola* Convoy, which was bringing their ground crews to join them; similarly, fighter pilots of the 34th Pursuit Squadron at Clark Field were waiting for their Kittyhawks, which were packed in crates on the *Meigs*.

Coming only hours after Pearl Harbor, Clark Field was a shambles that should never have happened; the War Department demanded scalps, but MacArthur covered up for Brereton and his chief of staff, Colonel Francis M. Brady, telling Washington: 'No unit could have done better. Their gallantry has been conspicuous, their efficiency good. You may take pride in their conduct.' This whitewash was not designed to save the careers of Brereton and Brady, but rather to protect MacArthur himself from criticism.

In private, he raged against his air chiefs as 'bumbling nincompoops' and it would be many months before he would trust the air force again.

Meanwhile, the Joint Army Navy War Board in Washington ordered the *Pensacola* Convoy to return to Hawaii to reinforce the garrison against further Japanese attacks. However, General George C. Marshall, chairman of the Joint Chiefs of Staff, although dedicated to Roosevelt's 'Germany First' policy, believed that MacArthur was entitled to some help. He put this view to the President at a meeting in the White House on the morning of 10 December and Roosevelt backed his Chief of Staff. That afternoon the Joint Board met again and, countermanding its original order, instructed the *Pensacola* Convoy to press on towards the Philippines, though by a less direct route. To avoid carrier-borne Zeros and the threat of a Japanese blockade, the relief ships would now sail to Manila via north-eastern Australia, which Colonel Dwight D. Eisenhower had recommended to his superiors as the most suitable region in the south-west Pacific for military operations against Japan.

Marshall approved Eisenhower's plan to establish an American military presence in Australia and appointed Lieutenant-General George H. Brett as commander.

Australia had been playing a small but vital role in aiding the Philippines ever since Captain Floyd S. Pell, a member of MacArthur's staff in Manila, had conducted a survey to find a landing strip with a long enough runway to act as a refuelling stop for B-17 Flying Fortress bombers on their way from the United States to Clark Field. Pell had located a rough but suitable strip at Batchelor Field in the wilds of Australia's Northern Territory and, after September, the big four-engined bombers had been touching down there, refuelling and taking off again for the Philippines.

Marshall's directive to send the *Pensacola* Convoy to Manila via Australia proved to be a wise precaution. Howard Steffy's diary recorded: 'The ship's radio bulletin reports that the Japs have sunk HMS *Prince of Wales* and HMS *Repulse* off the Malayan coast and that the Philippines have been invaded.'

The convoy crossed the International Date Line some time during the night of 9 December and lost an entire day; in the morning, it was already Thursday 11 December. His diary shows Bill Heath was in a reflective mood: 'Here I am in the middle of the Pacific Ocean, Pearl Harbor burning behind us. Destination? Who knows? Like everyone else, I am scared. There's no fear worse than the fear of the unknown.'

At a meeting with his officers in the *Republic*'s saloon, the commanding officer, General Barnes, designated the *Pensacola* Convoy as Task Force South Pacific. He had received a message from General Marshall making him Commander of US troops in Australia until the arrival of George Brett and his orders were to set up the first American base in Australia to be used as a staging post for getting US reinforcements through to MacArthur.

In good seas, the *Pensacola* was capable of a maximum speed of 32.5 knots, but the convoy had spread out on a zigzag course to avoid Japanese submarines and the slowest ship determined the overall rate of progress. The big cruiser, under the command of Captain Frank L. Lowe, switched from one flank to another, sometimes going off on her own for an hour or more to investigate a submarine alert. She launched her aircraft on continual reconnaissance flights and the first sign of trouble was when one plane went out and did not return. Its fate is unknown; it simply disappeared into the ocean.

The national guardsmen knew nothing about that mishap, just as they were kept in the dark about everything else, including their new destination. Bill Heath said: 'Meals were cut to twice a day. Bread moulded, meat spoiled and drinking water tasted salty. The weather became very warm and humid. We had no idea where we were headed. Rumours slowed to a trickle with the realisation that our destiny was completely out of our hands.'

On the afternoon of 13 December two British planes escorted the convoy into Suva, the capital of Fiji, to take on fuel and fresh water. Shore passes were issued to all troops, then abruptly cancelled and only officers were allowed to leave the ships.

Mark Muller went ashore as an acting provost marshal to keep the troops in line. 'At the dock I met an English policeman named Inspector Hunt,' he said. 'A Fijian member of the local constabulary stood beside him, seven feet tall, all muscle, with large bushy hair, and dressed in a skirt. The inspector insisted that I had to be welcomed in the traditional Fijian manner. He produced half a coconut filled with amber fluid. "You drink this without stopping, then clap your hands twice and say 'Bullo!' " It tasted foul and, to be quite honest, I was glad to get it over with.'

The convoy sailed the following day, 14 December, and as the ships pulled away from the docks a group of Fijians sang 'Now is the Hour'.

At sea once again, pilots in the *Republic* were pressed into service as lookouts because it was reckoned they had near-perfect eyesight. After scanning the horizon for enemy activity from one of the gun turrets that night, Byron Wilhite wrote: 'There was no moon. The sea was as black as the lowest depths of despair. Far below in the troughs and now on the crest of the waves little marine creatures flashed their phosphorescence in defiance, like little stars fallen from grace on high. The wind whistled through the rigging like the cry of lost souls. The gates of hell were opened and the devil himself roamed the night . . .'

Indeed, somewhere among the sea creatures was the blackened hull of a Japanese submarine. 'One or more enemy subs had been trailing us for part of the way,' said Bobb B. Glenn, who was on the *Republic*. 'The *Niagara* was, for some reason, a day late in leaving Suva. This gave the enemy sub a chance to catch it and it sunk the *Niagara*. This was out of sight of the convoy, but we heard about it unofficially.' Lee Van Atta later claimed that the *Pensacola* had sunk the Japanese submarine and, although other members of the convoy disputed this to us, it was a fact that the convoy was not troubled by the submarine again.

Also, the weather was improving.

'During the following days, the air had become somewhat cooler and we were able to sleep without awaking to find ourselves bathed in a puddle of sweat,' Byron Wilhite noted. 'For the first day out from Suva we sailed due south and it looked as though we might be heading for New Zealand. The course was then changed and a course taken up that led in the direction of Australia. After a few days, it was more or less a certainty that Australia was to be our destination; some said Sydney, some said Brisbane.'

America's Minister to Australia, Nelson T. Johnson, had informed the Australian Prime Minister, John Curtin, 'in utmost secrecy' a few days earlier that US troops would be arriving in his country. Three warships were despatched from the Australian and New Zealand navies, HMAS *Canberra*, HMAS *Perth* and HMNZS *Achilles*, to meet the convoy near the French island of New Caledonia and escort it to the Queensland coast. First contact between the Americans and the Australians was made by a Walrus seaplane which was launched from the *Canberra* to locate the American ships in a heavy swell.

Howard Steffy recorded on 22 December: 'We have reached Australia and our destination is now generally known as the entire convoy is anchoring in Moreton Bay, which I understand is the entrance to the Port of Brisbane. General Barnes, with an advance party in charge of Colonel Alexander Johnson and Major Abraham G. Silverman, are going ashore tonight to make arrangements for the debarkation of the troops tomorrow.'

The Texan Hollis Allen puzzled over the pronunciation.

'Say what?'

'Say Brisbane.'

'Bris-*BANE*? Okay.'

Chapter Three

Eucalyptus Eden

December 1941

THE first American casualty in Australia was Milt Kaslow. He was fatally injured in a road accident soon after the sun went down, and it was a typically beautiful sunset that day. Upstream towards the City of Brisbane, sunlight bathed the weeping fig trees with a warm, golden glow and, in the lee of the troopships, oilslicks seeping from the bilges were turned into little rainbows on the incoming tide. It seemed an unlikely place for a soldier to die, but death does not always cast a shadow before it.

Lieutenant Milton Kaslow was on the *Republic*, one of the ships in the *Pensacola* Convoy that had come sailing up this big, broad river that morning. When he had left San Francisco, it had been almost winter; greatcoat weather, with icy winds whipping in off the fog-cloaked bay. Here, it was already high summer and the lawns of Newstead Park were spread out on the small headland at Breakfast Creek like a tobacco-stained mantle.

The date was Tuesday 23 December 1941, and the *Pensacola* Convoy had brought the first contingent of the million American servicemen that came to this eucalyptus Eden.

Future US infantrymen would be known as GIs (an acronym of Government Issue), but these national guardsmen were still the doughboys of old and, judging by the wild reception they received, the inhabitants of the river city were delighted to see them. It was as if, in a generous moment, Uncle Sam had granted them the Christmas present of their dreams and they couldn't wait to take off the wrapping.

Although this impression was real enough, the spectators on the river bank did not know anything like the whole story. The voyage had been long and uncertain, accompanied by secrecy and danger; plagued in its most critical phases by dissension at the very top of the United States high command. But on this hot, clear, memorable day, the politics and the physical hardship of the journey were swept aside as the troops crowded the decks and jostled one another for a better view. Whatever lay in store in Queensland had to be infinitely better than dodging Japanese bullets in a Philippine jungle.

And yet, just when the danger had passed and the odds should have changed in his favour, there was the simple tragedy of one man's death.

If Hollis G. Allen wondered what Brisbane was like, another member of the Allen clan could have told him a thing or two. Fred Allen, an American comedian, had passed through Brisbane during World War I and lived to regret the experience. Fred was a comedian who juggled balls while he cracked jokes, a feat that usually attracted applause, but he had the misfortune to tour the Australian vaudeville circuit in 1915–16 when America was still neutral in the hostilities of the Great War.

Fred Allen was booked for a six-day engagement at a theatre in Toowoomba, some 90 miles inland from Brisbane. With newspaper columns filled with the names of Australian casualties who had fallen in the Gallipoli campaign, many of them Queenslanders, the good folk of Toowoomba were affronted by America's hesitancy in coming to their aid. They took it personally and, in the absence of any American of military or political rank, made their feelings clear to Fred Allen, the juggling comedian.

Audiences neither laughed at his jokes nor applauded his act and he left the stage in complete silence. Nor did anyone speak to him in Toowoomba or Brisbane when they discovered his nationality. He was, he felt, fortunate to have escaped a tar-and-feathering.

But expatriate Americans also had a few well-chosen words to say about Australians. Mack Mathews, an American who resided in Australia for four years in the late 1920s, wrote in the *American Mercury* in March 1931: 'Whenever Yanks foregather, privately, may be heard an enlightening recital of Australia's obsolete business methods, obnoxious social customs and general economic instability. A popular toast goes: "To Australia—the land where the flowers have no fragrance, the birds no melody and the women no virtue." '

It was obvious to anyone in Brisbane that Mathews was referring to the southern big shots who lived in the smugly self-important cities of Sydney and Melbourne; he had clearly never set foot in Queensland, a veritable sub-tropical paradise where the womenfolk upheld the purest traditions of the British Royal Family as they were perceived in those days through the pages of the *Australian Women's Weekly*.

Neil Keeler of the 7th Bombardment Group spoke for many of the soldiers in the *Pensacola* Convoy when he remarked: 'Australia, before I got there, was kangaroos and teddy bears, although I also knew about the first settlers being English convicts.'

Aborigines of the Yugarabul language group had lived in the Brisbane region since before the end of the last ice age, at least 30,000 years prior to the arrival of Europeans. The first British settlers did not arrive until 1825 when a detachment of 30 convicts, guarded by 20 troopers under the command of Lieutenant Henry Miller, negotiated the sandbanks and mud islands around the river's tidal estuary in the brig *Amity* and, sailing 25 miles upstream, established a settlement at North Quay on the present site of the City of Brisbane. Like the river itself, the settlement was named after the Governor of New South Wales, Sir Thomas Brisbane.

The convicts were obliged to build their own prison barracks out of blocks of stone quarried from high cliffs rising above the mangroves at the river's edge at a place named Kangaroo Point.

Moreton Bay was opened to free settlement in February 1842 after a town plan had been mapped out to develop Brisbane as a frontier post of the British Empire. The main centre was on the northern banks of a thumb-shaped peninsula in the winding river, with streets named after Queen Victoria and members of her family: Queen, Edward, Albert, George, William, Ann, Adelaide, Elizabeth, Charlotte, Mary, Margaret and Alice. Streets in the less fashionable area of South Brisbane across the river were named after British politicians of the period: Stanley, Grey, Russell, Melbourne and Glenelg.

By the time Queensland was proclaimed a colony separate from New South Wales in 1859, Brisbane's free settlers numbered 5000 souls, all white and mostly male, scattered along unsealed roads in a collection of cottages, slab huts, rough hostelries and tents. The only substantial buildings were those that had been built in the stone called Brisbane tuff by convict labour: the barracks, the commissariat and a flour mill, complete with sails and a treadmill, on Wickham Terrace. There was no sanitation, no running water and the stink of tanneries hung heavily in the humid air. It was not an auspicious beginning.

Had the convicts returned at the tail end of 1941, they would have found a predominantly Anglo-Saxon city that had buried its lowly origins beneath the foundations of a sturdy Empire loyalism. Brisbane had developed into an Edwardian provincial centre that looked as though it had been transplanted, brick by brick, from some northern English vale; banks, insurance companies and government offices were located behind filigreed stone facades, with Grecian columns and carved pediments. There were Latin inscriptions above the porticos and revolving doors of solid bronze led into vestibules with tiled mosaic floors and moulded cornices.

It was typical of Brisbane's civic pride that the tallest structure should be the clock tower of the dome-roofed, neoclassical Brisbane City Hall.

The vast majority of business premises—the stores, hotels and restaurants—were mainly timbered buildings with iron-laced verandahs and wooden awnings, enabling southerners to remark unkindly that Brisbane was just a big country town masquerading as a city. No one, though, could deny its natural beauty. Since the advent of spring, jacarandas had turned whole blocks into avenues of purple blossom, and bougainvillea and hibiscus flowered everywhere. The city's emblem was the red poinsettia.

Brisbane's sub-tropical character was clear in its sprawling suburbs of weatherboard houses, built on stilts, with iron roofs and wide verandahs, shaded by camphor laurel, hoop pine and every variety of palm, fig and eucalyptus. In December 1941 the only visible concessions in the suburbs to the wartime emergency were blacked-out windows and an air-raid shelter in every backyard.

In the city, however, the entrances of public buildings had been fortified by sandbags and storefront windows were criss-crossed with masking tape as a precaution against bomb blast. Soldiers on leave from army training camps crowded into the city centre to drink Fourex or Bulimba beer in the Grand Central Hotel or the Gresham or the National, while senior officers adjourned to the colonial elegance of the Bellevue or the art-deco splendour of Lennon's Hotel, the city's newest hostelry.

It was during one such day the previous year that Australian troops, aggrieved over poor conditions in their camps, had rioted through the city centre. Shop windows were broken, traffic disrupted and trams halted while the vastly outnumbered civilian police force made a tactical withdrawal, allowing the troops the freedom of the city. But the police were out in force the following night when the troops reassembled in Adelaide Street with the intention of marching through the city.

Don Whitington, a reporter on the *Courier-Mail*, said: 'Every shop doorway along the street held plainclothes police. The moment the first files moved the police swooped, wielding batons. The unarmed troops were completely helpless. They were routed very quickly.'

The rioters were members of the 2nd Australian Imperial Army, the prestigious successor to the 1st Australian Imperial Force which had fought with great valour against the Turks at Gallipoli in the Dardanelles campaign and against the Germans on the battlefields of France. Conscription for overseas military service had been the hottest political issue in Australia arising from World War I and it was symptomatic of the country's attitude towards the draft that there were two armies: the all-volunteer 2nd AIF, which could fight the country's enemies anywhere in the world, and the Citizen Military Forces, which consisted of conscripted militiamen who could serve only within the boundaries of Australia or its adjacent territories. The diggers of the AIF considered themselves an elite force and rarely mixed with the militia, whom they disparagingly called 'chocos' after the Oscar Straus operetta *The Chocolate Soldier.*

The cream of the AIF, four divisions containing the best-trained officers and men, were serving overseas. The 6th, 7th and 9th Divisions had fought in the Middle East with distinction before the 6th was detached to take part in the doomed British expedition to Greece in April 1941 and the equally disastrous retreat to Crete. The 8th Division, under the flamboyant Major-General H. Gordon Bennett, was about to engage the Japanese in Malaya.

According to one source, AIF soldiers in World War I had been 'egalitarian, resourceful, engagingly disrespectful of authority, superb fighters and unfailing mates'. Members of the 2nd AIF soon discovered that, while legends were wonderful things for a young country to have, it was impossible to live up to them. Yet that was what was being expected of them, and more. In Malaya, General Bennett stated: 'The yellow Huns of the East will get the same reception that their brother Huns in Europe got from the old AIF in the last war. One AIF soldier is worth six Japs.'

He neglected to mention that the cemeteries of France and Belgium were sown with the bodies of Australian dead and that even Gallipoli had been a major Allied defeat. Nor, as time would tell, was Bennett the gung-ho hero he pretended to be.

Brisbane's main thoroughfare, Queen Street, was the site of the big department stores Finney's and Allan & Stark, and air-conditioned picture palaces such as the Regent and the Wintergarden. The theatres were dimmed in accordance with emergency regulations, but banners urging people to invest in war bonds were festooned gaily across their facades, alongside posters advertising the latest movies. The chief mode of transport was the tramcar, with a motorman at the controls and a conductor collecting the fares. The conductor wore a Foreign Legion *kepi* that made him look like an extra in one of the latest movies, *Beau Geste.*

It was largely through Hollywood that Brisbanites had formed their main impressions of America and Americans. Gangsters like Al Capone and James Cagney came from Chicago and blondes like Betty Grable came out of a bottle. American children were like Shirley Temple, Judy Garland and Mickey Rooney, and couples were either Katharine Hepburn and Spencer Tracy, or Roy Rogers and Trigger. Or so the Hollywood legends went at the time the *Pensacola* Convoy entered the Brisbane River between the army lookouts at Fort Lytton and the soldier crabs patrolling the mudflats at Bulwer Island.

The first Australian civilians to greet the Americans were in the SS *Koopa*, a little pleasure steamer that took holidaymakers from the Customs House pier on the Brisbane River to Bribie Island in Moreton Bay. Joan Staines, an 18-year-old secretary, said: 'We came out of the river and suddenly saw all these huge ships at anchor. My father said, "Cripes, it's the bloody Yanks." We'd had no warning that they were coming and it was a complete surprise to see them.'

While the smaller US ships proceeded upstream to New Farm Wharf, the heavily loaded *Republic* ran aground on a sandbank in the outer harbour. 'A lighter had to come to the side to pump excess fuel out of the hold in order to refloat her,' said Mark Muller.

Bob Firehock's first impression of Brisbane was 'of all these houses up on stumps. We'd never seen architecture like that anywhere before in a modern city. We'd seen pictures of native villages in the South Seas with houses on stumps, but nothing to this extent. I was born in New Jersey in a little town called West New York on the Palisades opposite New York City, so it was a complete change for me.'

As the *Republic* approached Brett's Wharf at Hamilton, Firehock realised from the sight of huge, waving crowds that they were being greeted as heroes. 'The people thought we were their saviours,' he said. 'They were obviously very pleased to see us.' Ben Greer, a law graduate who was serving as a ship's writer, said: 'Everybody was up on top of the roofs and the porches waving sheets, blankets and flags—where they got the American flags I don't know. It gave us a great feeling that we were welcome.'

The people of Brisbane had equipped themselves with the Stars and Stripes back in March of that year when a squadron of seven US ships, the cruisers *Chicago* and *Portland* and the destroyers *Clark*, *Reid*, *Conyngham*, *Cassin* and *Downes*, had made a goodwill visit. A quarter of a million out of the city's population of 345,000 had turned out to hail American sailors and marines as they marched nine abreast through a blizzard of confetti from Fortitude Valley to the City Hall, where the Queensland Governor, Sir Leslie Wilson, took the salute in the uniform of the Royal Marines. Many women in the crowd became so excited that they surged through the police lines for a better view of 'the gorgeous Yanks'.

Now the Yanks were back and although censorship had kept news of the convoy's arrival out of the local newspapers, the *Courier-Mail* and the *Telegraph*, word of mouth quickly spread that American ships were coming up the river and many of the theatres, hotel bars and department stores were soon stripped of their pre-Christmas crowds. The Carlton newsreel theatrette in Queen Street was advertising Paramount news coverage of 'The Bombing of Singapore . . . the Fortress of Hawaii . . . War with Japan', but why watch newsreels when the real thing was only a mile or so down the river?

The only grudge Brisbanites held against Americans was that they had not come into the war sooner, but that resentment quickly evaporated in the general euphoric feeling that they had come at all. Australia's total population in 1941 was just seven million people, many of whom had been severely buffeted by the chill winds of the Great Depression. In those tough times, Australia's armed forces were depleted of manpower and poorly equipped, yet they had been pitched into the war against Germany by Prime Minister, Robert Menzies, who was so archly Anglophile that he hadn't even bothered to ask parliament first.

Once the initial thrill of going to the rescue of the Mother Country for a second time that century had worn off, some harsh realities had set in. The phoney war had continued in the Pacific long after it had abruptly ended in Europe with the invasion of France, and Australians had come to realise, too late, that their resources were being drained away in Europe and North Africa while Australia itself was practically defenceless.

After Pearl Harbor, the abiding emotion throughout Australia was one of fear. As Queensland was closer to Asia than any other part of the island continent, the people of Brisbane were all too aware of the dangers of invasion. The meandering Queensland coastline was largely unprotected, apart from the natural fortifications provided by the 1250-mile-long Great Barrier Reef, but everyone knew that enemy ships could easily negotiate a passage through the coral reefs and land an invading force virtually anywhere.

One senior soldier, Major-General J. M. A. Durrant, stated after his appointment as head of Northern Command in September 1941: 'The most important area of Queensland, by far from a defence point of view, is the Brisbane area. Therefore we must be as certain as we can of retaining this in our hands by allotting the bulk of our forces to its defence. Should this area not be attacked, these troops could be regarded as a general reserve for eventual use further north, but only after adequate steps have been taken to secure Brisbane.'

The harshest reality of all was the price in human life that Australia had already paid in the Battles of Britain, Libya, Egypt, Greece, Crete and Syria. Thousands of Australian soldiers had been captured during the fall of Greece and Crete and were now languishing in German prisoner of war camps, while the wounded had started arriving home in frightening numbers from the Middle East.

One of them, 21-year-old Sapper James H. Skinner, who lost both hands, said: 'We heard Lord Haw-Haw on the wireless call us the Rats of Tobruk.' He was proud of that; they all were. Tobruk was already an Australian war memorial.

But these were battles in foreign lands, fought at Churchill's behest, while the emergency in Queensland represented clear and present danger to all Australians. Prime Minister Curtin, an avowed anti-conscriptionist who had been sworn in just two months before Pearl Harbor, frankly admitted that Australia lacked the manpower to defend herself. In that case, declared the Queensland Premier, William Forgan Smith, 'we must work like hell and fight like hell'. But with newspaper headlines and newsreels providing graphic evidence of the remorseless nature of the Japanese war machine, thousands of Queenslanders packed their bags and evacuated coastal areas for places like Toowoomba, while many others headed south to New South Wales and Victoria.

Brisbane was about to become a garrison city and by the time the *Republic* had docked around noon on 23 December it seemed to the excited throng lining the riverbank that deliverance was at hand. Mrs Elizabeth Harland, recently widowed when her husband of only a few months had been shot down over Germany while serving with the Royal Australian Air Force, said: 'I remember looking at those ships and the men on them and thinking that we had been saved. I thought, "Thank God for the Yanks."'

Under the blazing sun, the national guardsmen poured down the gangplanks in khaki uniforms and steel helmets, each man carrying an assortment of backpacks and duffel-bags, water bottles, canteen kits and gasmasks. On the docks, an Australian Army band struck up, 'While We Were Marching Through Georgia', much to the disgust of southerners in the American ranks.

'What's wrong with "God Bless America"?' asked one of the Texans.

'Guess they don't have the Kate Smith sheet music,' replied another.

The doughboys shouldered their semi-automatic .30-calibre M1 Garand rifles and marched past the crowds at the gates. They swung down Racecourse Road in the direction of Ascot racecourse, which the

Australian Army had already commandeered as a transit camp.

'What's this place?' one doughboy asked an Australian sentry at the gates.

'Askit Ricecourse,' replied the Aussie.

'You grow rice here?'

'Nah, mate, we run bloody ricehorses 'ere.'

Bob Firehock and his pilots ended up at Camp Ascot in the absence of any separate facilities for air crew. 'The Australians weren't expecting us, so we had cold lamb stew for dinner,' he said. 'Then we crawled up on the benches in the grandstands and slept the night there. The Australian soldiers were very admirable, very friendly; they did everything they could to make us feel wanted and at home.' Frank Fujita, however, said there was 'a near riot' among the Texans in the 131st Field Artillery when they realised they were getting mutton, not steak, after more than a month on sea rations.

'Stike?' scoffed one Aussie cook. 'It ain't Christmas yet, mate.'

Bill Heath and the 148th Idaho Field Artillery Regiment were camped in the middle of the racecourse. 'There were pyramidal tents for us to sleep in and even mattress covers filled with straw,' he said. 'It wasn't much, but it was summer, the air was sweet-smelling and every one of us slept better that night than we had for a long time. With the promise of fresh food in the morning and—what most of us wanted above all else, a glass of cold milk—Brisbane looked very good indeed. The next morning, we lined up for what we hoped would be a long-awaited, real breakfast. I held out my mess kit to the congenial cook, and plop! . . . a mutton chop with the grease already beginning to congeal. But the bread was fresh and plentiful and I thought maybe I'd get a good cup of coffee. Nope. Watered down tea with overly generous amounts of milk and sugar already added.'

Mark Muller found he had been appointed assistant signal officer at the new headquarters of the US Army in Australia and moved into the city's smartest address. 'After one night on the bleachers at Ascot, four of us piled into an army sedan and were driven to Lennon's Hotel located a few blocks off Queen Street,' he said. 'General Barnes and his staff had moved into the hotel the previous night and had already made plans to refuel and revictual the transports, reload them with the national guardsmen and send them north to the Philippines. The Kittyhawks and Dauntless divebombers would be assembled at airfields near Brisbane and then fly to the battlefront.'

This was wishful thinking. Three days earlier on Saturday, 20 December, Filipino and American defenders had been assailed by strong Japanese landing forces at Davao on the southern island of

Mindanao. Increased Japanese patrol activity was reported on the island of Luzon and there were bombing raids near Manila. On Monday 22 December the Japanese 14th Army, commanded by Lieutenant-General Masaharu Homma, launched its main attack on Luzon. According to reports reaching Brisbane, at least 40,000 Japanese landed from 80 transport craft in Lingayen Gulf, 100 miles north-west of Manila.

As the Japanese tightened their stranglehold on the archipelago, Churchill arrived in Washington to hold his first summit meeting with Roosevelt about Allied war strategy. This meeting, codenamed Arcadia, endorsed the 'Germany First' policy that placed the defeat of Hitler and the Third Reich at the top of the Allied agenda, with the new Pacific war running a poor second.

Knowing that Roosevelt was committed to Europe, MacArthur's hopes of holding the Philippines were firmly pinned on the *Pensacola* Convoy. He insisted to the commander of the Asiatic Fleet, Admiral Thomas C. Hart, that American and Dutch naval units should go forward to provide safe passage for the convoy. Hart refused; he could not, he said, take responsibility for the convoy's safety with the limited forces at his disposal.

MacArthur argued.

Hart stood firm.

Stalemate.

On their first night in Brisbane, some of the American officers visited the city's picture palaces to see Gary Cooper in *Beau Geste* or Edward G. Robinson, Marlene Dietrich and George Raft in *Manpower*. The Hollywood queen, Betty Grable, was starring in *Hot Spot* at His Majesty's Theatre.

But the city possessed much more than celluloid images of their American homeland. Brisbane was surrounded by hills not unlike those they had left behind at San Francisco, and beside the wharves at Hamilton, stucco apartment blocks and weatherboard houses climbed up precipitous, tree-lined streets. On the crest of one hill, there was even a Spanish mission-style church. The brand new Story Bridge further upstream was a modest replica of the Golden Gate and, at that point on the river, the cliffs had been quarried into a passing imitation of the Fourth Chickasaw Bluff, the site of Memphis, Tennessee.

There was even a bridge at South Brisbane that had arches spelling out the letter M for Memphis, just like the De Soto Bridge over the Mississippi, while a mildly high-rise section of Queen Street was known locally as Little Chicago, which gave the men from the mid-west something to chuckle about when they saw its miniature skyscrapers.

But the most striking resemblance of all was in the wooden homesteads with shady verandahs, balustrades and wrought iron panels. Even Katharine Hepburn once said they were 'pure New Orleans, honeysuckle and all'.

The bigger houses, set in gardens behind hedges or palisades, had great four-panelled cedar doors with lion's head knockers in solid bronze. In the biggest, grandest residence, Government House, lived His Majesty's plenipotentiary, Sir Leslie Wilson, the English Governor of the State of Queensland. The presence of an unelected, vice-regal governor testified that Queensland was still very much an outpost of Empire. However, Sir Leslie was quite powerless to prevent the King's subjects from pursuing a rumbustious political life of their own. During the Depression, a mob of disgruntled farmers armed with batons and coils of barbed wire had occupied one of the chambers of Parliament House to demand a new deal from the ruling Labor government. They had been apprehended by the police, but no jury would convict them and they had to be set free.

The city's Lord Mayor was J. B. Chandler, a mild-mannered man whose main preoccupation at City Hall was to have his chambers redecorated in gentle pastel shades that were more conducive to his powers of positive thinking. But City Hall was not Brisbane's main political power base; that privilege rested elsewhere at union headquarters, the Trades Hall, where a meeting had been summoned that night to discuss a labour crisis created by the unexpected American 'invasion'. The local stevedores, the 'wharfies', had refused to unload military equipment from the transport ships, claiming that, as they hadn't been consulted in advance, there was no agreement on rates of pay for the job.

Faced with a walkout, American soldiers had been ordered to stay back at the wharves and start unloading the holds themselves. The wharfies' union, the Waterside Workers Federation, promptly protested against this use of non-union labour. When the Americans heard that the Trades Hall was known locally as 'the Kremlin', they quickly adopted the name and the stage was set for an epic struggle between organised labour and the US military.

Although none of these things made Brisbane seem too alien or unfriendly in American eyes, there was one big and, it proved, fatal difference. When Lieutenant Milton Kaslow ventured onto the dimly lit highway that night as the passenger in a two-seated, soft-topped command car, his driver, an Hispanic orderly, had to contend with the fact that he was steering a left-hand drive vehicle in traffic that drove on the left-hand side of the road.

Perhaps he was unsure of himself in these strange conditions or perhaps he was a little shaky after a month at sea. Whatever the reason, he cut back too sharply after overtaking another vehicle. The command car's tyres touched the edge of the asphalt, veered onto the soft shoulder and the vehicle overturned in a ditch. The driver was unhurt, but his passenger was thrown from the wreck, landing on his head and suffering a fractured skull.

Lieutenant Kaslow, just 22 years of age, the Army officer who had led the 8th *Matériel* Squadron off the parade ground at Fort Douglas, Salt Lake City, on its way to God-knows-where, ended his journey in a Brisbane hospital, where he died of a brain haemorrhage. He was buried under the eucalyptus trees at Lutwyche Cemetery with full US military honours.

The *Pensacola* doughboys were well received in those first few days in Brisbane. They had been given partial pay of $10 to spend over Christmas and were having trouble getting rid of it. Frank Fujita said: 'The Aussies were most hospitable and would not let us pay for our own drinks.' Sergeant Jack Allured said: 'We still had most of our money left; they wouldn't let us pay for anything.' Hollis G. Allen, unlike his juggling namesake, found that everyone wanted to talk to him. Slug Wright, who was put on provost duty outside a hotel where a wedding reception was taking place, ended up as a guest at the insistence of the Australian bride and groom.

This friendliness was shattered when Australian and American soldiers clashed at a dance in a downtown ballroom. Things were going well until one Texan decided to enliven proceedings. 'A private stood up and said he'd whip any sonovabitch in the house,' said Fujita. 'We found that if there was anything the Australians like better than beer it's fighting. All hell broke loose and when the going started to get a little tough, the soldier who'd started it went over to the nearest window and stepped out. He had forgotten he was on the second floor and wound up with a broken leg in hospital.'

In Manila, MacArthur ordered the newly mobilised Philippines Army to withdraw to defensive positions on the Bataan peninsula and prepared to declare Manila an open city in advance of Japanese occupation.

On Christmas Eve he left Manila with his wife, Jean, and son, Arthur, and the boy's Chinese *amah*, Ah Cheu, in the steamer *Don Esteban* for the island of Corregidor, just south of Bataan in Manila Bay. He moved his family into a small house in a fort above the Malinta Tunnel, the island's main fortification, and called his top echelon together to deal with an immediate crisis. More than 40,000 men, women and children—more than twice the anticipated number—had swarmed into the fortress and MacArthur had to halve the food ration from the beginning of the siege.

MacArthur sent coded messages requesting urgent assistance from the *Pensacola* Convoy to Base 3 USAFA, which had become operational at Lennon's Hotel only a few hours earlier. These cables were received at the second-floor communications centre, decoded by Bobb Glenn and passed to General Barnes. Since no automatic encryption equipment existed, Colonel Van S. Merle-Smith, the military attache at the US Embassy in Canberra, had travelled to Brisbane with the double transposition cipher codes. These were handed to Mark Muller, who encoded Barnes's replies to MacArthur as he dictated them. The encoded messages were then taken to the signal office of the Royal Australian Air Force for despatch to the Philippines via Washington. It was a roundabout way of doing things, but the best they could manage on Day One of the Australian operation.

The following day, Christmas Day, saw the officers and staff of the new Base 3 assembled in the hotel's dining room. As there was nothing he could do to alleviate the food shortages in the Philippines, General Barnes ordered his staff to relax and enjoy themselves after the hard work they had done in setting up the base in less than 24 hours. The meal was also in the nature of a farewell because Barnes was being posted to Melbourne to work with Lieutenant-General Brett, who was replacing him as commander of United States Army Forces in Australia on New Year's Eve.

Beside each place at the table was an elegant printed menu and beneath the name of the hotel and its crest someone had penned *Brisbane, Australia* just to remind the visitors where they were. With liberal amounts of French wine to accompany each course, the meal kicked off with a selection of *cantaloupe au maraschino*, royal oysters in cocktail sauce and *consommé au sherry*, followed by either poached schnapper in prawn sauce, or *noisette d'agneau Renaissance*.

The main course was roast turkey gobbler with chestnut seasoning, roast sucking pig and apple sauce, and York ham ('This wasn't an either/ or offer—you got all three,' said one guest), all served up with French beans, green peas, baked, boiled and straw potatoes, and *asperges frappe sauce verte*. For dessert, there was Christmas plum pudding with brandy sauce, sweet mince pies and cream, Lennon's iced Christmas pudding with caramel custard and cream, devilled almonds, muscatels, ginger, cheese straws and, finally, *café noir*.

Among the diners was Bill Heath, whose unit had been invited by

Barnes to join the festivities. Barnes knew that the national guardsmen were heading for the Philippines in a couple of days and he wanted to share the meal with at least some of them. After his greasy lamb chop experience, Heath couldn't believe his eyes: 'What a feast! What a contrast to the canned meat and mouldy bread on the *Holbrook*! Who picked up the tab? I'd like to think maybe Uncle Sam did. More likely it was the generous management of Lennon's Hotel.'

When the guests gathered round the piano to give voice to the Christmas spirit, there was a faint echo far away in the night skies. Three thousand miles to the north the doomed of Corregidor were singing 'Silent Night'.

Chapter Four

◄○►

Rebel Gunner

RUGGED UP inside his tent near Tripoli on the Lebanese coast, Gunner Edward Sidney Webster from Millmerran, a township on the Darling Downs, wanted to go home. He'd had a bellyful of flies, rocks, the intense heat, lousy food, Arabs, being shot at. Now he was snowed in; yes, snowed in—that too! The last thing Ed Webster wanted or needed that December was a white Christmas.

Apart from the occasional huddled figure of a digger shuffling through the snowdrifts with wood for the fire, the only thing that moved across that ancient biblical landscape was the wind, sighing and moaning as it explored every inch of frosted canvas for a point of entry. Webster shivered and took a slug from a bottle of French brandy he'd liberated in Beirut during one of his forays among the Arab population after the cease-fire had been called.

One of Webster's comrades, Lieutenant (later Major) Bill Thomas, said: 'We had a very good time in Beirut. The city hadn't been damaged during the fighting and some of us stayed at St George's Hotel in great style.'

Beirut was a bit too Frenchified for the likes of Ed Webster, who found its expatriate French citizens stand-offish. The Allied victory in Syria and Lebanon in July 1941 had thoroughly trampled the little that remained of Vichy pride into the Levantine dust. Nevertheless, the city was still open for business and Webster enjoyed eating in the sidewalk cafes, drinking in the bars and going to the modern theatres to see the latest film releases.

He avoided fleshpots like the Kit Kat Club and the Lido, where the champagne flowed and officers danced with dark-eyed, scantily clad hostesses. Webster peered into this Middle Eastern *demi-monde* and, although he had to admit that Madame Mareka and her girls were humdingers—cheap, too, if a man was interested—he had other things on his mind. Like going home.

Webster's outfit, the 2/2nd Anti-Tank Regiment, 7th Division AIF, was camped at a place called Bssama on the rugged plains inland from the port of Tripoli. After the gunners had roistered in suitable style, it was back to work blasting defensive positions out of limestone rock in case of a German invasion through Turkey. Excavation had ceased in November when the seasons changed and winter announced its presence with heavy downpours that inundated the worksites. Then the snowstorms had blown in all the way from the Russian steppes and the troops were forced to retreat under canvas.

'As the weather became colder we were issued with extra blankets and, of course, we always had our greatcoats,' said Lieutenant Ronald Shea, one of Webster's officers. 'We were in winter battle dress and reasonably well equipped to deal with the cold. They got rations through the snow to us after a couple of days and we had some Christmas goodies, puddings and so forth.'

The New Year was also ushered in by brass-monkey weather and Ed Webster found himself dreaming about Queensland, where it was high summer and people in shorts were cooling off with glasses of ice-cold beer on the verandah. Webster was not a native Queenslander, although he'd been brought up on the Darling Downs and considered Queensland his adopted State. He'd been born in New South Wales and had lived at the old Webster family home at Haberfield in Sydney before moving to Millmerran in Queensland when he was a boy.

Raised like all his contemporaries on the Anzac mythology of the Great War, Webster had worked for a relative on his sheep station at Yandilla, near Millmerran, as a young man during the Great Depression. In his opinion, there was nothing great about either the Great War or the Great Depression; people called them great to make themselves feel important—it was just so much bulldust and Ed Webster was dead against bulldust.

Had Webster known about the arrival of the Yanks in Brisbane a few days earlier, he would not have been surprised; very few things would have surprised him after his experiences in the Middle East. Like a lot of his mates, he'd greeted the news of Pearl Harbor with glee: now the Yanks would have to come out and fight the enemy instead of sheltering behind Lend Lease and a lot of pacifist baloney. And as they were on Australia's side, they wouldn't be shooting at him, not like every other bastard he'd run into since he'd come to this godforsaken place. No one had ever shot at him in Brisbane, and that was where he fully intended to go once it stopped snowing and his regiment could pack up and go home.

The 2/2nd Anti-Tank Regiment consisted of headquarters plus four batteries; there were three troops of 30 men in each battery, each troop usually manning four anti-tank guns. The batteries were 5th, 6th, 7th and 8th; Gunner Webster was in 6 Battery. In the previous 12 months they'd fought against the famed Panzers of Rommel's Afrika Korps, tackled the French Foreign Legion and seen off assorted hordes of Moroccan Berbers, Algerians and Syrian Spahis. Webster had been awarded two campaign medals and he often wondered what they'd think about that on the Darling Downs: Gunner Edward Webster, war hero.

The Downs was nothing like the country outside the flap of Ed Webster's tent. At home in a good season the blacksoil plains produced fine harvests of wheat and there was an abundance of Mitchell grass to feed sheep and beef and dairy cattle. The land was originally divided between the squatters who built large homesteads and ran huge estates with thousands of head of sheep and cattle, and the selectors who farmed much smaller plots of land, or selections.

Millmerran was the centre of a mixed farming district embracing smaller places like Cecil Plains, Turallin, Yandilla, Pampas and Brookstead, with Moonie further west and then the flat spinifex plains stretching out to the cattle country around Winton in the dead centre of Queensland.

The spirit of the Outback and the western plains was firmly enshrined in the bush literary tradition. In January 1895, a few months before Mark Twain's visit to Australia, the poet Andrew Barton Paterson—'The Banjo'—wrote 'Waltzing Matilda' at a homestead near Winton. With its storyline about a swagman who stole a jumbuck and jumped into a billabong rather than be taken alive by troopers, 'Waltzing Matilda' was a powerful political allegory based on true events that had taken place during a shearers' strike in Queensland the previous year. Sung to the stirring strains of the Scottish sea shanty 'Craiglea', 'Waltzing Matilda' had become Australia's unofficial national anthem.

Despite his proximity to the Outback, Webster's own life was more akin to one of the works of the Melbourne poet C. J. Dennis concerning an anti-hero called the Sentimental Bloke, a rough diamond whom 'Crool Forchin' brings to his knees over his love for a girl called Doreen. There was a touch of the Sentimental Bloke about Edward Webster and his wife, Alice, had recognised it; his mates might call him 'Ed' or 'Webby', but to her he was 'Teddy', and, like Doreen, she had given her man a son.

Alice Webster said: 'I met Teddy in Millmerran when I was 20 years old. He was tall, dark and handsome and we were married in Millmerran in 1937. We had a son, John, and Teddy worked on the station for a while and then went transport driving. He enlisted in the army at a recruiting "do" in Millmerran when he was 30.'

The reason Webster had taken up truck-driving was that he'd injured his leg in a farming accident and the leg had withered. When the transport work had fallen off, money was tight, so he'd kissed Alice and John goodbye and gone to war as a five-bob-a-day private in the 2nd AIF. After enlisting in Millmerran, he'd got a lift to the big smoke and joined the 2/2nd Anti-Tank Regiment, which was formed in Brisbane in May 1940. He was 5 foot 10 inches tall with a broad chest, but his arms were not well developed and he walked on his wasted leg with a slight limp; one friend described him as 'a bit gaunt but nevertheless strong'.

Webster passed his medical examination despite the limp and donned the khaki tunic, the baggy pants with webbing belt, the blancoed anklets and big army boots and paraded in front of Alice. He wore the colour patch common to all 7th Division artillerymen: deep navy-blue and bright red triangles set against a silver-grey background. He had a patch on each shoulder, blue to the front, and an identical patch on the right-hand side of the headband on his slouch hat.

QX5862 Gunner Edward Webster had a uniform and a point of view, and the other recruits, most of them little older than schoolboys, gave him a good hearing in the barrack-room.

He talked about the bush tradition of mateship and held his grog like a man, saying that all his faults were on the outside for the world to see. Ed Webster had lots of little sayings like that, bush philosophies that he'd picked up in the rough hotel bars on the Downs and in the townships of the Brisbane Valley. They cut a lot of timber in the Brisbane Valley and one of the chips had landed on his rangy shoulders and stayed put. Some of the officers had him marked down as a troublemaker, a bolshy bloke who always argued the toss, but that was all right with Ed Webster; the brass hats could like it or lump it.

'Webby did have a bit of a short fuse,' admitted Lieutenant Shea. 'I used to see him reacting occasionally, particularly when he got an order he didn't like. He was the standard country bloke and not particularly fond of discipline. He was about 30 when he joined up, an old bloke by our standards; older than a hell of a lot of the troops we had at the time. I was 22 and the average age of the troops was about 20.'

The 2/2nd was an all-Queensland regiment and most of its gunners came from the Brisbane Valley where the recruiting officer had made a special effort to encourage young country men to enlist. 'It was still the Depression,' said Gunner Bruce Eglinton of 8 Battery, 'and a lot of men joined up for a bed and a feed. Five bob a day was a lot better than being on the dole.'

All the men were volunteers and a State examination pass in maths was one of the few academic requirements, although the officers included lawyers, accountants and architects. Several had gone to Brisbane Boys College, a private school which provided many of the city's top professional men. Along with the other new recruits, Gunner Webster had gone to Redbank, the big army camp near Ipswich at the southern end of the Brisbane Valley, for training from May to October 1940. At this relatively early stage of the war, Australian factories were working at half capacity and there was a lack of weapons for many of the new units that had been formed to keep pace with the carnage in the Western Desert. Twenty-four new field guns and half the machine gun carriers produced by Australian factories were earmarked for General Sir Thomas Blamey's 6th Division in North Africa.

Ken Blyth, sergeant of 1 Troop in 7 Battery, said: 'At Redbank, we had .303 rifles and one or maybe two two-pounder anti-tank guns and that was it.'

Thus, only partially trained, Ed Webster and his mates went down to Sydney by train on 17 October 1940, and were ferried out to the *Queen Mary* at Darling Harbour to go to war. Webster discovered that the *Queen Mary* was nothing like the luxury liner of the travel advertisements. Gunner Bruce Eglinton said: 'We were given a cabin several decks down and it stank of sweat. Seven of us went topside, sat down on the deck and refused to budge. An officer ordered us to go below, but we refused. He said we'd be treated as mutineers and courtmartialed. However, the regimental medical officer inspected the cabins and said they were a health risk, so we were allowed to sleep up on the decks—at least until 5 am each morning when the sailors swabbed them down.'

In Bombay, the 2/2nd changed ships and travelled to the Suez Canal on the Dutch freighter *Indoorpoura*, took a train to Gaza in the British Protectorate of Palestine, then went by truck across the Sinai Desert to Qastina, arriving in November 1940. Altogether, 10,918 newly arrived troops of the 7th Division were deployed in camps throughout Palestine.

Webster and his mates went sightseeing in Jerusalem, entering the old city through the Jaffa Gate and walking down the twisted alleys of the *souk* to the Via Dolorosa, the Wailing Wall and the Mosque on the Rock. Bruce Eglinton said: 'We also saw the Mount of Olives and the Garden of Gethsemane and went swimming in the Dead Sea.'

Headquarters and all four batteries reassembled at Qastina, then went down to the south of Palestine for five months' intensive training. They were in the old stamping ground of Ginger Mick, the Sentimental Bloke's cobber who had joined the 1st AIF and 'gone to flamin' war to stoush the foe'. Gunner Noel Glasgow of 5 Battery, who had enlisted in the 2nd AIF at 19, was very conscious of the Anzac tradition. He said: 'My father lost a leg fighting with the 1st AIF in France and died when I was quite small. I used to march on Anzac Day with my uncle, Major-General Sir Thomas William Glasgow, commanding the parade. We were aware that the old fellows who talked to us at school about Anzac Day had been in the Middle East, but these were entirely different times, although a lot of the young fellows repeated the same indiscretions—I mean, with women and suchlike. I wasn't keen to get mixed up in it myself; not only was I a young man, I was an extremely immature young man like so many of my generation and it just didn't feel like the right thing to do.'

There were still very few weapons with which the anti-tank crews could complete their training. Sergeant Ken Blyth said: 'We trained in Palestine without weapons other than Bren guns, using wooden mock-ups of anti-tank guns. The regiment took trucks down to Gaza on 6 April and a train from the canal to Helwan camp, just outside Cairo near the pyramids. We were there when things weren't going too well for our troops in Greece. We were going to go to Greece, but instead of sending two divisions, they only sent the 6th. We were issued with full war equipment and moved up the road to Mersa Matruh on 20 April 1941.'

The British had established a fortress at Mersa Matruh, a flyspeck on the Mediterranean coast well to the west of Alexandria and El Alamein, and a vital link on the old Egyptian road to the forts at Tobruk and Bardia in Libya. Lieutenant Shea said: 'Rommel had just driven the British forces out of Libya, apart from Tobruk, and we were anticipating the German invasion of Egypt. We—the 7th Division—all moved up into the desert and took up a defensive position in Mersa Matruh.

'Our job was to dig the defences and it was a constant job because the defence plan seemed to change every week. We'd dig a hole and then we'd have to go out and dig another one. But we grew pretty philosophical about it; we accepted that it was part of being in the army. We were a close-knit unit, partly because most of the officers were ex-artillery and had known each other in the Militia before joining the 2/2nd.'

Bruce Eglinton said: 'German planes came over and dropped bombs on Mersa Matruh and the British ground staff didn't like it at all. We wore boots and shorts while we worked and were burned pretty black. Whenever we could, we'd go down to the beach; it was glorious and the water was clear and lovely. A British naval officer saw us on the beach one day and said to one of our officers, "Tell me, where did your men get their white shorts?" '

Webster landed a cushy job as Shea's driver. 'He had a wasted leg, but he was a pretty good driver and a good mechanic who could keep a car going,' said Shea. 'He drove me around Mersa Matruh in a 1500-hundredweight Ford utility that we'd brought with us from Australia.'

The British forces at Mersa Matruh consisted of the 7th Australian Division and 6th British Division, although each had only two brigades. With the 9th Australian Division, the 18th Brigade of the 7th Division, and a force of British and Indian troops holding out at Tobruk, the panzers had swept eastward and taken Bardia and the key fort of Capuzzo on the road to Egypt. Shea said: 'Some of the units, including 6 Battery of the 2nd Anti-Tank, were moved up to the frontier where we had a quick stoush with the Germans and a very quick retreat. Webby was around there then. He was with the troops who were at Hellfire Pass on the border of Libya and Egypt.

'Fort Capuzzo was an Italian fort on the frontier and it guarded the head of this pass, Halfaya, which we called Hellfire Pass. We had what was later euphemistically termed a raid: we attacked the fort with the intention of capturing Bardia, but while we captured the fort we didn't get to Bardia.'

When the Afrika Korps retook Capuzzo, the British forces were left holding Hellfire Pass, the only gap in the hills where tanks could climb the escarpment and thus thrust into Egypt. 'We were using whatever we could get to keep them out,' said Shea. 'We had some two-pounders, some captured Swiss-made Socothurn anti-tank rifles, which were practically useless, some 18-pounders—anything that would fire and hit a tank.'

Lieutenant Lance Watts said: 'Our two-pounders could be fired as a portée from the back of a truck or unloaded and fired from the ground. In the desert, we got behind the sand dunes, fired and got out. But as the British discovered, our two-pounders were like a little popgun compared with what the Germans had—they were using anti-aircraft guns against our tanks.'

In addition, the 2/2nd had been trained to fight as infantry and used Bren guns, Thompson sub-machine guns and rifles against the Germans at closer range ... 'but the Germans came back with a very strong counter attack,' said Shea, 'and we were forced to move out.'

The 7th Division was withdrawn to its defensive ditches at Mersa Matruh, leaving Rommel to claim victory at Halfaya. The strategically vital port of Tobruk, however, was still holding fast and the German commander was determined to seize it. Lieutenant Shea said: 'The fact that we had Tobruk actually prevented Rommel from operating successfully in Egypt.'

The Luftwaffe dropped leaflets on Tobruk urging the defenders to surrender by waving white handkerchiefs. The Allied commander, Major-General Leslie Morshead, an Australian who was nicknamed Ming the Merciless because of his mandarin appearance, replied from his headquarters in the battered Town Hall that this was out of the question. 'Owing to the prevailing dust and the necessity to ration water for essential purposes,' said Morshead, 'there are no white handkerchiefs available.'

The Allied campaign in the Middle East went seriously awry when Churchill ordered the Commander-in-Chief, General Sir Archibald Wavell, to undertake an armed intervention in Greece. Churchill dreamed of forming a united Balkan front against Hitler, but lost his enthusiasm when Yugoslavia was invaded and even the Greeks opposed the plan. It was only Wavell who kept the campaign alive; an inarticulate man at the best of times, he seemed incapable of entertaining any doubts once his mind was fixed on a particular objective.

The Greeks eventually agreed to the intervention going ahead, but it ended abruptly in the teeth of a furious German onslaught. The Greeks surrendered, the swastika flapped over the Acropolis and the Allies were forced to withdraw to Crete, where they held out for only a few weeks before being overrun. Thousands of British and Australian soldiers were either killed or captured in the fighting.

Back in the desert, units of the 2/2nd Anti-Tank Regiment left Mersa Matruh on 23 May 1941, and travelled back to Cairo to prepare for Churchill's next campaign. 'We were in open trucks and the heat from the sun and the burning wind was intense,' said Bruce Eglinton. 'We sheltered under army greatcoats to keep the sun off our heads, but our motorbike riders collapsed from sunstroke and dehydration.'

The 7th Division crossed the canal into the Sinai desert, went through the village of Nazareth to Lake Tiberius and assembled on the border of Palestine and Syria for the invasion of Syria on 8 June. Shea said: 'The situation in Iraq had deteriorated because some bozo had overthrown the government and was trying to get German assistance to prop him up. The Germans were being very helpful and had started pouring aircraft and stores into Iraq through Syria; that is why we attacked Syria.'

The 'bozo' in question was the Prime Minister, Rashid Ali, head of an Arab Nationalist movement which had deposed the ruling, pro-British Regent in March. When the British defeated the Iraqis in the field on 31 May, Rashid Ali had fled and the Regency had been restored to power. However, Germany obtained an agreement from Vichy France, which had held on to Syria after the defeat of France, to refuel their warplanes at Syrian airfields and allow supplies to be sent through Syria to Iraq.

Churchill ordered a combined Allied force consisting of 18,000 Australians and 16,000 British, Indian and Free French troops to move against Syria and its mandate, Lebanon. This time Wavell opposed the campaign, but Churchill overruled him and, while the Syrian invasion was in progress, directed him to counter-attack Rommel in Libya. Wavell duly mounted Operation Battleaxe against the Afrika Korps on 15 June and was decisively beaten in just three days, losing 91 tanks. Battleaxe was Wavell's last throw of the dice in North Africa; Churchill replaced him shortly afterwards with General Claude Auchinleck, the Commander-in-Chief in India.

In Syria, however, the Allies scored a notable victory, even though they were opposed by 28,000 Vichy French and African troops and about 10,000 Lebanese and Syrians, all under the command of the Frenchman General Henri Dentz. For political reasons, Churchill later tried to draw a veil over the Syrian campaign and the Australians, who were in the majority among the Allied troops, never received due credit for their efforts.

The attack plan called for the invaders to move into enemy territory along three sectors: coastal, central and eastern. The Australian 7th Division, less the 18th Brigade which was still in Tobruk, was ordered to fight its way to Beirut via the coastal route, while other Australian and British forces moved towards Merdjayoun along the central route and the Indians and Free French struck out for the Syrian capital, Damascus, in the east.

At the outset of the campaign, an Australian patrol was sent in to prevent demolition of a section of the coast road. The patrol's guide was a young member of the Haganah defence force, Moshe Dyan. Although the patrol failed to prevent the road from being blown up, they succeeded in causing havoc behind enemy lines. Dyan helped to operate a captured mortar which lobbed bombs onto trucks bringing in Vichy French reinforcements. As Dyan was looking through his binoculars at one of the targets, the glasses were hit by a sniper's bullet and he lost an eye. The eyepatch he wore to cover the wound later became his trademark when he served as Israel's Minister of Defence.

Ed Webster, Ron Shea, Bruce Eglinton and the rest of the 2/2nd Anti-Tank Regiment went into action with various brigades and found themselves up against dauntingly superior firepower. Sergeant Ken Blyth said: 'We were instructed to wear our khaki felt hats into Syria to show we were friendly, but after about three seconds the French shot at us and we were in steel helmets.'

The Vichy forces had machine guns, artillery and tanks in forts and villages on the high ground, while the Australians had to attack uphill with bullets, shells and rock splinters flying all around them.

Blyth said: 'We fought the Vichy French, the Spahis and the Foreign Legion. The Spahis were big men in cloaks who rode horses with red saddlecloths, but we were also up against tanks and our anti-tank guns were well forward with the troops. Anti-tank guns were only armour-piercing if the armour was thin enough and they had an effective range of only 600 yards, so they were frequently used against machine gun emplacements. It was a short, sharp campaign and, as far as our regiment was concerned, we lost five guns and some men.'

Lieutenant Shea said: 'We had fair success against the French tanks, but that was mainly because Syria was a mountainous country and the tanks couldn't get off the narrow tracks. Most of the French troops we fought were colonial troops, the Berbers from Morocco, Algerians and two regiments of the French Foreign Legion. I was lucky—I did most of my travelling by motorbike, but the poor old infantry, of course, had only their two feet and had to do a lot of work on all fours climbing up the mountains.

'We thought we'd be held up longer than we were because there were some terrifically good defensive positions. It was an amazing campaign; we won it—the first time we'd won since the war started.'

The Syrian campaign is best remembered in Australia for the heroism of Rodin Cutler, the gunner who won the Victoria Cross (and lost a leg) in the fighting. But as Cutler, the most modest of men, knew only too well, there were many other unsung heroes at his side.

Bruce Eglinton took the central route with L Troop of 8 Battery, heading for Merdjayoun. He was caught up in the fighting for the key fort of Khiam and its adjacent village, both of which were heavily defended. Eglinton said: 'One of the officers, Hardacre, told us to go up this steep incline to attack the fort. As soon as we started up, a couple of enemy shells landed near us to alert the machine-gunners to our position and they opened up on us. I discovered that bullets coming close really do sound like bees.

'Even when we hit the ground with exhaustion, we were still quite open to this machine-gun fire and the chap next to me, Arthur Hack, showed me his tin hat which had been creased by a bullet. He looked so concerned, so hurt about it, that I burst out laughing, so he laughed too and that's what got us to the top.

'It was about midday when we got there and the others joined us on the outer perimeter of the fort some hours later after dark. We settled down for the night and it was cold, so we put our ground sheets over us. What we didn't realise was that there would be a heavy dew and in the morning sunlight we looked like shining pools of water. The next minute, bullets started landing on us and everyone scattered, except for the chap lying next to me. I thought, "Well, if he's not concerned, nor am I". Eventually, a couple of his mates came along and carried him off and asked me if I'd been wounded, too!

'We retreated and it took us two and a half hours to get back down to the starting line. We'd discarded our gas masks and other equipment to lighten the load in our haversacks on the way up, but we still had Primus stoves and made a mixture of biscuits, tins of Ideal milk and sugar—that's all we could get down our throats. The next minute all these aircraft came over, strafing the ground, and we thought that was lovely because we'd been told we had air superiority.

'What we didn't realise was that blue in the centre of the roundel was Vichy French, while our planes had red. These were blue and several of our chaps were wounded. I saw one of our planes hedgehopping with seven enemy aircraft chasing him. He disappeared from sight, there was a crash and he'd gone. We didn't see many of our planes at all; I gather they refused to fly because they were outnumbered; that, at least, was what the infantry was told.

'In the morning, a little biplane firing through the propeller like in World War I came round shooting up everything. I dived on the ground for my tin hat and he swung round and swooped straight down at me. You don't get time to get a fright in those conditions; I was quite interested to see what was happening. Instead of firing, he put his hand to his helmet, gave a salute, lifted his plane and flew off. He'd either run out of ammunition or he'd seen my beard and thought I was a Frenchman because Australian soldiers don't have beards as a rule.

'Hardacre made me a sergeant and told me to take over one of the truck crews manned by Irish Australians. We went out in four trucks— Hardacre in the lead in one truck, then two other trucks, then us. We went behind Khiam over towards Merdjayoun and, when shells started landing, I got our driver, Cec Casey, to swing around. We got our weapons out and took up a defensive position. Then we saw that the other three trucks had been abandoned with the weapons still in them; they'd just evacuated them, including Hardacre.

'The next thing I knew, Cec Casey jumped up, ran out, popped into one truck, started it up and brought it back. Then he went back for the second truck, which he had trouble starting, but brought it back anyway, then the third—and there were shells falling around him all the time.

'When we got back to the starting point, I went to Hardacre and asked him if he was going to recommend Casey for his action in retrieving the trucks. He looked very uncomfortable, but I kept at him. Eventually, he had to admit that he'd misunderstood his orders and we shouldn't have been there in the first place; we should have stopped below the fort. He said that, if he recommended Casey, he'd have to give details about time and place and they'd know he'd made a mistake. So Casey never got his medal.

'We took Khiam again when the infantry from the 2/33rd Battalion under Captain Ferguson went in with fixed bayonets against the French defenders—Senegalese, great big men—and we followed them in. As we went in, there was an Arab offering us drinks of water. He disappeared and we later learned that he was the French colonel who'd stayed to assess our strength and then he counter-attacked and drove us out. There was a hell of a mortar attack that night and the ground was all rocky and the rock splinters were almost as lethal as shrapnel. It was the most frightening thing I ever encountered; mortars are much worse for infantry than artillery fire.

'Fort Khiam finally fell after a heavy artillery bombardment, but we'd already moved on to the Merdjayoun sector. The enemy had blown a bridge over the Litani River outside Merdjayoun and the water was beautiful. Chaps were swimming and picking out little bits of shrapnel and rock splinters from each other's backs. The enemy had evacuated Merdjayoun and we drove through there with our lights out, but they closed in behind us and later there was a hell of a fight to take Merdjayoun—that was where Cutler [Arthur Roden—later Sir Roden—Cutler of the 2/5th Field Regiment] won the Victoria Cross.'

Merdjayoun, Jezzine and Damascus all fell to the Allies in rapid succession and General Dentz sought an armistice to prevent needless bloodshed. A ceasefire was called on 12 July. When the shooting stopped, units of the 2/2nd gathered at Saida, and proceeded up into the mountains behind Beirut to treat their wounded and regroup.

Lieutenant Shea said: 'The Lebanon mountains are full of these little resorts. One place was called Beit Mrouj, which consisted of a very good hotel, the Bois de Boulogne, with a few stores to complement it. The convalescent camp was in the hotel and I convalesced in there, suffering from sandfly fever. The terrain was rather rugged, but there were a few trees and they were the only trees we saw in Lebanon apart from the cedars high up in the mountains.

'The regiment were based a few miles away at Dhour Choueir and, after about four weeks, we went down to Bssama and started the diggings—or, rather, the blastings, because the ground was solid limestone—at Tripoli at the northern end of Lebanon to keep the Germans out if they came that way.'

Bruce Eglinton said: 'We were at Bssama for quite a while; it was an awful place, bleak, and that's when the snow came—by God it snowed! We were living in tents and at Christmas one part of the encampment completely disappeared under the snow. There was nothing else to do so a lot of us just got on the grog.'

Ed Webster celebrated along with his mates. It was Christmas and, besides, the booze helped to take away the pain in his leg.

There was nothing to celebrate in Asia that Christmas. Hong Kong fell to the Japanese on Christmas Day and Manila was being systematically pounded into submission. Carlos Romulo, a Pulitzer Prize-winning journalist, reported to the free world: 'Bombs fell on Manila's famous old walled city at 11.30 am on Sunday 28 December while ambulance men were still digging Saturday's dead and wounded out of the ruins . . .'

While the war hung in the balance that weekend on all three fronts—Middle Eastern, Russian and Asian—the national guardsmen of the 2nd Battalion, 131st Texas Field Artillery, the 147th South Dakota Field Artillery and the 148th Idaho Field Artillery left Brisbane and went to sea again in a small convoy consisting of the *Bloemfontein*, *Chaumont* and *Holbrook*, under the protection of the *Pensacola*.

Bill Heath wrote in his diary: 'We left this land with its summer when winter should be, with its milk and honey and pretty girls, with its cold beer and steak and eggs, with its fabulous Lennon's Hotel. We marched back to the docks and back to the stinking old *Holbrook*. We sailed out into the Pacific Ocean, turning north and crossing the Tropic of Capricorn past the Great Barrier Reef (all 1250 miles of it), angling north-west through the Coral Sea. Slowly we swung around to the west, through Torres Strait, past Cape York and into the Arafura Sea. Where the hell are we going?'

The mystery deepened on 3 January when the *Pensacola* handed over its escort duties to the cruiser USS *Houston*. Named after the Texas city when launched in 1929, the *Houston* was already a legend in the United States Navy. Before the ship was transferred to the Asiatic Fleet in Manila, President Roosevelt had undertaken four long voyages and made no secret of the fact that it was his favourite ship in the United States Navy. Since the *Houston* had slipped away from Manila in December and sailed to Java, the Japanese had claimed to have sunk her so many times that the cruiser was known in the navy as 'the Ghost of the Java Sea'.

Houston's main araments were nine 8-inch guns housed in three turrets of three guns apiece, two forward and one aft. There was a secondary battery of eight 5-inch anti-aircraft guns amidships, as well as .50-calibre machine-guns in waist hatches on both the main and foremasts, and four quadruple mounts of 1.1-inch guns mounted on either side of the signal bridge and amidships.

When the crew of the *Pensacola* caught sight of the *Houston*, she was in the company of three destroyers, *Alden*, *Whipple* and *Edsall*. Walter G. Winslow, the pilot of one of *Houston*'s four-scout observation planes, said: 'Those aboard the *Pensacola* were amazed to see the *Houston* and the four-funnel destroyers with us—they didn't believe there were so many ships left in the Asiatic Fleet. Their misinformation resulted from believing Radio Tokyo.'

New Year's Eve was a subdued affair on board the *Houston*, according to Winslow, with 'no horns, no champagne, no pretty girls, no bright lights, just a blacked-out ship and people fretfully attempting to sleep in the equatorial heat'. The same lack of celebration was also evident in Brisbane; although people were relieved to see the end of 1941, they greeted the prospects of the New Year with a sense of mounting dread.

Such gloom, however, did not extend to Lennon's Hotel or to its very important guests. The hotel's manager, Mrs Margaret Byrne, a vivacious middle-aged redhead, invited all American officers and an assortment of war correspondents to a traditional Hogmanay celebration.

'The table was loaded with food and the ceremony opened with a prayer for Australia and America,' said Mark Muller, one of the guests. 'Then a huge Scotsman appeared dressed in a kilt and piped in the haggis. When the piper stopped, a formal toast to the King and Queen was made. Next a toast to the President of the United States. I was feeling no pain as each toast represented a glassful of brandy. By the time the seven-course meal concluded, I could hardly stay awake.'

American war correspondents who had drifted into Brisbane from India, Asia and the United States gravitated to Lennon's, where they were briefed by Base 3 staff, usually by means of authorised press releases. 'The bar in Lennon's was the focal point of all activities because that was where everyone got his or her handout,' said Mark Muller. 'Some of the most beautiful women I have ever seen made their alliances with the Yank officers and correspondents there. The drinking and carousing went on until the bar closed because of curfew at midnight.'

Elsewhere in Brisbane, liquor sales were limited to a couple of two-hour swills each day, provided the daily beer quota lasted that long. Towards closing time, small groups of hardened drinkers would have as many as 40 beers lined up in front of them, while latecomers were told, 'Sorry, that's the end of the quota. Come back tomorrow.' Public holidays were cancelled and horse race meetings were restricted to the sand track at Albion Park because the army still had transit camps at

Ascot and Doomben. Milk and bread supplies were zoned, retail trading hours shortened and daylight saving was introduced, only to be abandoned after a short trial period.

The January heat was oppressive and so little rain had fallen during the previous 12 months that water restrictions were in force: there was a ban on showers and sprinklers and only five inches of water was permitted in the bathtub. Around the city, fortifications began to appear with a greater sense of urgency. Brick aprons were placed around government office doorways, water mains carrying river water were laid along the kerbs of main streets in case of incendiary attack. The blackout was enforced; school classes were restricted.

Around the city's fringes and in the country, new airfields were opened to receive squadrons of American warplanes, and secret storage spaces were found for explosives, ammunition and petrol in the disused tunnels of remote gold mines. 'We had a magazine depot for the navy in a big gorge at Mount Coot-tha, with torpedoes hidden under the branches of trees,' one US naval rating said. 'We had our own trucks pick them up at the docks, but we also needed to use some civilian vehicles. These had charcoal burners attached to the backs because of gasoline rationing, and it was touch and go whether they'd make it up the hills.'

The torpedoes were serviced at a monumental stonemason's yard in Fortitude Valley before being loaded onto submarines or destroyers in the Brisbane River. 'They made gravestones at this place out of marble and sandstone, and we took it over because it had cranes which we could use to hoist the torpedoes onto the work benches,' said the rating. 'The irony of working on a live torpedo surrounded by gravestones was not lost on us.'

Field ambulance services and search-and-rescue units were activated in the event of air raids. Igloo-shaped Nissen huts to house supplies sprang up in the suburbs from Eagle Junction and Nundah to Coopers Plains and Archerfield airfield. Searchlights from anti-aircraft batteries scanned the night skies and anti-aircraft batteries were manned round the clock.

It would not have helped the people of Brisbane to know that, in a Tokyo studio, Ida D'Aquino, a.k.a. Tokyo Rose, was learning to pronounce Queensland names like Camooweal and Charleville for her propaganda broadcasts. The Japanese already knew from spies on the Australian mainland where the new airfields were being sited.

The Rising Sun scorched ever further southward. More territories were added to the Greater East Asia Co-Prosperity Sphere whether they wanted to join or not. Two days into the New Year, the Japanese flag

(*Hi-no-maru*) fluttered over Manila. The Malay Peninsula provided stepping stones on Japan's path to the Dutch East Indies, allowing forces to leap-frog from Borneo and Celebes to Sumatra. The islands of Java, Bali and Timor were next in line, then New Britain and New Guinea and finally Australia.

Australia's only preparation to meet the invaders head-on had been to send the 2/22nd Battalion AIF to Rabaul, New Britain, to protect its forward airfields. Even though the Australian chiefs of staff knew this token force stood no chance of withstanding the Japanese, they were determined 'to make the enemy fight for this line, rather than abandon it at the first threat'. Rabaul fell on 23 January when an entire Japanese division swept ashore and, after encountering some stout resistance, had massacred most of the garrison.

Australia's Deputy Chief of General Staff, Lieutenant-General Sydney Rowell, privately commented: 'It's not the first time a few thousand men have been thrown away and it won't be the last.'

Australians were appalled when survivors reaching New Guinea described the slaughter of their comrades, and there was widespread concern at the proximity of the Japanese. The chiefs of staff secretly believed that the invasion of Rabaul would be followed by attempts to occupy Port Moresby and New Caledonia as a prelude to an attack on mainland Australia. Although American forces in Australia now numbered some 10,000, their presence had been kept secret, but not even that revelation would have prevented fear from spreading throughout the civilian population.

Unlike Australians, the Japanese public had been carefully conditioned for war. A three-year National Spiritual Mobilisation Movement had been launched by the Japanese government in October 1937 under which symbolic economies were encouraged, such as the Rising Sun lunchbox (*Hi-no-maru bento*), a pickled red plum on a bed of white rice reproducing the pattern of the national flag. When those three years were up, the government announced the New Order Movement to reorganise domestic society into more tightly controllable segments.

Progress had also been made on the international front to secure Japan's territorial demands from Russia and China. Japan's armed forces had been triumphant against the Chinese in Manchuria, then renamed Manchukuo, and hundreds of thousands of Japanese troops had been blooded in readiness for action in other theatres of war.

The Japanese soldier, committed to the Samurai warrior code of *Bushido*, became a figure of fear throughout Asia. When the militant Tojo became Prime Minister in October 1941, he adapted the martial mysticism and harsh discipline of *Bushido* into a code which promoted the ideology of conquest into a total commitment on the part of the soldier to winning, regardless of personal cost. Young soldiers going into battle were urged to fight fearlessly 'so as not to shame the spirits of the departed'. Talk of defeat was blasphemy; surrender a source of dishonour. It was a soldier's duty to die in battle rather than suffer the ignominy of capture, and any soldier who failed to uphold this principle had his name struck from official records, while his family faced public humiliation and ostracism.

Allied generals were forced to concede that the Japanese campaigns of December 1941 through the early months of 1942 had produced some of the most devastating victories in military history. With battles still raging in China, only 11 divisions had been devoted to the southward expansion, but Japan had ranged these limited forces against successive targets with such bewildering speed and to such stunning effect that British, Dutch and American prestige in Asia sank to a low point from which it never recovered.

In Japan, each new triumph of the Japanese Army was greeted by outbreaks of mass hysteria. 'Victory disease', it was called, and it spread like a virus.

Tojo claimed that this expansion was necessary to bring 'a new stable order in East Asia'. Japanese troops were indoctrinated with the belief that they were on a divine mission from their emperor-god Hirohito to liberate their Asian brothers and sisters from white tyranny. According to a political pamphlet handed to Japanese soldiers on their way to war, the colonial powers' 'greatest fear is that, with the help of a powerful Japan, the peoples of Asia will work together for independence. The aim of the present war is the realisation, first in the Far East, of His Majesty's august will and ideal that the people's of the world should each be granted possession of their rightful homelands.

'To this end, the countries of the Far East must plan a great coalition of East Asia. Through the combined strength of such a coalition we shall liberate East Asia from white invasion and oppression.'

In reality, the Greater East Asia Co-Prosperity Sphere brought its nominal beneficiaries nothing but economic chaos, hunger, devastation, torture and political suppression.

On 3 January, General George Brett attended his first conference between the American forces in Australia and the Australian chiefs of staff with the aim of achieving a harmonious working relationship that would lead to new bases being established in Australia to support military operations in the south-west Pacific region.

The meeting, held at Victoria Barracks in Melbourne, agreed to set up a joint planning committee to work towards these objectives, but although Brett was prepared to tread carefully in the new alliance, he knew that time was against him, particularly in getting aid to MacArthur's forces in the Philippines.

General Homma, now ensconced in MacArthur's suite at the Manila Hotel, was an aristocrat of the old school and he gave his rival general a sporting chance to surrender. MacArthur's answer was to emerge from the Malinta Tunnel wearing his soft, gold-braided field marshal's cap, carrying his mother's walking stick and smoking a corncob pipe. Thus attired, he observed the Japanese shelling of his troops and then set off on a day trip to Bataan—the only visit he made there—driving around in a Ford staff car and exhorting his men to greater sacrifice.

Summoning up visions of the *Pensacola* Convoy, he said: 'Help is on the way from the United States. Thousands of troops and hundreds of planes are being despatched. It is imperative that our troops hold until these reinforcements arrive. No further retreat is possible.'

MacArthur then went back into his tunnel on Corregidor, where he issued a barrage of communiques, singling himself out in such a manner that it appeared he was leading his men into one desperate clash with the enemy after another. His name was the only one to appear in these communiques; no one else of military rank rated a mention.

Under different circumstances, such egomania would have made MacArthur a laughing stock, but the troops on Bataan were too preoccupied with staying alive to feel like laughing.

When the *Holbrook* dropped anchor, Bill Heath found himself not in Manila but Darwin, the main port of northern Australia. The order for the transports to abandon their mission to the Philippines had been issued by General Brett. As the Japanese blockade controlled all sea lanes around the Philippines, Brett knew it was pointless sending the ships to almost certain destruction. With a fair wind and a bit of luck, however, they might still make Java.

The Kittyhawk fighters that MacArthur desperately wanted had been unloaded onto the Brisbane docks in their crates and were being assembled with great difficulty. Lieutenant Bob Firehock said: 'We were stationed at the racetrack for a while, getting the aircraft and other cargo off the convoy, sorting it all out, then shipping everything out to Amberley airfield, where the planes were put together by the B-17 ground crew who had originally been bound for Clark Field.

'They were bomber mechanics and it was like someone who'd been working on a Mack truck doing an MG: they missed out on some of the fine tunes. There were 12 pilots and only some of them had ever seen a Kittyhawk before. Most had never flown one and, of course, we had lots of problems. The P40s [Kittyhawks] had a Rolls-Royce inline engine and required Prestone [a brand of anti-freeze liquid coolant] and we had only four gallons here in Australia. We'd put it in a plane, send it up, fly around getting time in the air, land and then drain the radiator, get the four gallons and then put it in the next aircraft. In fact, they found a 44-gallon drum of it down in Adelaide, so they got a DC-3 to fly to Adelaide and pick it up, and one day we got six aircraft in the air at once. We had quite a problem getting the chemical formula for Prestone. It was a Shell patent and they wouldn't give it to us, so we had to put pressure on them through the British Government to give us the formula.

'There were also some Dauntless dive-bombers on the convoy and they were put together at Archerfield airfield in Brisbane. Quite a few of the aircraft that were sent to Darwin crashed on the way because none of the pilots had any experience in navigation. When they got to Darwin, RAAF Hudson bombers led them to Indonesia, heading for Java, but they got separated every once in a while from their bomber, lost their lead and crashed on the beaches or in the ocean when they ran out of fuel.

'Some of them landed in Java during air raids and were strafed before they could get out of the way. They didn't have any munitions on board to defend themselves because they needed all the tonnage they had in order to have enough fuel to get there. Every one of the planes from the *Pensacola* Convoy either crashed or was shot down in the first few months after we got them together.'

At Amberley, Byron Wilhite was put on administrative duties until a plane could be spared for him to fly, but he found it difficult to adjust to desk life. 'Headquarters in Brisbane, Base 3, is always riding me,' he wrote in his diary. 'They threatened to court-martial me the other night. I was talking on two phones at once and got so mad I hung up on Lieutenant Berry of the personnel office at Base 3. When I was next in Brisbane, I called at Lennon's to make the peace with Berry, but found the personnel office closed for the day. It was a little late for those boys to be open. We stay on duty until the small hours, but that's too much to ask of them.'

Wilhite talked to some of the American pilots who had flown down from Manila in search of new planes to take back. 'They include 1st Lieutenant Boyd "Buzz" Wagner, America's first ace of World War II,' wrote Wilhite. 'They've been giving us some instructions on combat flying. They let us gather that the Jap Zero is no toy, but try to make us believe that American planes with experienced pilots are more than a match for them. But where are the experienced pilots? The ones we have here are kids just out of flying school—kids just like me. It sort of gives us an empty feeling in our guts. There is no doubt we have underrated the Japanese pilots.'

Matters between Wilhite and the Base 3 brass came to a head when one of the pilots at Amberley, a Lieutenant Hamilton, was killed in a training accident. After he had landed his Kittyhawk, Hamilton had climbed onto the wing to inspect some damage and the wing of a second plane, coming in low on its landing approach, struck him in the middle of the back, killing him instantly.

In front of Wilhite, Colonel Alexander Johnson, commanding officer of Base 3 since General Barnes's posting to Melbourne, said: 'Second lieutenants are expendable.' To which Wilhite replied: 'Everything is expendable in time of war, Colonel.'

In recounting the episode in his diary he added: 'I gave him a look that implied more than I actually said. He has planned a big party to celebrate his promotion to general, but he hasn't gotten it yet and I hope he won't. I have never seen such a conglomeration of stupid, ignorant nonentities as him and his staff. When they have to make generals out of pricks like him we are in a very sad state indeed.'

In the Philippines, MacArthur celebrated his 62nd birthday on 26 January, which also happened to be Australia Day. Festivities for both anniversaries were cancelled, owing to war. President Quezon asked Roosevelt to declare the Philippines neutral, which would enable him to demand that America and Japan both withdraw their forces from his country. Roosevelt, however, urged Quezon to fight on, but gave MacArthur permission to surrender if the position became untenable. General Marshall wanted MacArthur to evacuate his wife and son by submarine, but he declined, declaring that he and his family intended 'to share the fate of the garrison'.

In Brisbane, Mark Muller was at his desk in the signal centre at Lennon's Hotel when Major-General Patrick J. Hurley, a former United States Secretary of War and great friend of MacArthur, strode in.

'I felt someone's presence and looked up,' said Muller. 'Standing in front of me was a very tall and impressive individual wearing the insignia of a one-star general. He was almost 6 foot 4 inches with a stern face complete with handlebar moustache.'

'Are you the signal officer in charge?' asked Hurley.

'Yes, Sir.'

'Do you have a safe I can lock this up in?' The general held up a large briefcase.

'Yes, Sir, and I can have a guard in the hall allow no access to the room overnight.'

'That's not good enough, Lieutenant. I want you to lock the safe, and sleep in front of it *and* have the guard outside.'

Muller spent the night on a bed in front of the safe containing Hurley's briefcase, while a guard patrolled the hallway.

At 7.30 in the morning, the general was back. 'I opened the safe and handed the case to him,' said Muller. 'He placed it on the desk and snapped open the locks. My eyes almost popped out of my head. The case contained bundles of high denomination Federal Treasury banknotes.'

Hurley told him: 'I don't take anything for granted. I check this case every time it's locked up. There are several million dollars here to hire relief ships to send to General MacArthur in the Philippines.'

When Hurley was satisfied that everything was in order, he set off for the airport, where his personal B-17 was waiting to take him to Java via Darwin and Kupang, Timor. Hurley would not have been surprised to learn that all three places were prime targets on the Japanese war map, but he was determined to get supplies through to MacArthur.

His plan was to bribe the skippers of merchant ships to run the Japanese blockade, regardless of the risk to the crews.

Chapter Five

—◁◦▷—

Provost Marshal

NORBERT J. Grant, a native son of Wisconsin, had no intention of becoming a provost marshal when he was drafted into the US Army as recruit number 36246528. Grant was as surprised as any of the other members of his intake when they were ordered to report to Fort Sheridan, Chicago, to join the 738th Military Police Battalion.

The battalion had been activated on 1 February 1942, and was fairly evenly split between draftees, national guardsmen and regular army men. There were five companies in the 738th, A, B, C, D and Headquarters; Grant was in C Company along with 140 other men under the command of Captain George V. Cockburn. Some of his comrades were equipped with good police-sounding names like Richard A. Hoover, Steve W. Maddox, Burr F. Monroe and Earle S. Stange.

One of the recruits, Alton C. Jensen, said: 'Prior to January 1942, the army, as a rule, did not have military police battalions. They had military police companies which were part of a division and it wasn't very satisfactory because many of the men who were in those companies were misfits. Then the War Department set up a group of officers at Fort Sheridan to work out a table of organisation for the military police and on 1 February 1942 various MP battalions were designated with numbers in the 700s, of which we were one.

'The military police companies that were already in existence consisted of small cadres of semi-trained men who did patrol work around Chicago. They had been culled from cavalry and infantry divisions and— from the ones I knew—a lot of them were misfits who had been thrown

61

out simply to get rid of them. A lot of them were from the south and they had to be moulded into shape as good military police people, but before that happened they were in all kinds of trouble.

'I was a teacher at a public school in Grantsburg, Wisconsin, and I was drafted on 11 June 1942, along with a whole bunch of other men from Wisconsin, Illinois and Michigan. We were put into the 738th to fill out the battalion's nucleus. Although I was 32, most of the new draftees were young men, some as young as 17 who weren't supposed to be in—you were supposed to be 18—but many were also lawyers, civil engineers, teachers and bankers in their twenties or thirties and we even had some bartenders who were 40 years old.'

The 738th's commanding officer was Colonel William Kester, an old campaigner from World War I whose main preoccupation in his leisure time was playing bridge. Kester was gratified to discover that the average IQ of his troops, which had stood at a lowly 85 owing to the 'misfit factor', had shot up 20 points to 105 after the influx of the draftees from Wisconsin, Illinois and Michigan.

Jensen said: 'There were two forms of military police: those who were supposed to stay in the States and those who could be shipped anywhere around the world. We were drafted into the ones who were supposed to stay in the States and then, lo and behold, they needed military police in Australia so they got the order changed because some of our people— the misfits—were considered to have been trained already. In fact, we were already under overseas shipment orders when we got to Fort Sheridan and that's absolutely unheard-of because the army says you've got to be trained before you go overseas.

'We had a couple of lectures on the duties of the military police, but most of us were still doing basic military training and we did very little of that. We were not taught about military law as such and there were no lessons in unarmed combat; the main thing we found out to start with was that we were going to be doing street patrol work. We were given MP armbands, dark blue or black with white letters, to go with our khaki uniforms and we had regular peaked caps instead of steel helmets. Then, after only a month in the army, we were sent overseas. What the army wants to do and what the army says they're going to do are two different things. The army does what it wants to do in times of war.'

The United States had mobilised its 18 undermanned and poorly equipped national guard divisions during 1940 in response to the war in Europe. According to an official army estimation at that time, 'It was largely an army of amateurs in which many officers were occupied chiefly in learning how to be officers, and the men were being trained with scant equipment, and without realisation, on their part, of the dead seriousness of the task ahead. The vast majority had not completely buckled down to business; they did not conceive themselves as future fighters. Their eyes were still on an early return to civil life rather than on the conflict steadily enveloping greater and greater portions of the globe.'

One of the first divisions to be called to active service was the 32nd, which, like the new 738th Military Police Battalion, had its feet firmly planted in Michigan and Wisconsin. The division had been created in 1917 and built around four regiments of national guard infantrymen, two from Michigan and two from Wisconsin. There were also three artillery regiments, one from Michigan and two from Wisconsin.

Under the command of Major-General William G. Haan, the 32nd had gone to Europe as part of the American Expeditionary Forces during World War I and fought German troops on the Western Front, often forming flying wedges to break through enemy lines. The AEF's commander-in-chief, General John J. Pershing, noted in his diary on 2 September 1918: 'Our 32nd Division has done splendid work in attack as part of the French Tenth Army.'

The division returned to the States with the names of four big engagements—Alsace, Aisne-Marne, Oise-Aisne, and Meuse-Argonne—stitched to its battle streamers. The 32nd sustained no fewer than 13,500 casualties, 3000 of whom had either been killed in action or had died of wounds. For their valour, each of the infantry regiments was awarded the *Croix de Guerre avec Palme* by the French Government.

French soldiers who fought side-by-side with units of the 32nd in the crossing of the Vesle and Aisne rivers against heavy German bombardments gave them a nickname: *Les Terribles*.

At the end of the war, each division in the AEF was ordered to choose an identifying symbol and Major-General Haan decided that a barred red arrow was more emblematic of the division's character than the existing red circle. Haan said: 'I chose the barred arrow as the division symbol because we pierced every line the Boche put before us.' Thus the men of the 32nd became known as the Red Arrows, although older members were still respectfully known as *Les Terribles*.

In February 1941 the 32nd was transferred to Camp Livingston down in the Red River country, where Wisconsin units had fought with distinction during the American Civil War. The whole division took part in the biggest peacetime manoeuvre in the history of the United States Army when more than 400,000 men of the 2nd and 3rd Armies were pitted against each other in the swamps of Louisiana and the rough terrain of eastern Texas. The 32nd were among the 270,000 men of the

3rd Army under the command of Lieutenant-General Walter Krueger who slugged it out for eight weeks against 130,000 men of the 2nd Army. Krueger's chief of staff at the time, Colonel Dwight D. Eisenhower, noted that 'the beneficial results of that great manoeuvre were incalculable'.

The most immediate benefit was that General George Marshall had a chance to assess the performance of the guardsmen's senior officers, many of whom were political appointees, with the result that he sacked a large number of generals and colonels and replaced them with regular army officers. The war games had also made it depressingly obvious to Marshall that the guards divisions were a long way from being ready to confront an enemy in armed combat.

On 9 February 1942, Major-General Edwin Forrest Harding took command of the 32nd, which had been reorganised into a triangular division based on three infantry regiments and renamed the 32nd Infantry Division. Harding was then 55 years old and had served in China, the Philippines and Hawaii. When he received orders from the Pentagon to rebase the 32nd at Fort Devens, Massachusetts, it looked as though he was going to add one of the European theatres of war to his wide-ranging record. The Combined Chiefs of Staff, representing the United States and Great Britain, had in fact decided to send the 32nd to Northern Ireland, but events unfolding in the south-west Pacific changed all that with shattering consequences for the Red Arrows.

Singapore was broiling hot and saturatingly humid. Gentlemen of the Oriental Raj wore tropical suits with starched shirts, collar and tie, and perhaps a panama hat; ladies took tiffin under the swaying punkahs at Raffles Hotel in summer cotton dresses and large, wilting straw bonnets. Cricket and polo were popular sports; bridge was practically compulsory.

But these trappings of colonial life disappeared from December 1941 onwards with the same rapidity as the Japanese advance down the Malay Peninsula. None of the British bureaucrats who ran Singapore had seriously believed that the colony was in any real danger. Malaya could fall and the island fortress would still remain impregnable; even the Japanese must know that—everybody else did.

Since Admiral Jellicoe had chosen Singapore as the base of the British Far Eastern Fleet in 1919, the colossal sum of £60 million had been spent on fortifications, culminating in 1938 with the installation at Changi naval base of 15-inch cannons that fired armour-piercing shells capable of sinking any ship afloat.

At the time of the Japanese invasion, air and land defences of the peninsula and its island fortress had been in the trembling hands of Air

Chief Marshal Sir Robert Brooke-Popham for just over a year. In the 'jobs for the boys' manner in which Britain ruled its empire, Brooke-Popham had been appointed Governor of Kenya and commander-in-chief of the armed forces after his retirement from the RAF in 1937. Arriving in Singapore in late 1940 to take up his awesome new posting at the age of 62, he found himself incapable of adapting to either the political or equatorial climates and snoozed through many crucial meetings of the Defence Committee.

Brooke-Popham knew there was a chronic shortage of modern aircraft in Singapore and that many of the garrison's troops were non-combatants, yet he went to Sydney in February 1941 and assured the Australian War Cabinet that Singapore could defend itself for six months, giving a British battlefleet ample time to arrive and protect it from a Japanese invasion. Privately, he doubted that this was true and later admitted that he had given the Australian Government 'a less than comprehensive survey of his view of the situation'. In other words, he had deliberately misled them. One must not appear hesitant among the colonials.

In the absence of sufficient men or *matériel* to defend the island properly, British strategists clung to the belief that an attack would come from the heavily defended seaward direction and very little was done to defend the causeway side bordering the Straits of Jahore. The key to stopping the Japanese was air power and Brooke-Popham, knowing that Churchill's main priority was to provide new fighter planes to Stalin on the Eastern Front, kept quiet about his desperate need for up-to-date bombers and fighters. His stiff upper lip might have trembled when Alfred Duff Cooper, Churchill's special envoy to Asia, urged him to make fresh demands, but he remained obstinately mute. According to Duff Cooper, Brooke-Popham 'sometimes seems on the verge of nervous collapse'.

One of the few liberated women in Singapore was Brooke-Popham's secretary, a young army wife, Beryl Stevenson. A few games of bridge with a British brigadier during a Kiplingesque cruise across the Bay of Bengal had taken the attractive Australian brunette into the heart of the British high command in Singapore. Her husband, Lieutenant John Drysdale Stevenson of the Manchester Regiment, was stationed in the colony, but the couple had been forced to separate shortly after their wedding because wives of British army personnel were banned from living there.

No such regulation applied in India, however, and when 'Steve', as Beryl's husband was called, was sent to Poona on an officers' training course in 1941, she flew from Sydney to join him. 'We had a wonderful seven or eight weeks in Poona and then Steve was booked on a ship to go back from Madras to Singapore,' she said. 'We decided I'd go down with him to Madras and after he'd sailed I'd fly back to Sydney on the first plane.

'We were delayed for a week in Madras, one of the world's sweatiest, most teeming cities. There was one air-conditioned pub, the Connamarra Hotel, with a great avenue of royal palms leading up to the entrance. Every Caucasian within riding distance dined at the Connamarra Hotel and, by one of life's miracles, we met the captain of the boat that was to carry Steve back across the Bay of Bengal to Singapore. The captain felt sorry for me and found a cabin for us on his ship, a dirty little P&O steamer out of the pages of Kipling. Our cargo was raw onions in the lower hold and raw Indian recruits on the decks. On the captain's small deck there was the postmaster-general of Kuala Lumpur and his wife, and two brigadier-generals from Fort Canning, the centre of the British army command in Singapore.

'There was no room for this handful of passengers even to walk, so we played bridge all the way across the Bay of Bengal. Whenever one of the brigadiers played with me, he won, so he got the impression I had a brain. When I got to Singapore, I had to report to the police and it was made plain to me that there was a plane leaving for Sydney on the third day and I had to be on it. On the morning of the second day, this brigadier rang me from Fort Canning and said, "Put on your best bib and tucker. I'm taking you out to the naval base to introduce you to the commander-in-chief. He needs a secretary." So I started to work for Air Chief Marshal Sir Robert Brooke-Popham, the man who mucked things up. It was May 1941 and I had both a job and the right to stay in Singapore.'

Beryl worked for Brooke-Popham for eight months until he was relieved of his command on 27 December and ordered home to England when it had become apparent that a major catastrophe was in the making. The sinking of the battleship *Prince of Wales* and the battle cruiser *Repulse* by Japanese planes off the Malayan coast earlier that month had shocked Australians, who seriously started to question Britain's defence strategy in Asia. While the British persisted in referring to the region as the Far East in relation to her own shores, Singapore and her Asian neighbours seemed to be drawing ever closer to Australia.

Prime Minister John Curtin had a sense of foreboding when he noted on 5 January 1942: 'The truth is that Britain never thought Japan would fight and made no preparations to meet that eventuality.' When he learned that the Defence Committee in London had debated the abandonment of Singapore, Curtin cabled Churchill on 23 January:

'After all the assurances we have been given, the evacuation of Singapore would be regarded here and elsewhere as an inexcusable betrayal.'

Even more unsettling was the comment of the new General Officer Commanding Malaya, Lieutenant-General Arthur Percival, that 'defences are bad for morale—for both troops and civilians'. Percival's fighting talk might have carried more weight had he been a more imposing figure himself, but he was tall and reed-thin, with buck teeth protruding from under a clipped moustache. Like many of the British officer class, he regarded the Japanese as racially inferior, myopic little men who could not be taken seriously as soldiers or airmen. This was to prove a fatal piece of xenophobia.

Curtin knew it was too late to make up for British folly and planned the defence of Australia from an entirely different perspective. In a cable to Washington, he said: 'From all reports it is very evident that in North Malaya the Japanese have assumed control of air and sea. The small British army there includes one Australian division, and we have sent three air squadrons to Malaya and two to the Netherlands East Indies.

'The army must be provided with air support, otherwise there will be a repetition of Greece and Crete, and Singapore will be grievously threatened. The fall of Singapore would mean the isolation of the Philippines, the fall of the Netherlands East Indies and an attempt to smother all other bases. This would also sever our communications between the Indian and Pacific Oceans in this region. The setback would be as serious to United States' interests as to our own.

'Reinforcements earmarked by the United Kingdom for despatch to Malaya seem to us to be utterly inadequate, especially in relation to aircraft and more particularly fighting aircraft. It is in your power to meet the situation. Should the United States desire, we would gladly accept United States command in the Pacific Ocean area. The President has said that Australia will be a base of the utmost importance, but in order that it shall remain a base, Singapore must be reinforced. In spite of our great difficulties we are sending further reinforcements to Malaya. Please consider this a matter of the greatest urgency.'

Roosevelt and Churchill had secretly reaffirmed their 'Germany first' policy at a summit conference in Washington over Christmas under which the bulk of America's war effort would be committed to Europe at the expense of Asia. But the President told Curtin that he and Churchill had given 'most urgent consideration' to Australia's request, while Churchill personally promised Curtin, in a bout of florid sabre-rattling, that he intended to defend Singapore 'with the utmost tenacity'.

This was pure bombast. After taking control of the air on the very first day of the Malayan campaign and routing the defending Indian troops on the Thai border, Japanese infantry had mounted up for the world's first 'blitzkrieg by bicycle', pedalling furiously southward through the rubber plantations, while their artillery and tanks followed along the peninsula's system of well-made roads. The Australian 2/30th Battalion of the 8th Division was waiting for them in Johore province and, at Gemas, staged a well-practised and devastating ambush. More than 1000 Japanese soldiers on bicycles were trapped in a ring of gunfire after the Australians blew up the bridge behind them. The Australians claimed that hundreds of Japanese were killed in the ambush at a loss of 76 Australian dead and wounded.

The diggers then contained the Japanese at the Muar River on the coast in what General Percival was moved to describe as 'one of the epics of the Malayan campaign'. After a week's heavy fighting, the defenders were cut off by flanking movements and had to make a fighting retreat towards Singapore, leaving their wounded at the mercy of the Japanese. As in Rabaul, their fate was horrific. They were 'herded together with kicks, curses, blows from rifle butts and jabs from bayonets', led away at sunset, roped or wired together, doused with petrol and burned alive.

Churchill, who had never believed that Japan would make war in the Pacific, was suddenly confronted with 'the hideous spectacle of the almost naked island and of the wearied, if not exhausted, troops retreating upon it'. Woefully late, he demanded to know from his defence chiefs why fortifications, barbed wire entanglements and gun batteries had not been installed during the two and a half years of war to protect the island from an attack from the mainland.

Churchill wrote angrily to General Hastings Ismay, Chairman of the Joint Chiefs of Staff Committee on 19 January: 'I must confess to being staggered. It never occurred to me for a moment that the gorge of the fortress of Singapore with its splendid moat half a mile wide was not entirely fortified against an attack from the northward. What is the use of having an island for a fortress if it is not to be made into a citadel? How is it that not one of you pointed this out to me at any time when these matters have been under discussion?'

Fifty-one Hurricanes, 24 British pilots and thousands of British troops were rushed to Singapore in the last convoy to reach the besieged island. The Hurricanes (not the latest model) were unpacked from their crates, rapidly assembled and sent into action harassing the Japanese forces in the plantations at the southern tip of Johore. Although they inflicted casualties, most were shot down in dogfights with the technically superior Zeros.

Meantime, Percival ordered the destruction of fuel and ammunition dumps that hadn't already been destroyed by relentless Japanese bombing, in which thousands among the colony's Chinese population had been killed or wounded.

The exodus from Singapore turned into the most hazardous evacuation of the war, with Japanese planes strafing and bombing any craft that left Keppel Harbour. Hundreds of ships set out for Sumatra and Java, partially obscured by clouds of black smoke rising into the air from blazing fuel dumps, but many were sunk before they had a chance to leave the protective cover of shore-based, anti-aircraft batteries, and many others did not get much further than the entrance to Banka Strait. The Japanese allowed inbound ships to proceed into port on the basis that the supplies they were carrying would simply add to the size of their booty when the island fell.

Rohan Rivett, a 23-year-old Australian reporter working for the Malaya Broadcasting Corporation, described the scene as he escaped from Singapore in a dilapidated Yangtze riverboard: 'Silhouetted by the surrounding fires, watching the labour and planning of many years and the fruit of millions of pounds of expenditure disappearing into clouds of smoke before one's eyes, one would indeed have needed to be mineral or vegetable to remain unmoved.

'Here was being enacted the last scene of one more major human tragedy, its very splendour underlining the magnitude and bitterness of our own defeat. No Australian could suppress feelings of bitterness and disgust at the thought of the difference between the impregnable fortress depicted for, and believed in by, the people of Australia, and the virtually defenceless island on which our troops, with their British and Indian fellow-soldiers, were now making a last stand.'

One of the ill-fated vessels was the *Vyner Brooke*, a small steamer which was attacked and sunk off the Sumatran coast. Twenty-two nurses and a number of wounded men survived the shipwreck and managed to reach Banka Island, where they were discovered by a Japanese patrol. The men were dragged into the undergrowth and bayoneted to death, then the nurses were ordered to walk into the sea, where they were all shot. One nurse, Sister Vivian Bullwinkel, feigned death after being wounded and later crawled out of the surf; although she was recaptured, she survived the war to tell the world about the atrocity.

Beryl Stevenson was among the last European women to be evacuated from Singapore and her husband 'Steve' waved a forlorn farewell from the quayside at Keppel Harbour. 'I sailed on a small boat, the SS *Anking*, with a friend, Elspeth Evans, whose husband was an officer in Steve's battalion,' said Beryl. 'I had Brooke-Popham's GHQ records in my possession and we went to Java, where the new headquarters was being set up.'

A new unified command with a title as improbable as its projected aims—the American, British, Dutch and Australian Command, ABDACOM for short—was established at the upland resort of Lembang, near the capital of Bandung in the Javanese interior. Churchill and Roosevelt had thrashed out the details of ABDACOM at the Arcadia summit meeting in Washington and come up with the absurd expectation that Wavell, who had been appointed Commander-in-Chief at Roosevelt's prompting, would defend a line stretching 4000 miles from west to east without the assistance of a battlefleet or control of the air. Wavell's deputy in this vainglorious enterprise was the genial American, General George Brett, who had come up from Melbourne to serve with him. Australian officers, however, were excluded from senior posts in the new command structure because it was still taken for granted that Britain spoke for Australia.

Beryl Stevenson was at the heart of the operation. She said: 'The war couldn't really start in Java until the office got there, as it were, and when we arrived in Batavia it was all pretty haphazard and a bit chaotic. We were put up in fancy hotels for a few days before being transported to Lembang. Once headquarters was set up, Wavell arrived and I worked mainly for his chief of staff.

'Our office was on the Bandung side of the building and although all the bigwigs were there, there were very few Indians; handfuls of generals and air marshals, but no Indians. So although I was officially the chief of staff's secretary in the office next door to Wavell, I was doing work for people all down the line, including the poor ciphers officer who was a fortnight behind [with his work]. Oh, what a sham! General Brett's office was within the headquarters, even though most of the American work was done at Andeer, the airport down the hill.

'The first time I saw Brett was when the President's representative Patrick J. Hurley arrived for a visit. Hurley was obviously a big shot and the Americans had a dinner party for him at a hotel down in Bandung. Women were in very short supply, so they scraped up the half dozen women who were around headquarters to decorate the occasion. Elspeth Evans and Louise Mowat, an English woman I hadn't met until that point, and I received invitations. On the day of the dinner party, to our amusement, corsages arrived for us to wear with our dresses—it was our first introduction to the American scene.'

The last time Beryl had heard from her husband Steve was when she received a card from him for her birthday on 14 January; she would not hear another word from him to say he was alive for more than a year. Singapore, the Gibraltar of the Orient and cornerstone of an Empire upon which the sun never set, went down in a blaze of ignominy when the British capitulated on 15 February. At the Ford motor works on Bukit Timah Hill, Percival handed over the Union Jack to the Japanese commander, General Tomoyuki Yamashita, as well as the lives of 85,000 Allied troops, including 14,972 Australians, mainly members of the 8th Division.

Singapore was renamed *Syonan* (Sunny South), the bronze statue of Stamford Raffles disappeared from its plinth in Raffles Square and the clocks were put forward 90 minutes to correspond with Tokyo time.

Beryl said: 'I took a walk that day out of the office and up onto a nearby hill through the wild briar roses and the tall grass. I remember the smile of a little Javanese girl whom I encountered on the track. We didn't have a word to exchange, but I have a vivid memory of that little girl among the wild roses. I didn't know whether my husband had been killed in the fighting or been taken prisoner, but I remember that walk because I knew to some extent what was ahead.'

The same fear gripped many thousands of Australian families whose menfolk were either in the 8th Division or with one of the other services trapped in Singapore. In Brisbane, 15-year-old Estelle Runcie (now Mrs Estelle Pinney) was worried about her cousin Darcy, who was in the Royal Australian Navy. 'At 15, one of my ambitions was to have a Singapore sling at Raffles Hotel,' she said. 'We knew the British had Singapore, so everything was supposed to be all right up there. Then we listened to the wireless for news and the fall of Singapore came as a terrible, collective shock.

'It finally filtered through to me what a disaster it was when I heard about my cousin Darcy. He was bombed on one ship, got onto a raft, was bombed again but got off that. We heard he had been taken prisoner of war, but then we were told he was missing, believed dead. We never saw him again.'

There was no shortage of high-ranking candidates to blame for the greatest military defeat in British history, but in the end the poor bloody infantry were singled out for the lion's share of odium. According to British military historians, Brooke-Popham was 'unjustly attacked' and Percival 'unfairly blamed', while Duff Cooper was similarly exonerated of any guilt.

However, Major-General Gordon Bennett, commander of the 8th Division who had escaped from Singapore after the capitulation, was a prime target for criticism, which he quickly deflected elsewhere. Safely back in Sydney, he laid the bulk of the blame on the 'low morale of Indian troops', although he could hardly be described as an impartial witness.

Wavell was certain about one thing: he was not going to take the blame. In his official report of June 1942, he said bluntly: 'For the fall of Singapore itself, the Australians are held responsible.'

This was as unfair as pinning the blame on the Japanese for invading in the first place, but fairness was not uppermost in Wavell's mind. It was true that once the Allies had failed to halt the Japanese advance, a number of Australians deserted their posts and commandeered boats to make a getaway. But this was also true of British and Indian troops; furthermore, the Australians had incurred 73 per cent of the deaths in battle although they comprised only 14 per cent of the Commonwealth land forces in Malaya. Privately, Wavell wrote to his former secretary Joan Bright Astley: 'I feel I ought to have pulled it off, but the dice were rather heavily loaded and the little yellow man threw them with considerable cunning.'

The ultimate responsibility, however, went full-circle back to London and landed on Churchill's desk in the War Cabinet bunker in Whitehall. For all his fiery, well-honed rhetoric about 'Fortress Singapore', Churchill had to admit that 'the possibility of Singapore having no landward defences no more entered into my mind than that of a battleship being launched without a bottom.'

Yet it was Churchill himself who had demanded huge cutbacks in Singapore's defence spending when he had served as Chancellor of the Exchequer in Baldwin's government.

The real legacy of the fall of Singapore was that Australia was pitched headlong into her wartime union with the United States. Thousands more American soldiers started to stream down the gangplanks in Brisbane, Sydney and Melbourne.

One of them was Private Edward J. Leonski, a 24-year-old New Yorker, a six-footer with fair hair, a well-developed chest and muscular arms. Leonski had left San Francisco with the 52nd Signal Battalion in the Matson liner *Mariposa* on 12 January and reached Melbourne on 2 February. He had been sent to an army camp at Royal Park, where he was put in tent No. 16 in an area assigned to headquarters company of the 52nd Signal Battalion.

Leonski did not want to be there. The day the battalion had left Fort Sam Houston in San Antonio, Texas, according to one of his bunkmates, 'he started crying and several of the men packed his bags for him. The night before we left, he was drunk. He did not want to come to Australia.' Leonski hated the army because it had separated him from the two women in his life: his mother, whom he worshipped, and his sister-in-law, with whom he was in love. Both women were in New York City, where Leonski had been drafted, and he had not seen either of them since he was posted to boot camp. In particular, Leonski was tormented by his separation from his sister-in-law. 'Every time he started to think of her, he would go out and get drunk,' said one of his buddies, 'and once he had a few beers in him, he always wanted to head for the west side.'

The west side was the red light district of San Antonio, where Mexican prostitutes were cheap and plentiful. It was during one of these trips into the *barrio* that Eddie Leonski met a girl called Beatrice Sanchez. In the darkness, he tried to strangle her.

Major Hayford O. Enwall of the US Army commented: 'It was unfortunate that the young woman apparently did not wish to press her assault charge which might have terminated Leonski's army career.'

Leonski went drinking in the bars around Royal Park and was soon showing off in front of the other customers. He'd gulp down a cocktail of beer and whisky spiced with chilli peppers, ketchup and mustard. His favourite prank in tent No. 16 was to heave a sleeping man out of his bunk and dump him on the floor, hoping it would provoke a fight. Colonel Spencer B. Eddy said: 'Eddie Leonski lived in a world of fantasy. He was crazy as hell. He should never have been taken into the army.'

In primly conservative Melbourne, Leonski's lack of chivalry marked him out among the other uniforms. No other soldier grabbed young women in the street and made them kiss him the way Leonski did, then insist they said 'Prunes' before he would let them go.

His drinking buddies regarded these gaucheries as the horseplay of a socially inept lout, but, unknown to them, one evening Leonski tried to strangle a young married woman in her flat in St Kilda. Overcoming blind panic, she managed to break free and run out into the night. It was the first of several attacks on women that would cast a long shadow over the city.

Gunner Edward Webster's progress back to civvy street was proving more difficult than he had expected. He had embarked with other members of the 2/2nd Anti-Tank Regiment at Port Tewfik at the southern end of the Suez Canal on 31 January, but his hopes of a trouble-free passage home soon evaporated and there was every chance he might find himself back in action again—this time fighting the Japanese.

Lieutenant Lance Watts said: 'We reached Bombay in the liner *Mauritania* on 6 February and changed over to the tramp steamer *Egra*, which was a bit of a comedown. The *Egra* had been built in Belfast in 1911 and was showing signs of old age. The captain was only half-joking when he told us, "Careful you don't knock off any paint or we'll leak".

'We set sail for Singapore on Friday the thirteenth of February, but it fell before we got there. Then we were diverted to Batavia in the

Dutch East Indies and we were only about four hours out of Batavia when the Japs beat us to it. One of our boats in a second convoy, the *Orcades*, did get into Batavia and unloaded pioneers and machine gunners there. They tried to get across Java down to the southern end, but most of the villagers were on the side of the Japs and they all ended up in the clink. However, a lot of Dutch people got out of Batavia on the *Orcades*—that's why they put our troops off the ship; they replaced them with civilians.'

Bruce Eglinton wrote in his diary on 15 February: 'Damnably hot now and we feel dirty and clammy all day. The news I've been awaiting came through today: Singapore has surrendered to the Japs. Perhaps it will be interesting later to read what things look like now. Seems a certainty that we shall go to Java. The chances of landing safely are quite good, as I see it, though most of the chaps think this convoy will have some excitement first. As for Java, methinks we will be in an evacuation yet if we go there. Air and sea support were the reasons Singapore fell, I think, and that will be why we won't be able to hold any island like Java. Perhaps this is the worst moment so far of the war, yet the result of the fall of Singapore seems to be that the war will last years longer now.'

The *Egra* headed back into the Indian Ocean to await further orders, which were slow in coming through owing to a serious political dispute between Churchill and Curtin. Lieutenant Bill Thomas said: 'We did a 12-day circuit of the Indian Ocean while Curtin and Churchill had a disagreement over where we should go.' The troops sweltered in the clammy heat of the wet season, played cards, wrote letters, watched dolphins at play and scanned the airwaves for any news that might throw a light on their ultimate destination.

After the fall of Singapore, Curtin had become involved in a battle of wills with Churchill over the placement of the 6th and 7th divisions in new theatres of war. 'Curtain and Churchill were at it, arguing over what to do with us,' said Lieutenant Watts. 'Curtain wanted us to come home and Churchill wanted us to go to Burma, and at one point we *were* going in the direction of Rangoon. We were sailing merrily along, then the next day we'd turn around and go south, the next day north again. It was quite a hectic trip, although we didn't know anything of this on the boat; we were more or less kept in the dark.'

Australia's Chief of General Staff, Lieutenant-General Vernon Sturdee, had a reputation for unflappability, but he believed that the troops offloaded in Java would probably be lost and he threatened to resign unless the government pressed Britain for the AIF's immediate return to Australia.

Even couched in diplomatic language, the cables exchanged between Curtin and Churchill at the height of the crisis showed the ferocity of the argument. Curtin wrote angrily to the British Prime Minister: 'It appears that you have diverted the convoy towards Rangoon and had treated our approval to this vital diversion as merely a matter of form. By doing so you have established a physical situation which adds to the dangers of this convoy, and the responsibility for the consequences of such diversion rests on you.

'We have already informed the President of the reasons for our decision, and, having regard to the terms of his communications to me, we are quite satisfied from his sympathetic reply that he fully understands and appreciates the reasons for our decision. Australia's outer defences are now quickly vanishing and our vulnerability is completely exposed. With AIF troops we sought to save Malaya and Singapore, falling back on the Netherlands East Indies. All these northern defences are gone or going. Now you contemplate using the AIF to save Burma. All this has been done, as in Greece, without air support. We feel a primary obligation to save Australia not only for itself, but to preserve it as a base for the development of the war against Japan.'

Churchill's cable explained: 'We could not contemplate that you would refuse our request, and that of the President of the United States, for the diversion of the leading Australian division [the 7th] to save the situation in Burma. We knew that if our ships proceeded on their course to Australia while waiting for your formal approval they would either arrive too late at Rangoon or even be without enough fuel to go there at all.

'We therefore decided that the convoy should be temporarily diverted to the northward. The convoy is now too far north for some of the ships in it to reach Australia without refuelling. These physical considerations give a few days for the situation to develop, and for you to review the position should you wish to do so. Otherwise the leading Australian division will be returned to Australia as quickly as possible.'

Curtin's firm stand had dramatically altered Australia's relationship with Britain, prompting Churchill to grumble that Australians came from 'bad stock'—a cheap shot at the country's convict origins.

Lieutenant Watts summed up the outcome: 'We went back to Colombo to revital [sic] and refuel and then we set sail for Australia under battleship escort.'

Australian troops returning home from the Middle East found the population in an edgy mood. The last illusory shred of innocence had been ripped from their eyes with the bombing of Darwin on

19 February. This was the first time in history that the Australian mainland had been attacked and it had been a salutary lesson. Refugees from Darwin had fled to other Australian cities with horror stories of the raid; of the failure of the air-raid warning system; of the panic among civilians; of the cowardice of some Australian servicemen; of the brute force and savagery of the Japanese.

If Pearl Harbor had been an American calamity and Singapore a British disaster, Darwin was Australia's very own debacle. With the enemy known to be advancing to within air striking distance, the town's lack of readiness amounted to criminal neglect. Resistance was so low that, when the smoke cleared, one RAAF officer remarked that 100 Japanese armed with frying pans could have occupied Darwin that day.

The Japanese high command had approved plans for an air raid on Darwin immediately after Pearl Harbor using the same task force that had struck the American Pacific Fleet. Reconnaissance showed that the town was an ideal bombing target. Its wide, open harbour was packed with Allied shipping on its way to reinforce Timor, and the planes lined up on its airstrip were due to fly to the defence of Java.

Bill Heath had noted the harbour's vulnerability when the *Holbrook*, *Bloemfontein* and *Chaumont* arrived on 5 January: 'We went in with the tide; with 28-foot tides, there was no other choice. When it was out, ships rested on the bottom of the harbour and were sitting ducks to enemy air attack.'

The three battalions of American troops in the convoy were allowed to go ashore for a few hours that evening and were depressed by what they found. As a town, Darwin had not evolved very far: there was a post office, four banks, one hotel (the Victoria, of course), a hospital, a railway station, Government House, a Chinese-run general store, a curio shop, several pubs, some weatherboard houses and the Star Theatre.

Most of the women and children had been evacuated and the remaining civilian population numbered only 3000. The 147th and 148th had only a few hours of leave to bemoan the lack of facilities before they were bounced down winding dirt roads to set up camp some miles from the township in rugged bushland. While they were digging slit trenches in case of air attack, the Texans of the 131st reboarded the *Bloemfontein* which headed for Java.

As an omen of things to come, a severe cyclone forced the harbour to shut down for six days. From the hotel bars, the workforce could do little except watch puddles of dirty water form in craters on the unsealed roads, while tents at the army camps were ripped to shreds by the wind, equipment was waterlogged and the soldiers drenched to the skin.

After the weather cleared up, the men of the 148th were trucked back to port on 14 February to board two ships which were to form part of a new convoy, codenamed Sparrow Force, heading for Timor to defend the airstrip at Kupang, a vital link in the lifeline to Java.

Waiting for them in the harbour, and looking slightly the worse for wear, was the *Houston*. Since the men had last seen her, the Japanese had claimed yet again to have sunk the Ghost of the Java Sea. Her rear gun turret had been knocked out by a 500 lb bomb with the loss of 48 hands during an air–sea battle in the Flores Sea. The blast had also blown a hole 12 feet in diameter in the steel deck just forward of the turret and near misses had sprung some of the plates in her hull.

The *Houston* had limped into Tjilatjap, a pestilential port on the south coast of Java, buried her dead and patched up the damaged deck as best they could. Admiral Hart, who inspected the cruiser, could have withdrawn her from active service, but instead ordered her back to escort duty to cover the movement of Sparrow Force to Kupang.

Apart from a slow leak and some structural damage, the *Houston*'s commanding officer, Captain Albert H. Rooks, had one even more potentially dangerous problem to contend with. Seventy per cent of the 400 5-inch shells that had been fired by the *Houston*'s gun crews at Japanese bombers in the Flores Sea had failed to explode due to faulty detonators. Rooks was vastly relieved to discover that the US cruiser *Boise* had off-loaded 500 good 5-inch shells during a refuelling visit to Tjilatjap and he was able to replenish his magazine with effective ammunition.

Headquarters, A Battery and the Service Battery of the 148th were to travel to Timor in the MV *Tulagi* under the command of Colonel James C. Patterson; B and C Batteries were in the SS *Portmar*, under Major George A. Whitely. After their ordeal in the *Holbrook*, the men had high hopes of receiving better living quarters, but they were out of luck; one of the freighters had been carrying pineapples and sugarcane, and the other cattle, and the stench of rotting vegetation and cowdung was nauseating.

An Australian contingent consisting of the 2/4th Pioneer Battalion AIF and a troop of anti-tank gunners were packed into two other transports, the *Meigs* and *Mauna Loa*, and the convoy set sail into the Timor Sea on 15 February escorted by the *Houston*, the elderly destroyer USS *Peary* and two Australian sloops, *Swan* and *Warrego*.

Sparrow Force had no air cover for the simple reason that none had been available when the convoy departed. It was put at risk because the political imperative insisted that the United States and Australia had to be seen to be supporting the Dutch, even if that meant sacrificing the lives of Allied soldiers.

Bill Heath commented: 'In retrospect, the entire mission was ill-conceived. The convoy had to cross more than 400 miles of open ocean with no air support, then establish a beachhead on an island that might be already crawling with Japs. The whole venture had all the earmarks of a disaster, along with the frightening prospect of losing 1800 men in the attempt.'

The convoy was making only nine knots on its first day out from Darwin when it was spotted by a Japanese flying boat on a routine patrol. The *Houston* unlimbered her guns. At 11.17 the following morning, the Japanese attacked the convoy with 35 Mitsubishi 'Betty' attack bombers and nine Kawanishi 'Mavis' armed flying boats from their base at Ambon in the Celebes.

Four flights came at the convoy from different directions in perfect V formations. The first flight was spotted at 20,000 feet off the *Houston*'s starboard beam with the clear intention of sinking the cruiser and then picking off the transports. In a remarkable show of seamanship, Captain Rooks dodged enemy bombs as they splashed into the sea on all sides of the *Houston*.

To lessen the risk of fire on the decks, one of *Houston*'s SOC-3 seaplanes, piloted by Lieutenant Jack Lamade, was catapulted into the air with orders to make for Broome in Western Australia. When he was safely clear of the ship, the chief gunnery officer, Commander Arthur Maher, ordered the *Houston*'s anti-aircraft batteries to open up. Firing 930 5-inch shells in less than 45 minutes, the blazing barrels of the pom-pom guns made the ship a 'sheet of flame' from end to end. Although many of these salvos reached only halfway up to the bombers, they had the effect of ruining the bombardiers' aim, and whenever the attacking planes lost height to improve their chances of hitting the *Houston*, they came within range of her guns. Twelve enemy aircraft were hit by shrapnel, five of them ditching in the sea. Walter Winslow said: 'Our new anti-aircraft shells proved to be much more effective than the old ones.'

Captain Rooks followed the incoming planes through his binoculars and, judging the altitude of the planes and mentally determining the time it would take for their bombs to land, he shouted orders to his helmsman, who swung the cruiser to port or starboard accordingly.

This evasive action had been worked out after the near-fatal attack in the Flores Sea and it worked perfectly. The *Houston* succeeded in avoiding a single direct hit, although several near misses swamped her decks with water.

'I thought she was gone,' said Lieutenant Lloyd V. Henrichs in the *Portmar*, 'but she bobbed up like a cork, still firing.'

The *Meigs* put down a smokescreen to protect *Portmar*, but 23 bombs landed within 200 feet of the vessel, popping the rivets in her plates. Sergeant Jack Allured of the 148th said: 'Our turn came when a formation of bombers came straight over us. The sound of falling bombs was new to us, but once heard is never forgotten. It starts out as a faint gush that turns into a hiss, becoming louder and louder until it sounds like an escape valve going off on a steam engine. The rumble and shock of the underwater explosions caused the old freighter to quiver from stem to stern.'

All four transport ships sprung leaks as a result of near misses, but after an hour the Japanese broke off the attack and returned to base. The *Houston* steamed abreast of the *Tulagi* and *Portmar*, and Captain Rooks dipped his ship's flag. The Task Force Commander, Colonel Patterson, returned the salute, while the men of the 148th cheered the heroic cruiser. 'She had literally saved our lives,' said Lieutenant Henrichs.

None of the convoy's ships had been sunk and casualties numbered only 29, including one fatality. However, the *Houston* and the other escorts had run short of ammunition and it was judged suicidal for the convoy to proceed on its journey. The ships straggled back to Darwin, arriving through the heads on the evening of Wednesday, 18 February— the same day that Vice-Admiral Nagumo's flagship *Akagi* entered the Timor Sea with a battlefleet of 16 ships, including four aircraft carriers.

The *Houston* was refuelled and rearmed in a matter of hours and left Darwin for the Java Sea that night. With the *Meigs* and *Mauna Loa* taking first place at the small main dock to unload the Australian troops, the 148th had to remain on the *Tulagi* and *Portmar* overnight, a situation which filled the men with foreboding because they knew Japanese surveillance planes had probably trailed them back into port.

Jack Allured wrote home that night: 'How one outfit could have as much good luck as we have had is more than I'll ever know. It sometimes makes me wonder how long that luck will last.'

At daybreak the next morning, Japanese carriers launched a strike force of 188 aircraft, consisting of 81 level bombers, 71 dive-bombers and 36 Zero fighters, all under Commander Mitsuo Fuchida, who had planned the attack on Pearl Harbor. These were followed by a second strike force of 54 land-based bombers from bases at Ambon and Kendari in the Celebes.

At the time of the attack, 52 vessels were at anchor in Darwin harbour, including the four transports that had just returned with the Timor convoy, seven other transports, two tankers and a hospital ship. At 12,568 tons, *Meigs* was the largest ship in port, and although she and *Mauna Loa* had finished unloading troops, they were still carrying the battalion's

Bren gun carriers, trucks and 3-inch mortars. The US destroyer *Peary* was there, as well as 32 Royal Australian Navy craft, including two sloops and five corvettes, plus a number of flying boats.

At RAAF Darwin airfield there were 10 Hudson bombers, 10 Kitty-hawks of the new USAAF 33rd Pursuit Squadron and one B-17 bomber. This was the personal aircraft of Major-General Hurley, who had just arrived back from Java with his briefcase of currency to bribe local Darwin skippers into running the Japanese blockade. Two ships, the *Don Isidro* and the *Florence D*, were already sailing along the coast of Arnhem Land on their way to the Philippines with wads of Hurley's banknotes stuffed into their skippers' back pockets.

At 9.15 am, Lieutenant Bob McMahon took off from RAAF Darwin with the nine other Kittyhawks of the 33rd Pursuit Squadron to follow the lone B-17 to Kupang airfield in Timor on the first leg of their journey to Java. McMahon was the artist who had sketched the *Pensacola* Convoy from the deck of the *Republic* and his plane, like the other Kittyhawks, had come to Australia in crates on the deck of the *Meigs*.

Soon after take-off, the squadron ran into bad weather and the commander, Floyd Pell, recently promoted to major, aborted the mission and ordered his pilots back to Darwin. Mindful of the mistakes at Clark Field, air-traffic control ordered half the returning fighters to circle overhead while the others landed. When a coast-watcher on the northern tip of Melville Island reported to RAAF HQ that he had seen a 'large number of aircraft' heading in the direction of Darwin, control interpreted this as possibly referring to the Kittyhawk formation, even though Melville Island was north of the route they had taken.

Similarly, a second message from Father John McGrath of the Catholic Mission on Bathurst Island at 9.37 am that 'an unusually large air formation [is] bearing down on us from the north-west' was also the subject of debate and conjecture rather than any positive action. The RAAF men who received these alerts knew that the Sparrow Force convoy was sitting in the harbour and that a follow-up raid could reasonably be expected at any time. In truth, liaison between the RAAF and the army was abysmal and no one on duty was prepared to take responsibility for sounding the alarm. So despite two clear sightings of suspicious aircraft approaching Darwin, no advance warning was given of the first Japanese air raid on the Australian mainland. This was timed at 9.55 am—18 minutes after Father McGrath had radioed his alert.

The first Japanese fighter to reach Darwin was flown by Yoshikazu Nagahama, who saw five Kittyhawks patrolling the airspace above the airfield. He dived to attack the leader, Lieutenant Robert G. Oestreicher, who had no idea that hostile aircraft were anywhere near him until he saw flames spurting from the cannons of Nagahama's Zero.

Oestreicher jettisoned the belly tank that had been fitted for the long haul to Timor and threw his plane into a dive. The other Kittyhawk pilots saw what was happening and attempted to follow suit, but Nagahama was on top of them, cannons blazing, and, in quick succession, shot down Lieutenants Jack R. Peres and Elton S. Perry before turning his guns on Lieutenant Max R. Wiecks and shooting him down as well. Wiecks managed to bale out and land in the sea, where he could only watch as Nagahama caught up with Lieutenant William R. Walker, who was shot in the shoulder.

Walker managed a crash-landing back at the base, and Wiecks spent many hours in the water before struggling ashore. This left only Lieutenant Oestreicher out of the original five Kittyhawk pilots to tackle the approaching bombers, and he bravely did so, shooting one down in flames before making his escape into the clouds.

Major Floyd Pell then led Bob McMahon, Charles W. Hughes, Burt Rice and John G. Glover in attempting to take off in the five Kittyhawks still on the ground at the RAAF base. However, more Zeros swooped down on them before they were airborne and Pell's plane was hit. He baled out at 70 feet, but his parachute barely had time to open before he crashed to the ground. Grievously hurt, he attempted to crawl to safety, but the Japanese fighters followed through on a strafing run and shot him dead.

Hughes had failed to take off and was strafed and killed in his cockpit on the runway, but Bob McMahon was airborne and managed to come up behind three Zeros. His gunfire missed the first, but he believed he hit the second. His undercarriage then dropped down and, unable to manoeuvre his aircraft properly, he was at the mercy of another Zero, which shot his plane full of holes. He was hit in the leg.

Ack-ack fire, which had opened up from the harbour area, forced the Zeros to break away, giving McMahon an opportunity to nurse his burning aircraft towards the airfield. There, he spotted a Japanese dive-bomber, opened fire and saw the rear gunner slump over his gun. McMahon baled out at 700 feet and landed safely, while his plane crashed in the scrub.

Meanwhile, the big Japanese bombers, 'shining like silver with a red sun and a burst of red-and-gold stripes', were bombing the harbour. Two ships unloading explosives at the pier and an oil barge blew up together in a single, terrible explosion that rocked the whole area. Twenty-two out of 70 waterside workers taking a break on the dockside were killed instantly. The *Meigs* was hit 20 times, caught fire and sank. Two bombs went through the open hatch of the *Mauna Loa*, breaking her back. The hospital ship *Manunda* suffered one direct hit and other bomb damage; 12 people were killed and 58 wounded, but she stayed afloat and was able to receive many of the injured.

The greatest potential for mass slaughter was at the back of the harbour, where the *Tulagi* and *Portmar* were anchored. They were still packed with American servicemen who had been unable to get ashore the previous night. When the bombers came at them, machine gunners from the 148th opened fire with their .50-calibre weapons, while the rest of the troops remained below deck to avoid alerting the pilots to the fact that the troopship was still loaded with men. James M. Wofford and Elmer Belknap of Battery A were manning a machine gun on the fantail of the *Tulagi* when Japanese gunners opened up. Wofford was killed outright and Belknap badly wounded.

On the aft deck, Martin Likkel and Wilbur Meade, also of Battery A, were operating a gun together when Meade was hit by a bomb fragment and killed. He had discharged himself from hospital, where he was being treated for dengue fever, to join the Timor expedition. Horace Brown went down with a shrapnel wound; Lloyd Henrichs took a bomb fragment in the calf of his leg; Major Whitely suffered a severe wound in the arm; another 10 men from the 148th were also injured in the attacks on the *Tulagi* and *Portmar*.

The 3289-ton freighter *Admiral Halstead* succeeded in staying afloat, although she was damaged by a near miss and had her rigging shot away. Her skipper unceremoniously dumped her cargo of 14,000 drums of aviation fuel over the side of the ship and they floated ashore. The *Peary*, however, was doomed. She took five direct bomb hits and, though blazing fiercely, kept firing her guns until the last one fell through the deck. 'I saw a big bomb hit the *Peary* amidships,' said a witness. 'There was a terrific explosion and the ship sank in five minutes or less.'

A total of 172 men were killed or badly wounded on the ships in harbour and another 300 were injured.

After the level bombers had done their damage, the dive–bombers and fighters came in for the kill against the town and the airfield. There were 52 deaths among civilians and servicemen in town and at the airfield; five were women operating the town's manual switchboard, four were post office staff. The post office, Darwin Hospital, the Victoria Hotel and the Bank of New South Wales building were all badly damaged.

Just as the marauders were about to break off, a dive-bomber made a final attempt to sink the *Tulagi*. 'He was firing his machine guns and he had one bomb left which he hoped to drop on the deck,' said Louis H. Kohl. 'Sergeant Merrill G. Hulse and Private Roylie Sam, both of

Headquarters Battery, valiantly continued firing their machine guns, forcing the enemy to bank and drop his bomb near the side of the *Tulagi*.' This near miss damaged the vessel sufficiently for the captain to beach her. 'We were ordered to abandon ship,' continued Kohl. 'Some jumped into the water, others went down ropes. We swam and floated on anything that would support us.'

'Watch out for sharks!' the captain called out to Dudley L. Smith.

'To hell with sharks; let them look out for themselves,' shouted Smith.

A small boat was manoeuvred alongside the *Tulagi* and one of the crew called out to Colonel Patterson to jump into the water so they could fish him out. Patterson declared that he would stay on board and share the ship's fate with the captain. When they heard this, Henry Bartol and Clarence Kemp grabbed the colonel and tossed him overboard. 'We waited for the boat to pick him up, then jumped into the water,' said Bartol. 'We tried to swim to shore, but the tide took us out to sea. We were in the water for three hours, taking turns holding on to a length of two-by-four until two Aussies rescued us in a motorboat.'

The *Portmar* was riddled with 98 holes and the men abandoned ship as she started to sink, but she got up enough steam to make it to the beach. As they were departing over the coast of Arnhem Land, the Japanese raiders spotted the *Don Isidro*, which was taking ammunition and other supplies to the Philippines. She was hit by dive-bombers; so too was the *Florence D*, which had picked up a distress call from the *Don Isidro* and was going to her aid. The *Don Isidro* was beached, but the *Florence D* went down with most of her hands.

Bill Daly of the 147th South Dakotans, who were still camped outside Darwin, recorded events in his diary: 'At the present time, we are having an air raid and I'm writing this while squatting in a narrow slit trench. At first we thought the planes were US air reinforcements, but they were flying unusually high, and they were silvery, glinting in the sunlight. They were too high for the naked eye to see any insignia.

'Our camp is located about 15 miles south east of Darwin and the first three flights of nine bombers each circled around to the south of us and then there were more and more and more. I counted about 75 passing towards Darwin. In the distance, we began to hear explosions, the sharp crack of the ack-ack guns, the dull ground-shaking boom of the exploding bombs and we realised this was really it, our first air-raid. Some of the boys were hard to convince; Big Gehring, for instance. He said, "Hell, those are American planes and the guns are just practising . . ."'

Later that day, Daly continued his report: 'The 148th FA was out in the bay getting ready to come in and unload when the attack occurred. They beached the ships and most of them got off. Poor devils, they really have been through it. All afternoon the road past camp was almost continually filled with refugees, driving cars or walking with a few personal belongings. A pitiful sight. It's the same old story, just as in Malaya and Singapore . . .'

The men of the 148th struggled back to camp under the gum trees on the outskirts of Darwin. Five Silver Stars and 34 Purple Hearts were later handed out for gallantry, but there were many more heroes than medals.

Somewhere in the Timor Sea that night, the crew of the *Houston* heard about the raid on Radio Tokyo. Walter Winslow said: 'We listened in grim silence as the Japanese commentator claimed, once more, that the *Houston* had been sunk at her mooring.'

The Australian War Cabinet suppressed most of the details of what had happened in Darwin, the Prime Minister telling the nation: 'In this first battle on Australian soil, it will be a source of pride to the public to know that the armed forces and the civilians comported themselves with the gallantry that is traditional in the people of our stock.'

While it was true there had been individual acts of bravery by nurses, seamen, civilians and the ack-ack gun crews, Australians would have hung their heads in shame if Curtin had told them the real story. In the township, there had been pandemonium. Believing a Japanese invasion was in progress, deserting Australian troops joined civilians in fleeing inland towards the settlement at Adelaide River. Bicycles, horses, a road grader, a sanitary truck, even an ice-cream seller's bicycle cart were used in the mass getaway.

Jim Kelly, a long-time Darwin resident, said: 'What the fuck were we supposed to do? There were Jap planes flying all over the place dropping bombs . . . wait in town for them to land? As soon as the bombing stopped I got on my bike that quick I was in the Adelaide River before I realised the chain was broken.'

Many of those who remained behind, including a large number of Australian soldiers, systematically looted the stricken town, claiming that they were doing so to prevent the goods from falling into Japanese hands.

'The shock of Australia being bombed was widespead enough, but we had no idea of the devastation or the panic up there,' said Estelle Runcie. 'We simply weren't told; the government censored the whole thing— there was almost nothing in the newspapers or on the wireless—and there was a lot of anger later on when we found out. I mean, Darwin was terrible; it was the first time we felt Australia had actually been violated.'

In the Philippines, Carlos Romulo took a boat across Manila Bay and joined the besieged garrison in the Malinta Tunnel on Corregidor. 'There wasn't enough room, enough bedding, enough of anything in the tunnel except smells, bedbugs and flies,' said Romulo. 'Colonel Bowler had charge of mess and bedding. He was constantly harassed in his struggle to find enough bedding to go around. "When this war ends," the colonel told me, "I'm going home to manage the Waldorf-Astoria. After the tunnel it'll be a breeze!" '

Romulo worked with Colonel LeGrande A. Diller, whose friends called him Pick, in setting up the Voice of Freedom radio station to broadcast morale-boosting bulletins from the Rock. 'I would confer with Colonel Diller on the topics for our three daily broadcasts—morning, noon and night. Courage! We clarioned that message through the Voice of Freedom.'

PLUM refused to fall into Japanese hands, but Java was a succulent piece of tropical fruit just waiting to be plucked from the tree. This island of 42 million people was the last bastion of Dutch rule in Asia, a teeming expanse of rice paddies, rich valleys, dense jungles and spectacular volcanic mountains. The main city, Batavia (later Jakarta), was the administrative centre for 3000 islands whose oil, rubber, timber, rice and spices provided the colonialists of the Netherlands East Indies (now Indonesia) with a inexhaustible supply of wealth.

When Holland was occupied by the Nazis in the summer of 1940, Churchill and Roosevelt prevailed upon the Dutch government-in-exile to hold out. Many promises of military aid were made but few kept, with the result that the Dutch found themselves in a precarious position after the outbreak of hostilities in the Pacific. Their army consisted of mainly Javanese soldiers whose loyalty to the motherland was suspect owing to the cruelty of many Dutch traders and farmers towards the local population; there were few warplanes and even fewer trained pilots to fly them; and the Dutch Navy had no hope of guarding the thousands of miles of jagged coastline.

The valiant Texans of the 2nd Battalion, 131st Field Artillery Regiment, became the first and only United States ground combat unit to reach the Netherlands East Indies when they landed at Surabaya in the *Bloemfontein*. The Texans were despatched to guard a grass airfield at Singosari, near Malang, a densely populated locality set in a green valley of palms and terraced paddies. They secured their camp and guarded B-17s of the 19th Bombardment Group, which had flown to Java after the debacle at Clark Field. On leave the Texans frequented the movie houses, brothels and bars in an adjacent village, where the last remaining Dutch settlers bemoaned the passing of colonial rule. Then the battalion was split up, E Battery staying in Malang and D Battery going westward to reinforce Bandung.

The *Orcades* reached Tanjong Priok, the port of Batavia, on 17 February and Wavell insisted on disembarking many of the troops in order to preserve British prestige in the area. The following forces were ordered ashore: the 2/3rd Machine Gun Battalion, minus their Vickers machine guns and vehicles which were in another convoy and less some 200 men; the 2/2nd Pioneer Battalion; the 2/6th Field Company; the 2/2nd Casualty Clearance Station; the 105th General Transport Battalion, and a platoon of the Australian Guard Battalion.

Having botched the defence of Singapore, it was obvious the British intended to put up a fight for Java. The Texans of D Battery, the 131st Battalion, joined Australian troops in forming "Blackforce" under the command of Brigadier A. S. Blackburn, commanding officer of the 2/3rd machine gunners.

While Blackforce was marshalling its meagre resources, the Japanese landed near Kupang in Timor to prevent any further reinforcements reaching Java. In a confidential memo to General Marshall, Patrick H. Hurley wrote: 'I am convinced that if the Japanese should make an all-out attack on Australia . . . the situation would be immediately critical. It may be pointed out by the optimistic that Japanese landings in New Zealand and Australia would over-extend long supply lines and thus enable us to break them, but when I stated this proposition to one of our Generals, he replied, "Break them with what?" Unfortunately, his question is significant.'

Wavell was informed by the Combined Chiefs of Staff that Java should be defended to the last man. Wavell himself, however, was instructed to withdraw his headquarters from the island and set it up at a safer location somewhere else, like Burma. Not wishing to be made the scapegoat for yet another fiasco, Wavell argued that ABDACOM should not be withdrawn but dissolved altogether and all Allied forces in the Netherlands East Indies placed under the control of the Dutch. This suggestion was readily accepted in London and Washington and many of Wavell's headquarters staff just had time to pack their bags and scramble aboard the *Orcades* before she sailed for Australia.

Thus on 25 February Beryl Stevenson found herself jobless and cut off when ABDACOM ceased to exist. Beryl said: 'It was what I'd call a "quick quit" by the British at Lembang. Nothing was destroyed ahead of the Japanese coming in, but perhaps there wasn't time. One night we had a meeting of the heads running the show, nutting out what they could do with the equipment they had and what was coming in. I stayed on to transcribe my notes and the transcription went into the safe at 1 am. I was back again at seven o'clock in the morning, all alert, waiting to see this [plan] implemented. As far as I know, it's still in the safe. Nothing was done because it was such a shambles at that point.

'Wavell was there, walking along the ouside verandahs with his aide. Wavell had lost an eye in the First World War and he'd chosen an aide who'd lost an eye in the Second World War. He took a rather jocular view of this; they walked along with their two blind eyes in the middle so that they had a good eye on either side. Then Wavell was gone and the place was empty.

'A Scottish major was left to do the handover to the Japanese. Can you imagine anything quite so British? He came to the window of my office, putting a cheerful air on it, to say goodbye and wish us well. What happened to him God alone knows. The attitude of the British was quite out of this world; leaving an officer behind to hand over to the Japanese!'

Wavell sailed in the *Orontes* on 28 February for India, where he was to become commander-in-chief of the armies in India and Burma. The previous day the Australian chiefs of staff had come to the reluctant conclusion that Japan was 'now at liberty to attempt an invasion of Australia should she so desire'. Wavell's deputy, General Brett, was heading back to Australia to resume command of the US forces there, but before he departed he performed an act of chivalry towards the four women on the ABDACOM staff.

Beryl said: 'It was George Brett who got me out of Java. He arranged for me, Louise Mowat and two American women who were working at the airstrip at Andeer to be flown to Australia. At first, I turned him down because I didn't think we should be leaving Java. I felt we'd run too far; there was only New Guinea left and I knew it had no ports, no airfields: how were we going to fight the Japanese behind Java? I said this to Brett, but he said, "I don't want you four women to be taken prisoner of war by the Japanese". He quite probably saved our lives.

'Louise and I left Lembang with Brett's driver and Brett's aide, who was armed with a tommy gun, in Brett's car—khaki, long wheel-base, very distinctive. After picking up the two American women at Andeer, we were leaving Bandung for Tjilatjap and there was a flight of Japanese planes coming across, presumably to bomb Bandung. One of them saw the general's car, veered away from the flight and strafed us from the front. Suddenly, I was lying on my belly in a paddy field beside the road, but I have no recollection of getting there. The aide was popping away with his tommy gun, and instead of turning round and coming back, the Jap plane rejoined his flight. We arrived at the port looking pretty filthy and got into the Qantas *Circe*, which was going to Broome.

'It was the last plane out of Tjilatjap.'

After their adventures with the *Pensacola* ships, there was no respite for the 1000-strong crew of the *Houston*. The American cruiser churned through the jade-green waters of the Java Sea to Surabaya, where a combined naval force consisting of eight cruisers and 16 destroyers had assembled under the newly created Dutch command. This was led by Vice-Admiral Conrad Helfrich, who had relieved Rear Admiral Hart. Plagued from the start by farcical communication problems between its Dutch and English-speaking components, the new Combined Striking Force was destined for a savage ending.

When two Japanese convoys were spotted making towards the Java coast on 27 February, the Dutch commander, Rear Admiral Karel Doorman, sent a message from his flagship *De Ruyter* to the cruisers *Houston*, *Java*, *Exeter* and *Perth* and nine destroyers: 'Am proceeding to intercept enemy units. Follow me. Details later.' While searching for the easternmost convoy that afternoon, the Combined Striking Force ran into four Japanese cruisers and 14 destroyers, and the stage was set for the Battle of the Java Sea.

Doorman drew the Japanese within range of his 6-inch guns, only to discover that he had made his own task force vulnerable to torpedo attack. The cruiser *Exeter* was badly damaged early in the action and broke formation, whereupon she was mistakenly followed by *Houston*, *Perth* and *Java*, who believed this was part of Doorman's plan. Amid mounting confusion, the Dutchman immediately counter-attacked and then, after losing a destroyer, quickly ordered a retreat under the cover of night. But, in the darkness, the Allied ships ran into more Japanese warships and *De Ruyter*, *Java* and three destroyers were sunk. Doorman never gave any more details about his plan of attack; he went down with his ship.

Once again, Captain Rooks's superior seamanship coupled with the marksmanship of her ferocious gunners under Commander Maher brought the *Houston* through the battle. Commander Henry E. Eccles, captain of the destroyer USS *John D. Edwards*, paid this tribute to Rooks in his official report on the battle: 'The manner in which *Houston* fought, the aggressive way in which she, at all times, carried the battle to the enemy with steady accurate fire, will long remain an inspiration to all who saw her.'

The *Houston* limped back into Tanjung Priok with the *Perth*, both cruisers critically short of fuel and ammunition and carrying many battle scars. But instead of allowing their captains time to repair the damage, Vice-Admiral Helfrich ordered them to leave port almost at once and sail through the Sunda Strait to Tjilatjap to re-engage the enemy. Dutch intelligence claimed that the Sunda Strait, a narrow strip of water dividing Java and Sumatra, was free of Japanese ships and they would have no trouble getting through.

In fact the Japanese aircraft carrier *Ryujo*, four heavy cruisers, three light cruisers and numerous destroyers were close to the northern entrance of the strait, escorting 56 transports that were due to land troops at Bantam Bay on the north-west tip of Java. Sunda Strait was a death-trap.

At 11.15 on the night of 28 February, the *Houston* and the *Perth* ran into the biggest amphibious landing yet attempted by the Japanese. After almost an hour of blistering exchanges, during which two enemy transports were sunk, torpedoes blasted into *Perth*. Only nine weeks earlier, she had been one of the two Australian warships which had welcomed the *Pensacola* Convoy off New Caledonia and now she was dead in the water and going down, with Captain H. M. L. Waller and 350 of her crew on board.

Alone once again and surrounded by enemy ships, the *Houston* turned her guns on anything in range as the Japanese closed in for the kill under the glare of searchlights and the blaze of bursting star shells. Such was the frenzy to get the Ghost of the Java Sea that the Japanese cruisers and destroyers opened fire indiscriminately. Walter Winslow said: 'We watched in amazement while the enemy, for a short time, fired heavily at each other and no shells so much as splashed near us.'

Houston's guns kept blazing, hitting many of their targets, but at 12.15 on Sunday morning, 1 March, a torpedo blasted through her port side. This was closely followed by another, which exploded against the starboard side just below the bridge. Number 2 turret took a direct hit and blew up, with appalling loss of life. A third torpedo ripped a great hole forward of the quarter deck and vast quantities of water poured in through the gash. With fires spreading out of control and shells exploding on the decks, Captain Rooks ordered the bugler to sound the order to abandon ship.

Seconds later, Rooks was wounded by a shellburst and died in the arms of one of his crew. His Chinese steward, Ah Fong, known as Buddha, refused to leave the body. He said: 'Captain die, *Houston* die, Buddha die.' At 12.45 am, they went down with the ship. Going into battle, *Houston*'s complement had been 1015 men; 655 were killed that night. The other 360 were washed up on Java's newly occupied shores and taken prisoner for the duration of the war.

Speaking for every man in the 148th Field Artillery Regiment when they heard about the tragedy, Sergeant Jack Allured said: 'The *Houston* was the best damned ship that ever rubbed noses with a whale.'

Chapter Six

-<o>-

Clark Gable's Cousins

B ERYL Stevenson had kept one step ahead of the Japanese in Singapore and Java, but her luck almost ran out when she reached the safety of Australia. 'I arrived in Broome the day before the Japanese laid waste to it,' she said. 'I spent the night sleeping on someone's verandah and took off again at first light in the morning just before the bombing started.'

The little port was devastated at 9.50 am on Tuesday 3 March 1942, in an air attack that destroyed 24 aircraft and killed 70 people, many of them Dutch women and children who had been evacuated from Java.

Lieutenant Jack Lamade had just taken off in his SOC-3 seaplane when nine Zeros came screaming out of the sun towards him. Lamade, it will be remembered, had been ordered by Captain Rooks to take his plane to Broome when the *Houston* had come under attack while protecting the Sparrow Force convoy in the Timor Sea.

Lamade had attempted to rendezvous with the *Houston* after she had returned briefly to Darwin for refuelling prior to departing for the Java Sea, but the orders giving him the rendezvous point in the Timor Sea had arrived too late for him to make it in time. Rooks had waited an hour for the little seaplane, then sailed on, and Lamade had been stranded in Broome. As a result, he missed the Battle of the Java Sea and its dreadful sequel in the Sunda Strait.

Lamade had just heard about the tragic loss of the *Houston* and the death of hundreds of his shipmates when his SOC-3 skimmed over the sparkling waters of the Indian Ocean and lifted off into the sights of the Japanese Zeros. Ironically, the raiders had taken off two and a half hours earlier from the airfield at Kupang, the same Timorese strip that was to have been defended by Sparrow Force.

Normally the home of pearling luggers, fishing boats and a few members of the beachcombing fraternity, the tiny port of Broome had been selected as a target because Japanese intelligence reports noted that it had become a major transit centre for planes flying thousands of refugees out of Java. Evacuees were given food and clothing while their aircraft refuelled for the long haul south to Perth. Many of the civilians passing through Broome that morning were the wives and children of Dutch naval officers.

The port had been buzzing since dawn with the loading of 15 big flying-boats in the harbour and five Fortresses and three Liberators at the airfield. Four of the bombers had already got away safely and most of the Dutch flying-boats were ready for take-off when Lamade's seaplane came under attack from a Zero piloted by Warrant Officer Osamu Kudo. Bullets ripped through the seaplane's fuselage and Lamade was forced to ditch in the sea, but he survived the crash and swam ashore.

In the next 15 minutes, the Zeros destroyed every aircraft at Broome, including the flying-boats containing Dutch families. One Dutch Catalina was strafed, set on fire and sank, with the loss of a number of passengers. A newspaper report of the tragedy said: 'There were distressing scenes as the dead and wounded were brought up from the jetty. Many of them were frightfully burned. Others had seen their wives and children killed or burned. All these women and children were Dutch.'

The hero of the hour was Lieutenant Gus Winckel, a Dutch pilot who grabbed a machine gun he had brought ashore from his flying-boat for repairs and, resting it on his forearm, fired at the attackers. He brought down the Zero flown by Kudo, killing him, and scored hits on five of the other Zeros. Although his arm was burned on the red-hot gun barrel, he kept blazing away until he ran out of ammunition.

The Japanese advance seemed unstoppable. On 8 March they landed at Lae and Salamaua on the north coast of New Guinea and set up bases for future expansion. The Japanese Imperial General Headquarters planned to capture Port Moresby in the Australian sector of New Guinea as well as taking over the southern Solomon islands of Tulagi and Gaudalcanal. After these conquests, they planned to isolate Australia by seizing Fiji, Samoa and New Caledonia.

General Barnes said: 'The entire situation in the South West Pacific area had reached the stage where successful defence of Australia itself was questionable, considering the force which the enemy could concentrate against it as soon as the situation was cleared up in the Netherlands East Indies.'

Beryl Stevenson and the other three women from Lembang finally reached Melbourne after a long train ride from the west and found a surprise waiting on the platform. 'Having rescued us, George Brett met us at Melbourne railway station and offered us jobs,' said Beryl. 'He was commanding USAFFE, and because the glamour of Wavell had rubbed off on me a bit, he gave me a job as his secretary. That was how my lot came to be cast with the Americans. I moved into a flat along Queens Road with a number of women and went to work for Brett in a building just across St Kilda Road from the Victoria Barracks. I was so busy setting things up in the office that a couple of weeks seemed like an aeon.'

Beryl had got out of Java just in time. The Japanese swarmed ashore at three different locations on the night of 28 February, with the central force sweeping aside Dutch resistance with tanks and infantry and pressing east towards Bandung. Brigadier Blackburn, commander of Blackforce, proposed to counter-attack with his tattered band of Australian, American and British troops. He placed the 2/2nd Pioneers in positions along the banks of a river, while the Texans were ordered to set up their artillery further along the road to Bandung. When Japanese troops massed on the other side of the river crossing, the Pioneers opened up, inflicting heavy casualties.

Blackburn's troops then fanned out along the river bank and out-flanked the Japanese as they tried to find safer crossing points. Wave after wave of Japanese were repulsed and, with the Japanese force stacking up on the riverbank, Blackburn ordered the Texans in D Battery to open fire.

The barrages from the American .75s effectively dispersed the main Japanese force and when the Texans ran out of ammunition they opened up with .50-calibre machine guns salvaged from wrecked B-17s. Black-force held off a third of a Japanese division for three days with the loss of 100 men killed and wounded, fighting with such ferocity that the enemy were convinced they were facing an entire division.

But it was only a brief respite. With the Japanese threatening to slaughter Dutch civilians in Batavia and with the Javanese population openly supporting the invaders, the Dutch caved in on 8 March and the Allies were forced to sign an unconditional surrender at Bandung four days later.

The Texan gunners were moved under guard to Tanjong Priok, then taken by train to a stinking, over-crowded concentration camp outside Batavia known as 'the Bicycle Camp', where they were joined by exhausted, oil-stained survivors of the *Houston* and the *Perth*. Rohan Rivett, the young Australian reporter from Singapore who had fallen into Japanese hands after his ship had been sunk at the entrance to Banka

Strait, said: 'It was odd that by the merest coincidence practically all the Americans taken prisoner in Java should have been Texans. The artillery boys looked after the *Houston* survivors in splendid fashion.'

The Texans in E Battery, which had been defending the airfield at Malang in eastern Java, had also been forced to surrender when the Dutch turned their machine guns on them and threatened to shoot if they didn't lay down their arms. Altogether, 532 members of the 2nd Battalion, 131st Field Artillery, went into captivity.

One of the Texans, Clifford Johnson, said, 'They sent us to Java as a political deal to help the Dutch. Sacrificed us is what they did.' Another gunner, Jesse Bumpass, said: 'We were stripped of everything—pride, dignity, hope. All we had were each other.'

The only man who was still at liberty among the original members of the Lost Battalion was the feisty Texan who had broken his leg falling out a window at a Brisbane dancehall after promoting a fight between Americans and Australians. He had turned up at the dock in a roll-away hospital bed, but had been declared unfit for duty. As far as anyone knew, he was still convalescing in Brisbane.

The day of the Darwin bombing, a 19-year-old Australian girl married a 23-year-old US Army cook in Melbourne. Australia's first war bride had met her husband two weeks earlier on his first morning in Australia. He had introduced himself to her in the street with the greeting: 'Hi babe, comin' truckin'?'

Those four words appeared in the *Australian Women's Weekly* in a report of the nuptials and confirmed the worst fears of many Brisbane mothers that the alien presence in their midst was delinquent and probably dangerous. Jive talk like 'Hi babe, comin' truckin'?' sent a shudder through middle-class sensibilities. With visions of young crewcut, gum-chewing doughboys scattering 'hi's' and 'babe's' through-out the house, and 'cutting a rug' in the lounge to that ultimate vulgarity, jazz music, many parents instructed their daughters to have nothing to do with the Americans. There were to be no exemptions, even for offi-cers who looked like Cary Grant and sounded like Clark Gable.

Pauline Eglinton, who had been educated at St Margaret's, a private girls' school at Clayfield, said: 'I was crossing Edward Street in the pouring rain one evening when this beautiful American officer came up to me and whispered, 'Can I share your umbrella?' I said 'Sissy!' and walked on. Poor baby! My family had more to do with the AIF than the Americans; my mother, my sister and I worked at the British Empire Club on Sundays, and I wrote to my boyfriend Bruce in the AIF every day. The Yanks were here but I never went out with one of them.'

With Queensland now firmly established inside the battle area, the trickle of American troops into the city had become a steady flow. Everybody called them 'Yanks', even after it was politely explained that many came from south of the Mason–Dixon line; crucial distinctions between north, south, east and west were ignored by the locals because it was easier to accept the Americans if they were regarded en masse as possessing identical national characteristics.

There was no doubt that the Americans looked different, sounded different and, as they used aftershave, an unknown commodity in Australia at the time, even smelled different. In the middle of wartime austerity, they brought promise of an exciting release from boredom, drudgery and endless restrictions. Many Brisbane girls loved their jive talk and wanted to learn jitterbugging steps like the 'jersey bounce' and the 'jig walk', eat hamburgers and drink milkshakes. They went to coffee inns, ate hot dogs and dreamed of a glamorous life in California with a swimming pool and a Cadillac, and Clark Gable living next door.

'There was a huge innocence around in those days,' said Estelle Runcie, who had finished her schooling at 14 and came to Brisbane with her mother from Cairns in North Queensland. She had a job as a photographer's assistant when she caught sight of her first American serviceman. 'You hear about Brisbane being like a Sodom and Gomorrah but it wasn't; there was a lot of innocence.' Temptation was likely to offer itself in the form of advertisements for jitterbugging contests; there were exciting swing bands to listen to, newly released 'flicks' to see at the American camps, nylon stockings to wear and new kinds of cosmetics to try out.

Lola Taylor, who danced with the Americans at the Trocadero in South Brisbane, said: 'After the Americans came, we used to all wear make-up—that puce colour, very purply, and lipgloss, rouge and lipstick, tons of it. I used to put it on very thickly indeed.'

The Americans were talkative and extremely polite, dropping 'yes, ma'am's and 'thank you, ma'am's in every other sentence. They had been brought up in close contact with the opposite sex, so it was only natural for them to seek out female company. 'American high schools were co-ed and we were used to mixing with girls,' said Sergeant Bill Bentson. 'In Australia in those years, boys and girls were generally split up after primary school; most boys went to all-male high schools and girls to all-female high schools. In the main, they were segregated during their teenage years, which was the opposite of the education system in the United States.'

In fact many young Australians never had the opportunity of going to high school at all. During the Depression it was commonplace for them to be thrown onto the labour market as young as 13 and 14; with many fathers out of work, the few pounds that a young girl could earn working behind a shop counter made the difference between making ends meet and serious deprivation. Boys were apprenticed to a trade at the same age, and would likely as not marry a childhood sweetheart, probably a girl from the same neighbourhood. If a young man took his girl to dinner at the Shingle Inn, followed by the double feature at the Regent, the chances were that the next stop would be the altar.

Brisbanites invariably entertained each other at 'keg parties' in their homes and at these parties segregation of the sexes was rigidly observed. Any man who preferred the company of women was regarded with cold-eyed suspicion as either a 'ladies' man' or a 'poofter'. The American presence brought these deep-rooted attitudes into sudden focus, and many Australian men found themselves compared unfavourably with their American counterparts.

The official war historian Gavin Long wrote in his diary: 'Australians have always treated their women a little worse than their dogs. Therefore the Americans, who have usually been taught to respect women and have displayed some tenderness towards Australian women, have stolen most of the pretty girls.'

And not only the girls. They brought flowers for mothers, cigars for fathers and candy bars for little brothers and sisters, 'as much stuff as they could pinch from the boats or the army camps,' according to Lola Taylor. 'They didn't bring you one chocolate but a carton—always a carton—not only that, but they brought you a corsage—a beautiful gardenia—about a foot long—they'd be gardenias or camellias. You'd always go out in a taxi and home in a taxi. We were thoroughly spoiled.'

'I was working at Crown Studios next door to Lennon's in George Street when I noticed these soldiers and I didn't know who or what they were,' Estelle Runcie said. 'They were in and out of Lennon's all the time, but they didn't look like soldiers to start with. Most of my girlfriends felt—and I felt the same—that the American uniforms didn't really look like military uniforms. Our boys had the best uniforms—you couldn't go past those jungle greens and those slouch hats and those little waists and little hips, those slim, lean bodies.

'Yet you hear that the American uniforms were one of the reasons that Brisbane girls threw themselves at the Yanks. Well, a lot of the Americans were a little bit podgy, but I'm talking from a young girl's viewpoint. But the other girls were after them and, when all's said and done, they were interesting and good-looking, especially the first lot that came out. They had beautiful teeth, that's what you noticed, their marvellous teeth, whereas a lot of our fellows had all their teeth pulled out when they went into the army and had dentures.

'The whole population was tied up with what we'd seen on American films and we wanted to know from nearly every one we met at first if they knew Clark Gable. Of course, they all said they did! Their accents were fascinating to listen to, but hard for me to understand. Four Texans came into the studio to have their identification photos taken and I couldn't understand a word they said.'

Brisbanites did not see themselves as insular or particularly narrow minded, and considered it was a misconception to say that Brisbane was remote from world capitals like London, Rome or Paris; it was the other way around—they were remote from Brisbane. Besides, Brisbane had all the advantages of Europe and none of the drawbacks, like Hitler.

The latest fashions were available at Finneys, T. C. Bierne's, McWhirter's or Allen & Stark's, the latest British and American films were showing at the Regent, the Metro or the Wintergarden, and taking tea in the Victorian environs of Rowe's or one of the other elegant tea shoppes was *de rigueur* for anyone with social pretensions.

Although there were definite class distinctions based on school and wealth, Brisbane had a certain easy-going egalitarianism. Where else in the world could anyone with the price of a train fare travel to the coast, swim at beautiful, unspoiled beaches, stroll on the tree-lined promenade, and eat fish and chips on the pier?

But even though it was fast expanding around the edges, Brisbane could not claim to be a metropolis. One of the biggest problems for out-of-towners, including Australians from other states, was actually finding the city centre in the drabness of the brownout. Ivan Bradshaw was a Victorian with the 46th Battalion of the 3rd Division who arrived in Brisbane in early 1942. 'I'd lived in the country at Yarrawonga, Victoria, but I'd been to Melbourne quite often on holidays and we knew what a big city was like,' he said. 'We got to Brisbane and boarded a tram for the city. When we went over the Victoria Bridge into South Brisbane, the conductor said, "Where do you fellows want to get off?" We told him to let us off in the city centre. "You've just gone through it," he said. We'd travelled the entire length of Queen Street and hadn't even noticed.'

Brisbanites were offended by such comments, particularly when they came from southerners. They believed that if Brisbane was lacking in glamour, or anything else for that matter, it was because the federal government invariably put the needs of Sydney and Melbourne first. The main source of contention was the so-called Brisbane Line, a defence strategy worked out by military advisers in Canberra that envisaged abandoning all territory above Brisbane in the event of a Japanese invasion. Although this was never admitted officially, the people of Brisbane believed that it was true, and regarded it as yet another example of southern perfidy.

Pauline Eglinton said: 'We in Queensland weren't told anything by the federal government; we were cut off from the rest of Australia. They were down there and we were the ones in the front-line. I even had to get letters of permission to cross the New South Wales border to visit my relatives in Tenterfield. We had nothing in Brisbane, everything was rationed. Oh, it was terrible, but we didn't know it was terrible—it was just the way life was.'

One American soldier summed up the situation: 'Brisbane people complained to me, "The bloody military's got everything. We just don't have it and we can't get it because the bloody military's got it". But the Brisbane Line also annoyed people terrifically. They knew they didn't have the military or naval facilities to protect themselves adequately and they knew that's why we were there.'

Estelle Runcie said: 'Sure, there were shortages but we had coupons for meat and we had the occasional roast. We always had enough butter and there was plenty of fresh vegetables and fish galore. The shortages were tinned food like ham, corned beef and fish, but they didn't really affect us. We came from North Queensland and there was a more multicultural population up there.

'My mother cooked Italian spaghetti, she cooked Syrian dishes and Chinese food like cabbage rolls. For people who were used to steak and Irish stew it was a different set-up, but we used to go into Nick's cafe in Adelaide Street and have a marvellous meal of steak, chicken and spaghetti for a very nominal price. And then you had the Chinese restaurant in George Street that was always going flat out. There were half a dozen cafes, so food was available.

'Once we got some dried fruit to make a cake. I made the cake and mother found some cellophane to wrap it in. The cellophane had been in a suitcase that had naphthalene in it. We didn't realise that and the naphthalene went all through the cake and we couldn't eat it. We even tried to steam it to have it as a steamed pudding but it was still full of naphthalene.'

One Brisbane woman thought the Americans were 'terribly, terribly extravagant; they seemed to have twice as much as we had—fruitcake with ice-cream! Ice-cream was something reserved for Sunday lunch; fruitcake was for Christmas.' But this was more of an admission about the true state of affairs in Brisbane prior to the American invasion than a criticism of the visitors.

In the aftermath of the Depression, money was tight and the basic family values that were stressed in high moral tones from the city's many pulpits did not promise much in the way of hope: work hard, pay tax and fear God. But temperate, God-fearing citizens were in a minority, and drinking and gambling were highly developed artforms in Brisbane. For many, regardless of denomination, the biggest wartime deprivations were restrictions on liquor sales and the suspension of activity at most racetracks. The result was that sly grog shops and gambling dens did a roaring trade in the tenderloin district of South Brisbane and other less salubrious parts of the city.

Brisbane's robust pioneering past had also spawned other outlets for licentiousness that remained secretly intact. Brothels were located only a short walk down Albert and Margaret streets, two blossom-filled avenues in the city centre, where the most rudimentary form of vice was available for £1 a time in one-storey weatherboard houses hidden from view by 10-foot high corrugated iron fences. The madam sat in an armchair on the verandah, chatting to her girls over her knitting or a glass of sherry. As the iron cladding indicated a penitentiary rather than a house of pleasure, the setting was well suited to the widespread concept that sex outside marriage was a moral, if not quite criminal, offence. These bordellos were known to the police as 'tolerated houses' and the degree of tolerance was determined by the size of the kickback to the Vice Squad.

Estelle Runcie said: 'Gradually the town became more and more filled with troops. The Americans and the Australians went their separate ways at night for entertainment. The Yanks went over Victoria Bridge to the Trocadero and the Australians were at other dancehalls like Cloudland. The only place they mingled was at the City Hall, which is where I went dancing. You made snap judgments of a person's character. When you think of all the young men we met, I never heard of anything bad happening to any of my friends. We used to walk home through Musgrave Park on the way home from the dances. Other women will tell you that no white woman was allowed over the bridge to South Brisbane during the war. That's a load of rubbish; the Trocadero was over there for a start.'

Until the Americans made their presence felt in the summer of '42, the greatest service rivalry was between the Australian Army and the Royal Australian Air Force. Bruce Eglinton said: 'I was working as a clerk for Dalgety's, the big wool people, and I had my heart set on joining the RAAF. I went to the recruiting office and they asked me some difficult mental arithmetic questions. I'd been to Church of England Grammar School and knew my maths, but the questions they asked me were impossible. I was turned down and I was very resentful towards the air force after that experience. I joined the army and became a gunner instead.'

Estelle Runcie said: 'The army and the air force really detested each other. The air force only accepted men with a university education, although I think that all went by the board after a while. They were so precious we called them the "Blue Orchids".' Outbreaks of violence between the two services were commonplace. Estelle witnessed one big fight in 1942. 'I was walking from the studio to catch my tram and saw that Queen Street at North Quay was just a milling of men, all fighting. One of the trams had been overturned and there was a fellow on top of it throwing prawn heads at everybody from a paper bag—I'll never forget that; he was throwing prawns at them.

'All the other trams were lined up as far as the eye could see. I couldn't cross the road, I just had to stand on the side of the road and watch it. I didn't have any feeling of fear; other people were just looking and tut-tutting while every Australian in a uniform was happily throwing himself into the fight. It was the army versus the air force. No Americans were involved; they didn't get involved in brawls when they first came here.'

Once the fighting started in New Guinea, Japanese propagandists seized on the fraternisation between American troops and Australian women. In her broadcasts, Tokyo Rose concentrated on telling Australian troops that Americans were seducing their women. Nor was this untrue. 'You could spot the women who were pick-ups for the Yanks,' said Estelle. 'They wore a lot of lipstick and stood around on street corners waiting to be noticed.'

As many American soldiers lived in camps, they used parks, shop doorways and empty air-raid shelters for intimacy. Vigilante groups of Australian soldiers were formed to let Americans know that this wasn't acceptable behaviour. Many suburban picture theatres had rows of canvas seats like extended deckchairs with no dividing armrests, and these were favoured by servicemen as 'passion pits'.

'There was always a head usher with a torch and he'd patrol up and down the aisle,' said one Brisbane woman. 'If he suspected something was going on, he'd shine his torch and break it up. Americans were always being slung out in the middle of the feature film.'

After many complaints, the US authorities issued orders forbidding servicemen from holding hands with their dates in public places, cuddling on trams, or even kissing girls goodnight in the street outside their homes. Provosts were empowered to cancel a soldier's leave if his behaviour was judged likely to cause offence.

Basil Veal was a 14-year-old schoolboy when the first US servicemen arrived in Brisbane. 'When the US fleet came on a goodwill visit in 1941, they got a terrific reception,' he said. 'I went to the Valley to watch them march past and everyone went wild. Then in 1942 it was different. The Americans moved into a camp at Victoria Park next to the golf course, near where I lived. The Australian Army had been there, but they moved out and the Americans immediately staged a massive building program.

'Huts were built overnight and barbed wire went up. There was a no-man's-land along a track between two stretches of barbed wire so that we could get to school. They had an open-air theatre on a hill beside the track and we used to watch adult movies on Friday night, sitting out of sight among the trees.

'As kids we tried to copy their hairstyles and clothes, but we didn't really get on with them. Some of the kids were caddies for them on the golf course and could spend their money in the canteen. One kid had a paper round and got chocolates from the PX. I joined the sea cadets at Kangaroo Point and we used to get the same goodies down there at the canteen. You couldn't buy these things in the shops. I used to get the ferry for Kangaroo Point from Petrie Bight in the city to go to sea cadets and I'd see Yanks drunk in the street. Fellows would knock off their wallets; I saw that a few times.

'There were brothels in Albert and Margaret streets and there would be queues a mile long. They were in old houses with high fences. We used to look through nail holes and see the girls sitting on the verandah. The mother of a friend of mine at Herston ran a brothel at her house. She had a few girls who worked there from time to time. She always had Scotch and chocolates from the Americans, and you'd see the same troops there whenever they came back on leave.

'The Americans really had an impact on Brisbane; they changed the whole system.'

Several thousand Aborigines lived in Brisbane, but almost all of them had been forced to the margins where they were effectively shunned. The question of colour had troubled the Australian psyche long before Federation and the fact that a proportion of American troops, about eight per cent, were black, or 'coloured' in official terminology, created a political dilemma.

All major political parties supported the White Australia Policy and the vast majority of Queenslanders agreed with the sentiments of the early Australian prime minister, Alfred Deakin, when he said: 'Unity of race is an absolute essential to the unity of Australia.'

In late February 1942, US Ambassador Nelson Johnson wrote to a friend in America: 'I get mighty discouraged with the Australian. He has no plans and no arms and won't work. Seems to expect us to do everything for him, fight for him and work for him.' Johnson blamed the country's 'artificial standards of living' which were created by high protective tariffs against foreign goods and a shortage of labour.

Australians saw their immigration policy largely as a matter of economics, believing that the importation of cheap Asian or black labour would catastrophically affect the living standards of white Australian workers. This attitude was so firmly entrenched that the Advisory War Council, which had been set up by Prime Minister Curtin to deal with wartime emergencies, even had the audacity to suggest to the State Department that only white troops should be sent to Australia. This 'suggestion' was passed on to the then chief of the war plans division of the War Department, Brigadier-General Dwight D. Eisenhower.

When Eisenhower referred the matter to the Secretary of War, Henry Stimson, he received a one-word reply back—'No!'—and the first Afro-Americans arrived in Queensland in March 1942. However, most of them were hastily shuffled off to far-flung country districts to build new airfields in the stifling outback heat.

In March 1942, Australia received 6346 black troops and the first mention that they had arrived appeared in the *Courier-Mail* on 20 March when the paper published a photograph of two black soldiers with the caption, 'Stalwart members of US forces who have arrived to do their part in the defence of Australia.' On 23 March, the *Truth* referred to the difficulties encounteed by US authorities in recruiting Australian labour to do menial work as a means of commenting on the Afro-American presence. The newspaper reported: 'Their inability to command labour here who could work to their standards ended in the importation of their own workers, most of them coloured boys, whose striking physique has captured the attention of street crowds.'

Two days later, General Brett cabled Washington requesting that no further black troops should be sent to Australia and that those already there should be returned to the United States or rebased in India or New Caledonia. Brett cited as his main reason the 'lack of understanding on the part of Australians of the relationship customarily preserved in Continental America and the consequent well-intentioned but ill-advised attitude of civilans towards Negro troops.' Bett warned that although every effort was being made to keep Negroes and Australians apart, 'the situation will inevitably lead to bloodshed'.

The War Cabinet and the American military authorities had come up with a plan to deal with the influx of black troops, but it hadn't really worked. Using primarily a policy of geographical isolation, the powers-that-be had tried to ensure that black Americans were sent to do hard manual labour, such as clearing scrub and building airfields in remote rural centres like Mount Isa, Cloncurry and Birdum. Mount Isa was a huge, dry, dusty, fly-infested mining town, but it had bars and brothels and some of the proprietors were only too willing to take the soldiers' money. Cloncurry was a more modest place with one of the most hostile environments anywhere in the world; blazing hot in summer, freezing cold in winter.

But it quickly became apparent that geographical isolation was only a partial answer to the problem. Labour was required in urban areas like Brisbane, Ipswich, Townsville and Rockhampton to unload the huge shipments of arms and equipment that were passing through the docks and railheads.

Residential zoning was introduced to keep black and white troops apart. US authorities designated certain areas as either 'white' or 'coloured' in accordance with practices in the United States, and the colour line was rigidly enforced by US provost marshals in exactly the same way as if they were serving in Mississippi or Alabama.

However, many of the Afro-American troops came from northern urban areas, such as New York, Chicago and Detroit, and had no intention of surrendering their hard-won rights and privileges. As the grandsons of former slaves, they were keenly aware of the freedoms at stake.

A lot of Americans carried weapons for protection and in one early brawl in Stanley Street, South Brisbane, black troops threatened white servicemen with knives. In the ensuing fight, the local civilian police acted with restraint, but US service police unhesitatingly broke up the fight with batons.

Prior to 1942, Brisbanites had rarely seen white women consorting with black men, and then only with Aborigines and Torres Strait Islanders around the streets and parks of South Brisbane. They had not anticipated that this situation would radically change once black troops got a chance to mix with Australians living in 'coloured zones'. The culture shock was immense. Black Americans had hitherto been protrayed in various sections of the press as 'wild-eyed Rastuses'.

When it was realised that this racial stereotyping was unfounded, many white girls found themselves attracted to black troops. Girls from 'respectable' families invited them home and attended dances with them. A hostile, racist edge crept into correspondence reaching the US War Department's General Staff files, one correspondent stating: 'You ought to see a big buck with his ribbons. You can imagine what a big shot he is with the women—their weak point.'

Pamela Davenport said: 'I did have a very soft spot for the American Negroes. They were always so cheerful and I loved their smiles—so white against their polished black skins. I remember my excitement when one night I answered the door to a cheerful Negro who seemed to a small child [to be] of mammoth proportions. He was the first I had seen. In a rich southern accent he asked for water because, "My automobile has boiled". What, I wondered, was an automobile and what was he doing cooking on the road?'

Many Brisbanites simply turned their backs on the situation. One said: 'They seemed so huge and black and up to that time we didn't have any dark races in Brisbane and very few of our own Aborigines. I guess we were antagonistic and prejudiced. I guess we just ignored them.'

Australian men who had already come off second best against white American males were now confronted with smartly dressed, well-paid and physically superior Afro-Americans. Intelligence reports sent back to Washington during 1942 emphasised that a main cause of friction between the Allies was the question of 'white women with coloured troops'. As one office of Strategic Services report commented: 'In many cases, white girls have associated intimately with coloured troops, and, of course, the effect is very bad.'

An official report on civilian morale in North Queensland conducted by Professor R. D. Wright and Dr Ian Hogbin, said: 'It is commonly believed in the southern States that there are licensed brothels in Queensland. This is not so, though police insist that girls living in certain houses, who are known to be prostitutes, shall have regular examinations. In Brisbane, there are some 20 of these houses. The American forces have set up several such places, with Australian girls, for the use of Negro troops, much to the disgust of many civilians.'

The Americans did indeed requisition whatever they needed, although not girls, using powers granted to them by the Australian government. Gloria Valentine (later Mrs Gloria Bradshaw) said: 'They confiscated all the Singer sewing machines from every business premise in Brisbane. I worked for a fashion designer, Mrs Caldwell, in an exclusive little salon in the Old Town Hall Arcade. We had four machines and the Americans just came in one day and took them.

'Then they said we could work for them; they'd taken over the Watson Ferguson stationery building in South Brisbane and put all the sewing machines they'd gathered from all over Brisbane on the first floor. We had to forget all about our fashion work and mend American Army uniforms. There were hundreds of girls working there from 7 am often until 7 pm and sometimes weekends, depending on when the big bales of torn uniforms came in.

'If you worked for the Americans, you had your little photo disc and you could go to the American Red Cross canteen opposite the Gresham Hotel in Adelaide Street and have your meals. So I lived pretty lavishly;

they had so many things you couldn't get in the shops like salmon and chocolates and Nestles tinned cream. The boys used to bring the girls nylon stockings—that was a real treat. The Americans had everything like that. They were very hard to work for, and you had to do a hard day's work, but they were very generous and the pay was very, very good.'

In addition to the sewing machines in Mrs Caldwell's salon, the Americans took over the best offices, the best hotels—the elegant old Bellevue as well as Lennon's—and even some of the best schools. When the GPO was unable to met an order for telephones, troops ripped the handsets out of public phone boxes near their bases and hooked up their own equipment to the lines.

Bob Firehock said: 'I became purchasing officer and I went to the Nash automobile agency and told the manager I wanted every one of his cars. I got six Nash sedans and just signed for them, but they were happy with that because I also bought a lot of toolboxes, towlines and other equipment.'

The air of urgency appealed to girls like Joan Staines, who had wondered what the Americans were like from the deck of the *Koopa* in December 1941. 'The Americans were can-do,' she said, 'and they had great *joie de vivre*.'

In common with Estelle Runcie and many other young Brisbane women Joan was about to meet a dashing American sweetheart.

Immediately after the loss of the *Houston*, Rear Admiral William A. Glassford Jnr ordered all US ships remaining at Tjilatjap, three destroyers and four gunboats including USS *Tulsa*, to make a break for Australia. The *Tulsa* was an old seagoing gunboat, PG-22, which had been part of the US Asiatic Fleet based in the Philippines, and she made it safely across the Coral Sea to the Queensland coast. Sailing south, she entered the Brisbane River and came to rest in a dry-dock at South Brisbane for repairs.

Estelle Runcie said: 'I lived in a flat at Dock Street overlooking the dry-dock behind the South Brisbane library. There was a ship in there being serviced, the USS *Tulsa*, and I met the captain, Bill Porter, and fell madly in love with him. I met him on a date set up by a friend of mine called Bob, who drove some of the American staff cars. He asked me if I'd have dinner with a nice man who'd just arrived in Brisbane and I was reluctant but finally agreed. I arranged to meet Bill outside Lennon's and said I'd be wearing a pretty hat with pink roses. It belonged to my cousin Bubbles and I'd borrowed it for the occasion.

'Bill turned up and we had dinner. He was 32 and a widower; he said his wife had been killed in a raid on Hong Kong and he had a little son. His family came from one of the southern states, where his father had been a general. After dinner, Bill said he'd take me home and, as his ship was in dry-dock at the bottom of my street, I let him. He rang up the next day and invited me onto the *Tulsa* for dinner. I didn't know he was captain of the ship until I was piped aboard and we went down to this beautiful dining room in his quarters.

'The table was set up with silver on a white tablecloth. He'd asked me in advance what I'd like to eat and I'd said curry and rice, so his Chinese cook brought out *rijstaffel* on this great big silver platter. There were so many different dishes I didn't know what to do. I was only 15 and I must have sat there open-mouthed because Bill found my reaction highly amusing. I saw a fair bit of Bill after that night; he used to look up at me in Dock Street through his telescope and give me a wave. He was a lovely fellow and a real southern gentleman.'

On a moonlit night, Ed Webster sniffed the air of the Indian Ocean off the port bow. The coast of Western Australia was over there somewhere, although you'd never know it. But when Webster went ashore at Fremantle, he soon felt at home. The streets were clean, the little cottages neat and tidy, and there were familiar sights and sounds; a man in a Jackie Howe shearer's singlet cutting the grass with scythe, Aussie accents in the shops, kids playing cricket.

The date was 23 March 1942, and Gunner Webster had made it home from the war along with 18,000 members of the 7th Division of the AIF. 'We landed at Fremantle and some of us had about six hours leave ashore in Perth,' said Gunner Noel Glasgow. 'We were the first AIF convoy to return and people had us in their homes and gave us a meal. Then we went back to the ship and took off before daylight for Adelaide.'

Webster spent his leave with his mates in the bars, drinking beer. This was what he had dreamed about for the past 18 months. He caught his first sight of Americans, a group of dashing submarine sailors.

Bruce Eglinton remembers one of the diggers saying: 'They say the Yanks are stealing our sheilas.'

To which another digger replied: 'Nah, they're just sorting them out for us!'

Everybody laughed; it was good to be back. If things had changed at home, well, they'd changed too; still the same salt-of-the-earth blokes who'd arrived in Palestine, but they had a harder edge now; knew more. Webster could feel the change deep in his guts. He'd learned what Ginger Mick and the other blokes in the first AIF were talking about;

cut from the same cloth, they were, peas in a pod. He knew about other races too, and how all men died more or less the same irrespective of rank, class or religion.

As the *Egra* rounded the coastline towards South Australia, Webster kept reminding himself that he'd be kissing the army goodbye before Easter. He'd be home, playing with Johnny and telling Alice the things he hadn't been able to put in his letters; that war was a mug's game, really, and he'd had a bellyful of it. He had a few quid coming to him from the army and he'd go back into the transport business, perhaps get a truck of his own. Just for once, Crool Forchin seemed to be smiling on him.

Lieutenant Lance Watts said: 'We landed at Port Adelaide and were due to go north to defend Darwin, but they put us on a train on the Victorian border instead and we came up inland New South Wales to Tenterfield. We disembarked there and stayed at London Bridge, just outside Tenterfield, for a few weeks. Then we went on to the Brisbane Line, as we called it, we were not told that originally, but it soon came out that north of the Brisbane Line was to be wiped out.

'The line ran from Caloundra on the coast, inland through the Glasshouse Mountains, through Kilcoy and Woodford. We were based at Caboolture to the east of the railway station in a big swampy area for two or three months. We had our equipment with us, mainly two-pounders, and we patrolled the beach and up through the pine forests as far as Kilkoy.'

Many of the gunners who had come from the Brisbane Valley were practically in their own backyards and beating a path through the bush tracks brought memories of hunting in the forests and fishing in the headwaters of the Brisbane River.

But some of their comrades had been killed in Syria and they remembered them when they saw familiar things, such as a young boy fishing in a shady pool, or a rusted plough abandoned by some old battler in an overgrown paddock: They knew the names and numbers of the fallen off by heart: QX768 Duckering G. E., QX 14967 Steinhardt H. R. C., QX990 Taylor E. J.

As Ginger Mick said:

An' the blokes that ain't returnin'—blokes that's paid the biggest price—
    They'll go singin', singin', singin' to the Gates uv Paradise.

Lieutenant Bill Thomas, who had been brought up in Brisbane, saw huge changes in the city when he went home on leave. He said: 'I'd been married just before I sailed for the Middle East and I found that my wife and the other locals had coped very well with the wartime restrictions and everything else that went with being transformed suddenly, almost overnight, from a city of 300,000 to a big metropolis. I went for a walk one night near my parents' home at Morningside and three streets away came across an entire regiment of American anti-aircraft gunners. There was no doubt in my mind that the Americans had taken over the place.'

Gunner Noel Glasgow said: 'I had the experience of coming home and finding my city was not mine anymore—the Yanks had it. That's how it appeared to us, but we steered clear of trouble with the American soldiers and their MPs. I was always well-behaved and so were my particular friends; we didn't go out and get drunk or cause any problems with the police or the Americans, but some of the fellows, particularly infantry fellows, enjoyed a fight.

'Yes, some of them went looking for trouble.'

Chapter Seven

◄○►

MacArthur's Kingdom

HOLED up in the Malinta Tunnel on Corregidor, General Richard K. Sutherland had no intention of surrendering to the Japanese. However, the last thing he expected in the midst of the Siege of Bataan, with food, ammunition and medical supplies running perilously low, was to find himself rolling in riches.

The windfall came unexpectedly when General George Marshall ordered MacArthur to evacuate the ailing President Quezon from Corregidor and smuggle him to the United States. Quezon agreed to go, but before departing decided it was time to honour a debt owed to MacArthur and his senior staff over the modernisation of the Philippines armed forces.

Ignoring the fact that MacArthur's military preparations were about to cost him his country, Quezon told him to draw up an executive order authorising a number of payments linked to a secret arrangement between the two men under which MacArthur and his most senior staff would receive a percentage of the Philippines annual defence budget, plus compensation for loss of salary and expenses in the event of war. The deal was legal under the terms of a letter that the US Adjutant-General had written to MacArthur in September 1935, granting him the right to accept such a payment from the Philippines government.

At MacArthur's instigation, Sutherland formulated Executive Order No. 1 of the Commonwealth of the Philippines, and Quezon signed it. MacArthur's entitlement was $500,000, making him rich. Sutherland, as chief of staff and therefore junior partner, was awarded the far from inconsiderable sum of $75,000. All the two men needed to do to collect was to get out of the Philippines.

The opportunity arose on 9 March when Roosevelt ordered MacArthur to leave Corregidor and make for Australia, where he was to take command of American forces in the south-west Pacific. MacArthur said that he wanted to fight on, but members of his staff, notably General Sutherland, urged him to leave. Three days later MacArthur, Jean, Arthur MacArthur IV, his amah Ah Cheu and 14 of his staff boarded torpedo boats and left Corregidor for Mindanao. MacArthur was in PT-41, commanded by Lieutenant Thomas Bulkeley, USN.

Arriving at Mindanao two days later after an extremely rough voyage, they proceeded overland to an airstrip at the Del Monte plantation to await three B-17s from Australia. However, only one aircraft, piloted by Lieutenant Harl Pearse Jnr, turned up for the rendezvous. MacArthur took one look at the youthful, 'inexperienced' pilot and, more particularly, the distressed state of his plane, a veteran of the Philippines and Java campaigns, and refused to fly in it. There were tin-can patches on the fuselage, the superchargers did not work and it had no brakes.

MacArthur was furious. He sent a blistering message to Brett in Australia and Marshall in Washington, demanding the three best B-17s in the Pacific and experienced pilots to fly them. Pearse loaded up his plane with air corps pilots and personnel from Mindanao and flew to Batchelor Field, the B-17 landing strip 40 miles inland from Darwin, touching down on virtually his last drop of gasoline.

Two serviceable B-17s eventually arrived at Del Monte and MacArthur and his family boarded one of them. The engine refused to start. The party was offloaded into the other B-17, piloted by Captain Frank Bostrom, which proceeded down the runway without mishap. The plane was so overloaded that it dipped slightly on take-off and just managed to clear the trees. MacArthur made the flight to Australia sitting nervously on a chair in the radio operator's compartment, while Jean, Arthur and Ah Cheu crouched on a straw mattress beneath the waist guns.

When they landed at Batchelor Field, Patrick J. Hurley was waiting to greet MacArthur. Hurley offered to fly his old friend to Melbourne in his own plane, but MacArthur had had enough of flying and opted to travel the 2000 miles to Adelaide by train. The battered old locomotive that was provided for him was the railroad equivalent of Pearse's patched-up B-17 and he had a miserable journey with his aide de camp, Syd Huff, trying desperately to make the best of a bad situation.

In Adelaide, wearing no ribbons, no gold buttons and no gold braid except for the scroll on his field marshal's cap, MacArthur launched into his famous 'I shall return' speech at an impromptu press conference: 'The President of the United States ordered me to break through the Japanese lines and proceed from Corregidor to Australia for the purpose, as I understand it, of organising the American offensive against Japan, a primary object of which is the relief of the Philippines. I came through and I shall return.'

However, MacArthur's bravado evaporated on the journey to Melbourne in a much smarter train when his deputy chief of staff, Richard Marshall, informed him that there were only 29,000 US servicemen in Australia, mainly air corps, anti-aircraft crews and service troops, with only a few thousand combat troops. Equally galling, there were only about 250 combat aircraft and many of these needed spare parts or repairs before they could go into action. The bottom line was that MacArthur would have to make a protracted stay in Australia while a big enough invasion force was painstakingly assembled to retake the Philippines. His expectations of charging back to Manila almost immediately at the head of a victorious army had been dashed at a stroke.

One biographer wrote that on hearing the news MacArthur 'turned deadly white, his knees buckled, his lips twitched. An officer who had known him for 20 years said later, "I have never seen him so affected. He was heartbroken". After a long silence, MacArthur whispered miserably, "God have mercy on us". Unable to sleep, he spent the whole night pacing the train.'

MacArthur had regained his composure when he stepped onto the platform at Spencer Street Station in Melbourne the following morning, 21 March. During the night, he had found time to sit down and compose a simple, statesmanlike address. He was greeted by a crowd of 4000, including 35 uniformed American press correspondents and a guard of honour of US and Philippines soldiers in full battledress. The Army Minister, Frank Forde, clearly overawed by the occasion, welcomed MacArthur on behalf of the Australian government with the astonishing observation that 'never in history has such a galaxy of uniforms and insignia been seen at Spencer Street Station'.

Reading from his prepared statement, MacArthur said: 'I am glad indeed to be in intimate co-operation with the Australian soldier. I know him well from World War days and admire him greatly. I have every confidence in the ultimate success of our joint cause. But success in modern war requires something more than courage and a will to die. It requires careful preparation. This means the provision of sufficient troops and material to meet the known strength of a potential enemy. No general can make something out of nothing. My success or failure depends primarily on the resources the respective governments place at my disposal. My faith in them is complete. In any event, I shall do my best. I shall keep the soldier faith.'

George Brett had arrived at Spencer Street Station at the head of the welcoming committee, but found himself relegated to the fringes. Beryl Stevenson said: 'General Brett went to meet him, but he snubbed Brett at the station. MacArthur had his peculiarities and his relationship with Brett was of that order for the whole of the time that Brett remained on his staff. They were two tall, magnificent, beribboned men like two bulls in a paddock when there was only room for one.'

It was Brett who had been given the task of telephoning Curtin on Roosevelt's behalf on 17 March to inform him that MacArthur would command all US forces in Australia, an appointment which the War Cabinet instantly greeted as an 'inspiration'. MacArthur, however, felt nothing but loathing for Brett and had no wish to work with him. Not only had Brett stopped the *Pensacola* ships from taking aid to the Philippines, he was also responsible for endangering the lives of MacArthur and his family by sending a patched-up plane to collect them at Del Monte. And there was more: Brett's first interview with the Australian press published on 17 March had contained inflammatory stuff about the stupidity of planes being lost on the ground, a not-so-veiled reference to the shambles at Clark Field, even though he actually referred to Java.

Brett said: 'I have not lost faith in Australians. They're not going to lose this country. No, Sir! Not in the least. You may have to take a little drubbing from the Japanese at the start. But so did England. And there's still an England. The whole strategy of air warfare today is to hit and hit hard and not sit anymore. You must never lose a plane on the ground. If you lose a plane in the air its okay. Don't let them be mopped up on the ground. That was one of the terrible things that happened in Java, where so many grounded planes were destroyed.'

MacArthur moved his family in to the sixth floor of Menzies Hotel in Collins Street where he silently brooded about George Brett, refusing to see him even to express his grievances.

Five days after his arrival in Melbourne, MacArthur was driven to Canberra, where he addressed the Australian parliament. He wore his four-star general's uniform for the occasion with a glittering array of medals pinned to his tunic. The politicians, diplomats and public servants of the federal capital, accustomed to a certain regal Empire pomp, treated him like visiting royalty. Prime Minister Curtin informed MacArthur that Roosevelt had awarded him the Congressional Medal of Honor, the United States' highest award for valour and announced that he would 'see him through until our flags float side by side in Manila'. What the

Prime Minister did not say was that to achieve this victory he was handing MacArthur the keys to the Commonwealth, giving him power to do more or less as he pleased. 'He was made dictator of the armed forces—air, sea and land,' noted one Australian commentator. It was little wonder that MacArthur wrote about Curtin with characteristically unconscious humour: 'We promptly came to a sense of mutual trust, co-operation and regard.'

MacArthur's faith in that 'mutual trust' might have been shaken had he known that Curtin, a former journalist, actually took members of the Australian press corps into his confidence at twice-daily briefings in Canberra. Don Whitington, then political correspondent for the *Daily Telegraph*, said: 'At those intimate talks we were told, long before most others knew, and long before it could be printed, of the departure of the AIF from the Middle East and its hazardous progress across the Indian Ocean to Australia. We knew of the bitter behind-the-scenes arguments between Curtin and Churchill when Churchill tried unsuccessfully to have the returning army diverted to Burma where, as events transpired, it would have been lost.

'We knew of the impending arrival of Douglas MacArthur, of the preparations being made for the hush-hush arrival of the first wave of American troops.' MacArthur regarded such fraternisation as inadvisable at best and dangerous at worst.

As for 'regard', the politician and the general actually held diametrically opposed views on just about everything except the war. Although they were from the same generation—Curtin was born in 1885, MacArthur in 1880—Curtin's father was an Irish-born policeman who had never risen above the rank of constable, and who had worked as a hotel manager after leaving the police force. As a young man, Curtin had left the Roman Catholic faith and taken up playing the cornet in a Salvation Army band. His main job before entering the House of Representatives was as a trade union organiser; politically, he was a socialist and a pacifist who had vehemently opposed conscription during World War I. He also had a drink problem which led him to binge on alcohol after long periods of painful abstinence.

MacArthur was cut from very different cloth. His father, Colonel Arthur MacArthur, was a hero of the American Civil War, holder of the Congressional Medal of Honor, and a former governor-general of the Philippines. MacArthur himself had topped his years at West Point, and had a distinguished role with the American forces in France towards the end of World War I. He had never had any reason to question his family's devout Republicanism.

During the Depression, he had led a detachment of troops against the

Bonus Army, a gathering of World War I veterans who had marched peacefully on Washington to demand payment of a bonus promised to them for war service. Riding on horseback at the head of 600 troops, MacArthur gave the order to disperse the marchers with tear gas. After that, many Americans regarded him as a symbol of right-wing repression, a natural enemy of men like John Curtin.

One of the few things the two men had in common was a love of football: Curtin followed the Melbourne Australian Rules club, Carlton, while MacArthur was devoted to the team at West Point, where he had been superintendent.

By nature, both men were reclusive. MacArthur had rarely attended social functions in the Philippines and Curtin's form of relaxation was to play a game of billiards at the Lodge with his chauffeur. A mutual loathing of Japan provided a strong enough bond to bring the two men together in an unquestioning, enduring and—as Roosevelt and Churchill would quickly discover—formidable partnership.

Curtin had officially acknowledged that American troops were in Australia on 17 March, welcoming them with a reminder about their white Anglo-Irish origins. He said: 'The warmth of [their] welcome will not be motivated by other than one of kinship with men and women who largely come from the same stock as ourselves.'

This must have come as a surprise to US troops of Norwegian, Swedish, German, Italian and African ancestry. MacArthur also picked up on the racial theme when he told Parliament of 'the link between our countries which does not depend upon the written protocol, upon treaties of alliance, or upon diplomatic doctrines. It goes deeper than that. It is that indescribable consanguinity of race which causes us to have the same aspirations, the same ideals, and the same dreams of future destiny'.

Despite his rousing words, MacArthur was deeply dispirited and the unusually cold weather in Melbourne did nothing to improve his outlook. The 'southerly buster' whistled in from Antarctica, bringing pouring rain that turned the army camps into freezing quagmires. Menzies Hotel lived up to its Scottish name with good malt whisky in the bar and fine cuisine in the dining room, and the unheated rooms had all the bracing grandeur of a remote Caledonian castle.

MacArthur set up his headquarters at 401 Collins Street, a few blocks from the Menzies, travelling there and back in a black Cadillac with four stars on the front bumper bar and the number plate USA-1 at the rear. Apart from those short trips to and from the office, he rarely went anywhere. Never one to socialise in Manila, after he'd paid his respects to the State Governor, Sir Winstan Dugan, he gave Melbourne society a shoulder as cold as the weather.

Jean MacArthur attempted to keep up appearances and drove herself to social functions in a Ford sedan with the number plate USA-2. She grappled with the pecking order of Melbourne's social elite, the Toorak Set, and did her best to overcome the language barrier. When she went shopping at the Myer Emporium, she asked an assistant if she could see some pocketbooks. The assistant had never heard the American term for 'handbag' and, thinking Mrs MacArthur wanted a diary or appointment book of some kind to keep in her pocket, escorted her to the stationery department.

The real reason for MacArthur's solitariness was not the weather, but his inability to influence events taking place in the Philippines. MacArthur was in mourning, not only for the men he had left behind, but also for the loss of his reputation. He hadn't even got his feet under his new desk before General Wainwright gave up the fight in Bataan rather than witness the mass extermination of his forces at the hands of Japanese tanks and artillery which had driven a huge wedge through his front-line defences. With Bataan gone, only the forces on Corregidor and Mindanao remained, leaving MacArthur with the forlorn task of trying to prise men and armaments out of the reluctant Roosevelt.

However, on 17 April Curtin informed MacArthur that the following day he would place command of the combat elements of the Australian defence forces in Australia in his hands. Australian commanders would be told that all orders and instructions issued by him were to be considered as having emanated from the Commonwealth Government itself. On 18 April, MacArthur issued his first general order as Supreme Commander of Allied forces in the south-west Pacific, specifying the following commands:

a. Allied Land Forces, South-West Pacific Area. Commander: General Sir Thomas Blamey, Australian Army.
b. Allied Air Forces, South-West Pacific Area. Commander: Lieutenant-General George H. Brett, United States Army.
c. Allied Naval Forces, South-West Pacific Area. Commander: Vice-Admiral Herbert F. Leary, United States Navy.
d. United States Forces in the Philippines. Commander: Lieutenant-General Jonathon M. Wainwright, United States Army.
e. United States Army Forces in Australia. Commander: Major-General Julian G. Barnes, United States Army.

However, MacArthur was far from happy with these appointments. Every one of them had been officially sanctioned by Washington and

Canberra before he had arrived in Melbourne and he deeply resented having them foisted upon him, particularly Brett's appointment as air force commander. When the right moment came he would act with great skill in despatching his enemies, but for the time being he worked hard to consolidate his relationship with the bedazzled Curtin, realising that fate had placed him in a position to seize political as well as military power.

At MacArthur's urging, Curtin asked the British government to send to Australia an aircraft carrier loaded with planes as well as a British infantry division and an armoured division. Churchill referred Curtin's request to Roosevelt, demanding to know whether MacArthur had 'any authority from the United States for taking such a line', and MacArthur was rebuked by Washington for making a request through incorrect channels.

It was obvious to Churchill and Roosevelt that Curtin was completely spellbound by his American commander-in-chief. In Canberra, it was already being said, in both hope and fear, that the new Curtin–MacArthur alliance would decide the future of Australia.

Inevitably, MacArthur's tactics produced results, although some of these could be measured only in terms of the heat they generated. Richard Sutherland never attempted to dissuade MacArthur from challenging the Joint Chiefs of Staff in Washington, even when his language was intemperate and his arguments flawed. As a result, Sutherland himself was inundated by the flow of irate replies from Washington and the files involved in assembling an Allied command virtually from scratch grew thicker and heavier.

Sutherland was a capable, hard-working chief of staff who dealt with the minutiae of his job, but still found time to socialise. Even in the midst of all this paperwork, he found himself thinking about a woman he had met at a party. He couldn't seem to get her out of his mind.

The Yale-educated son of a senator from West Virginia, Sutherland had slipped easily into the Toorak Set. At a party he was introduced to Elaine Bessemer-Clark, a married woman of 32 with a three-year-old son. With plain features and mousy hair, later dyed blonde, she could no more be described as a society beauty than Wallis Simpson, the American divorcee who had captivated Edward VIII. However, like Mrs Simpson, Elaine Bessemer-Clark was totally ruthless in getting what she wanted and, more than anything, she wanted to be at the hub of the power vested in MacArthur and his highly decorated minions. When she met Sutherland, the magnetism between them was instantaneous; she saw weakness, he sensed a dominatrix.

For all his bluster, Sutherland was a frightened man at heart, an ill-tempered bully with a yellow streak who acted out his faults in sexual gameplay. Flushed with the confidence that a sum like $75,000 could give a man, he now found himself knocked sideways by a woman he hardly knew, yet who seemed to know him so well. Ignoring his wife and children in America, he plunged headlong into a tempestuous affair.

As Elaine Bessemer-Clark's double-barrelled surname suggested, she was an aristocrat of sorts. Her father, Sir Norman Brookes, was a legendary figure in the Australian sporting world, having won the Wimbledon Singles Tennis title. Her mother, Dame Mabel Brookes, was a pillar of Australian society and tireless charity worker. But it was her husband, Reginald Bessemer-Clark, an English millionaire and heir to the Bessemer steel fortune, who had given Elaine class and wealth beyond the dreams of Toorak. Reginald Bessemer-Clark, however, was in no position to protest his wife's infidelity; he had been taken prisoner when Singapore surrendered and was in Changi prison.

Quite apart from the indecency of cuckolding a fellow officer, especially one held captive by the enemy, Sutherland was taking a considerable risk in a purely military sense: adultery, sodomy and fraternisation were strictly forbidden under the United States' Uniform Code of Military Justice and he would be court-martialled if an official complaint was made about his behaviour.

But Sutherland completely ignored the dangers. Although Elaine had never needed to work and was not trained for a career of any description, with breathtaking audacity he found her a job as receptionist at MacArthur's headquarters in Collins Street.

'Elaine Bessemer-Clark was a floozy blonde,' said one of the men who met her at GHQ. 'She wore so much perfume you could smell it eight floors up.' When the working day ended, Sutherland and his lover adjourned to the Menzies for dinner, then slipped upstairs to the privacy of his suite. MacArthur did not intervene. Sergeant Bill Bentson said: 'MacArthur knew what was going on, but he never did anything about it.'

For all his much-vaunted piety, MacArthur was in no position to lecture anyone on the subject of morality, having once been involved in a sex scandal with a 16-year-old showgirl named Isabel Rosario Cooper. He had installed Isabel, whom he had picked up in Manila, as his mistress in a suite at the Chastleton Hotel, Washington, until he had grown tired of her and then thrown her out. The story was hushed up to save his career.

But Melbourne was a straitlaced, Presbyterian sort of place and the sexual activity surrounding the khaki casanovas at the Menzies attracted much vitriolic comment. The novelist Henrietta Drake-Brockman said: 'At night, generals, colonels and lesser ranks made the white and gilt dining rooms look like a set for *Army Romance*. It was, of course, difficult to get a seat to view the spectacle if one was not in some way attached to the American Army.'

Another married officer to form an attachment to an Australian girl was Colonel LeGrande A. Diller, whose wife Harriet had been evacuated from Manila to the United States the previous year. Joy Foord was a brunette who worked in the staff office of the Myer Emporium, an only child who had left her parents' home in Ballarat at the age of 17 to head for the bright city lights.

'Every Friday night the girls at Myer's got together for drinks after work, usually at the Australia Hotel to meet the Yanks,' she said. 'This did not appeal to me, so one night I suggested we went to the Alexander Hotel at the other end of the city. When we got there, the bar was empty except for an enlisted man, who was on his own, and some officers at another table. The enlisted man asked if he could join us, which he did. His name was Eric Ives and he was a member of the Flying Tigers on leave from China.

'Then two of the officers asked the maitre d' if they could also join us and the maitre d' did the right thing and introduced them. I thought it was very strange because enlisted men and officers did not mix socially. Two of the officers were Colonel Diller and Colonel Harry Williams, a Brit who worked in press relations. Colonel Diller asked me to have dinner with him the following week at Menzies Hotel. This was how I met the love of my life. He was short, skinny and married—but life is never what we would like it to be.

'We had dinner and I started seeing him. Soon afterwards, the window dresser at Myer's wanted to do a display with the theme of "I shall return". They had a very large photo of General MacArthur, but there was no signature on it. The Myer's directors were trying to get the General's signature, but were getting nowhere because they had to pass General Sutherland.

'When I told my boss I thought I could get it done, they all laughed. However, I took the photo and asked Colonel Diller if he could get it signed for me. He did and it was quite a triumph, because thousands of people crowded around that window to see MacArthur's picture. A lot of the girls who met Americans worked for Myer's. They liked Americans because they gave them silk stockings, lipsticks and things we couldn't get.'

Escape from the rigours of Corregidor seemed to have activated the testosterone of many of MacArthur's male staff. One Australian woman who worked for the US Army said that, if an applicant was blonde and 'well-stacked', she would be shown a typewriter and a washing machine and, if she could identify the typewriter, she would be offered a job. There were, according to another Australian typist, those who 'held their jobs by their tails and ones who did their jobs'. One secretary claimed she was the only female working for the American colonels in Melbourne who did not have sex with her boss.

Colonel John A. Robenson, the officer who had almost been knifed by a Filipino steward on the *Holbrook*, turned up at an official function in Adelaide with his female stenographer on his arm and proceeded to behave like a pompous oaf. Robenson's new task was to get supplies through to the guerrilla forces on Mindanao. The American Consul refused to turn a blind eye to his conduct, and in an official report to MacArthur's headquarters, described Robenson's behaviour and stated that the officer had 'succeeded in insulting almost every Australian with whom he has come in contact'.

MacArthur had already annoyed his Australian allies by refusing to appoint anyone other than Americans to his staff. This included the 14 colleagues who had accompanied him from the Philippines known as the Bataan Gang. MacArthur told General Marshall: 'There is no prospect of obtaining qualified senior staff officers from the Australians.' No fewer than eight gang members were named in senior positions at Allied General Headquarters and the other six were already working for him in various capacities such as chief medical officer or *aide-de-camp*.

Only one senior position in the entire SWPA command had gone to an Australian, Sir Thomas Blamey, then 57, who had been Commander-in-Chief of the AIF in the Middle East, where had had to bow to the wishes of his British superior, General Auchinleck, even though Australian troops formed a majority among the Allied forces.

Blamey had arrived in Melbourne from the Middle East on 26 March to become Commander-in-Chief of the Australian Army. Soon afterwards, Curtin had informed him that he would also be serving as Commander of Allied Land Forces under General MacArthur. Thus Blamey found himself with two vital roles to play instead of one, a prospect that appealed immensely to his self-aggrandising nature, even if in one of those roles he had to serve a new master and an American one at that.

Blamey was a former Victorian police commissioner who had been the subject of a sex scandal when his badge of office had been found in a brothel. He was a domineering man with an explosive temper which he kept rigidly under control; not so his penchant for loose women, whom he pursued with the vigour of an old roué—but, then, Curtin had not been looking for a gentleman to fight the Japanese when he had chosen Blamey.

Short, fat and ruthless, Blamey was MacArthur's poodle from the start. 'He is an experienced military officer,' opined MacArthur. 'He is very courteous and comes to see me whenever I want to see him immediately.' Blamey would remain MacArthur's man until, having served his purpose, he would be dumped as ruthlessly as George Brett.

Sergeant Bill Benston went to work in the GHQ hornets' nest, even though he had never been to the Philippines and was not a member of the Bataan Gang. He said: 'I was serving as a sergeant in the Coast Artillery Corps based at Fort Stevens in Oregon at the time of Pearl Harbor. This was a reservist force, but I enlisted after the 9th Corps sent a message that they wanted a sergeant for overseas duty. I volunteered and was assigned to signals.

'After training, there were 35 of us and we went to San Francisco, the port of embarkation, where we were medically examined and fumigated. We were based in an old fort on an island near Alcatraz in San Francisco Bay. When they took us to the ship in ferries, we looked up and it seemed to be a mile long—it was the *Queen Elizabeth*, which had been converted into a troop carrier. So as a sergeant I was going to travel to Australia first class in a cabin that accommodated two, although other ranks among the 6000 troops on board were down among the bilges. There were two other ships in the convoy, the *Mariposa* and the *Coolidge*, and we had a cruiser for escort.

'We reached Sydney Heads on 6 April 1942, and stopped outside the heads while the *Queen Mary* came out—she had just come over from New York and both liners couldn't be in harbour at the same time. There were no facilities for ships of this size, so we anchored in the stream out near the old fort at Pinchgut. Daytime, it was beautiful—red tiled roofs, the Harbour Bridge; it was really a sight to see.

'We all went to bed that first night and were woken up at 11 pm to board ferries to go ashore to board the railway on the dock. It was after midnight before we set off and the train was packed. There was an entire regiment on board, the 163rd Infantry Regiment of the American 41st Division who'd arrived in our convoy. Men slept in the overhead luggage racks, on the floors of the compartments, in the passageways. The locomotive just made it up hills and rolled down the other side; it was real Casey Jones stuff.

'We stopped at Cootamundra for breakfast and the whole regiment was fed on the platform. We had tea, not coffee, and sausages and mashed potatoes, which we later found out were called bangers 'n' mash. There was a second stop at a station with a railway bar and everyone crowded in for a drink. We didn't have any Australian money, but they had big posters up showing each dollar bill with its equivalent in Australian currency and the barmaids held up the dollars to match them with the ones on the poster to give out the right change.

'When we got to Albury, everyone got off to change trains for the different gauges that operated in each State. We reached Melbourne at 11 pm on 8 April and it was darker than hell in the brownout. There were just 35 of us; the members of the 41st Division had got off at the big army camp at Seymour. We took an electric train to the camp at Royal Park, which had been named Camp Pell in honour of Major Floyd Pell, who was shot down at Darwin. You had to make your own mattress out of straw, but we just laid our gear down and went to sleep.

'In the morning, we heard lions roaring, monkeys screaming, elephants trumpeting and wondered what the hell was going on. It sounded like we were in the jungle, but we were near the zoo. The Aussies had a mess for breakfast and we had mutton stew with grease on top, no coffee, only tea.

'An American colonel came out to interview us and I was one of 13 who were assigned to MacArthur's staff out of the original 35. We were the first enlisted men to work at MacArthur's headquarters in Collins Street because, although he'd brought his officers with him from the Philippines, he had no enlisted men. We had to find desks and other furniture, but we had a high priority, so we got what we needed.

'The first time I met MacArthur, I literally bumped into him. I had a date with an Australian girl at 7 pm and I didn't want to miss it. I got into the elevator and ran right into the general: my face was in his ribbons. "You're in a hurry," he said. "Have you got a date?" I said, "Yes, Sir." "Where are you from, soldier?" "Oregon, Sir." I was called "Sergeant Oregon" after that.'

The last man out of Bataan, Carlos Romulo, reported to GHQ on 25 April. Romulo had made such a hurried exit from the Philippines that he was wearing a uniform he had borrowed from a private twice his size at Mindanao. General Richard Marshall and Colonel Stevenot greeted Romulo in the outer office.

'They didn't look like the same men I had last seen in the tunnel,' said Romulo. 'They looked wonderful—fresh-shaven and clean. I felt dirty, and I knew I looked like hell, but they pounded me on the back.'

Romulo had lost 29 pounds on Corregidor and was swimming inside the uniform when he was shown into MacArthur's inner sanctum. 'Carlos, my boy!' said MacArthur. 'I can't bear to look at you.'

Still attired in his baggy uniform, Romulo was taken to Menzies for dinner by Marshall, Stevenot and Diller. He ordered steak and mushrooms, followed by vanilla ice-cream. 'The tables in the big dining room were set with gleaming silver and white linen,' he said. 'There were men in dress uniforms and women in evening clothes. Yes—

women, beautiful in light chiffons and flowered dresses! I had forgotten women could look so beautiful. I looked slowly from table to table and saw that the officers were those who had worked in the advance and rear echelons, in the headquarters on the Old Wall in Manila, and in the murk of the tunnel on Corregidor.

'Suddenly, I couldn't take any more. There seemed to be with us in that handsome and comfortable room the men and women we had left to await the coming of the enemy on Corregidor. There were the soldiers, who had succumbed to disease and starvation; the thousands of Filamerican captives who were being marched through the streets of Manila in rags and even in their underwear—gaunt skeletons, half naked and half dead. Their haggard, dirty faces looked at me through the silver and glitter of that dining room. I pushed the steak away . . .'

Romulo overcame his revulsion after several days' rest and went to work in press relations with Diller. Sergeant Bentson said: 'I got him a uniform that fitted, and the next time I saw him he was wearing the insignia of a lieutenant-colonel.'

Communications were vital to the work at GHQ, particularly signal intercepts obtained by American and British listening stations in Honolulu, Melbourne and London. In mid-April, Admiral Chester Nimitz received a report from his staff at Pearl Harbor that intercepts of the Japanese naval code JN25 indicated seaborne landings at Tulagi in the Solomons and Port Moresby in New Guinea about 3 May.

Nimitz decided to send the *Lexington*, then near Pearl Harbor, and the *Yorktown*, then near Noumea, with five cruisers, 11 destroyers and three other ships to engage the Japanese invasion fleet. Rear Admiral Jack Crace's cruiser squadron the *Australia*, the *Hobart* and the American *Chicago* were ordered to join in, making a total Allied taskforce of 26 warships under the command of Admiral Frank J. Fletcher.

With the prospect of a Japanese invasion, the civilian exodus from Queensland had become a controversial issue. The *Courier-Mail* asked its readers in a challenging editorial: 'Rifles or running shoes—which is it to be? That is what most people north of the Tweed want to know, and the question is pressed more insistently the further north it is asked. During the last few weeks there has been much talk about evacuation plans, loose talk, and irresponsible talk. We want more fighting talk— because fighting is the only thing that will keep the enemy out of Australia or throw him out if he effects a landing.'

Nimitz had no way of knowing the full extent of the Japanese invasion plan, but his decision to engage the enemy in the Coral Sea between New Guinea and Australia would mark the turning point of the war in the Pacific. For the people of Queensland, deliverance was at hand.

Chapter Eight

◄◊►

Deliverance

I N the last hour of her life, Ivy McLeod sheltered from the biting wind that whipped in off the waters of Port Phillip Bay. As the nightshift at MacArthur's headquarters at 401 Collins Street hunkered down in the early hours of 3 May to await developments in the Coral Sea, 42-year-old Ivy was huddled in the darkened doorway of a shop next door to the Bleak House Hotel, a *faux* Dickensian hostelry just across the road from the waterfront at Albert Park.

After spending the evening at her boyfriend's flat, Ivy was waiting for an all-night tram to take her home to East Melbourne, when Private Eddie Leonski sauntered up. Melbourne was a law-abiding city, at least in terms of crimes against women, and Ivy hadn't thought to ask her boyfriend to accompany her to the tramstop, even though it was two o'clock in the morning.

Leonski had been drinking heavily that night in hotel bars in the Albert Park area. 'I saw a girl standing by a doorway' he said later. 'She smiled. We talked and she stepped back into the doorway and I grabbed her by the neck. I changed the position of my hands, so that my thumbs were at her throat and I choked her.'

Ivy McLeod's semi-naked, mutilated body was found in the shop doorway the following morning. Reports of her murder in the press over the next two days alerted Melburnians to the presence of a strangler in their midst, but there was no reason for police to suspect that an American soldier had committed the crime, nor was there any reason for it to arouse interest at MacArthur's headquarters. The staff there were on full alert monitoring the action that had commenced off the Queensland coast.

The Battle of the Coral Sea was the first aircraft carrier battle fought in the history of warfare and the fact that, in terms of losses, the outcome was inconclusive only heightened the tensions aroused in the breasts of those who took part. Documents captured from the Japanese cruiser *Nachi* in 1945 showed that the invasion of Port Moresby was part of an ambitious three-phase operation by Yamamoto to destroy the US fleet and prepare the way for the invasion of Australia.

The first step of the Japanese plan was for an invading force to capture Tulagi at the end of the Solomon chain on 3 May. The following day the 114th Regiment, 3rd Kure Naval Landing Force, was to leave Rabaul in 11 transports and head due south towards the eastern end of Papua, where they would rendezvous with the striking and covering forces that had been engaged in the Tulagi landing.

The striking force would consist of two large carriers, *Shokaku* and *Zuikaku*, with two cruisers and six destroyers in attendance; the covering force was to be provided by the smaller carrier *Shoho* and four cruisers. Leaving the covering force to fight off any US Navy ships in the area, the transports would slip through the Jomard Passage and be in place for the invasion of Port Moresby on 7 May. At the same time, *Shokaku* and *Zuikaku* would sweep down through the Coral Sea and launch air strikes against Allied airfields at Townsville, Cooktown, Coen and Thursday Island to hamper air retaliation from northern Australia. The only problem for the Japanese was that the strike-force commander, Admiral Takagi, had no idea that Chester Nimitz had sent two aircraft carriers into the area to stop him.

About 8 am on 3 May, the first Japanese invasion group made an unopposed landing on the beaches of Tulagi. Admiral Fletcher had taken the *Yorktown* to a position about 100 miles south-west of the nearby island of Guadalcanal and the following day his planes launched three attacks on the Japanese landing force, sinking one destroyer and several smaller vessels. *Shoho* and some heavy cruisers dashed back to the area to confront the raiders only to find that the US ships had melted away to the south-east under cover of densely overcast skies. The *Yorktown* group rejoined the *Lexington* group on the morning of 5 May and the American carriers refuelled from the tanker *Neosho*.

On 6 May, the Japanese pressed ahead with their Moresby operation with the invasion convoy approaching Jomard Passage. It was protected on the port side by the covering force, with *Shoho* providing an air patrol until sundown. The Japanese were in a bullish mood; they had been elated earlier that day by the news from Manila that Corregidor had surrendered. As Port Moresby had been softened up with bombing raids for three months and the garrison of one Australian brigade was known to have little air cover, Japanese intelligence reports were unanimous in suggesting that the New Guinea campaign would be a much easier proposition than the Philippines.

Everything was going Japan's way until, at 7.30 on the night of 6 May, Admiral Fletcher set a course which would bring his carrier-borne aircraft within striking distance of the enemy at dawn the following morning. In the next 48 hours, nothing less than domination of the south-west Pacific hung in the balance.

At 6.25 am on 7 May Fletcher ordered Admiral Crace's cruiser squadron of the *Australia*, the *Hobart* and the *Chicago* to attack the transports, while he sought out the big Japanese carriers. At this point, neither admirals Fletcher nor Takagi knew each other's whereabouts and, furthermore, Takagi still did not realise that he was up against the *Yorktown* and the *Lexington*. Japanese land-based aircraft had actually sighted the US carriers, but inexplicably this vital information had not been radioed to him. The Allied fleet, on the other hand, had a rare piece of luck. The pilot of a US spotter plane reported at 8.15 am that he had seen two carriers and four heavy cruisers slightly north of Misima Island. A total of 93 planes were launched from both US carriers and this force was well on its way to the target area when the scout returned and it was discovered that what he had actually seen were two cruisers and two destroyers. Then, quite by chance, another US patrol plane located *Shoho* only a few miles from the original target site and at 11 am on 7 May America made its first assault on a Japanese carrier.

Shoho was attacked by wave after wave of US warplanes and hit by no fewer than 13 bombs and seven torpedoes. She burst into flames and went dead in the water; the order to abandon ship was given at 11.31 am and the carrier sank five minutes later with most of her crew still on board.

At almost the same time, 11.30 am, Admiral Crace spotted a Japanese reconnaissance plane on the horizon and prepared his force for an air attack. At 3 pm Japanese land-based planes from Rabaul attacked Crace's three cruisers with torpedoes and bombs, but radical manoeuvres in the boiling waters saved them from a single hit, while Crace's gun crews succeeded in shooting down 10 enemy aircraft.

At 3.19 pm the *Australia* dodged more bombs from three huge aircraft which suddenly appeared overhead. These turned out to be American B-17 bombers which had been sent from Townsville to help the Allied fleet. Failing to recognise the Allied cruisers, they had returned to base and gleefully reported they had inflicted heavy damage on several Japanese warships.

A similar error in identification was made by a Japanese spotter plane, which mistook the tanker *Neosho* and her escorting destroyer *Sims* for the two US carriers. The Japanese command sent flights of bombers and dive-bombers against them. *Sims* went down with most of her crew after three hits, while *Neosho* took eight hits and, blazing fiercely, had to be abandoned.

The decisive actions in the Battle of the Coral Sea were fought out on the morning of 8 May when 121 aircraft from the two Japanese carriers overlapped in the air with 122 planes from the American carriers. The Japanese ships had the protection of clouds and rain squalls and *Zuikaku* took advantage of some hesitancy on the part of US pilots to slip into the enveloping mists. The *Shokaku*, however, was attacked by Dauntless dive-bombers, which made three hits on the carrier. The flight deck was severely damaged, with 108 men killed and 40 wounded.

By that time, Japanese planes had located the *Yorktown* and the *Lexington*, which had lost the cover of bad weather and were exposed under clear blue skies. The Japanese first attacked the *Yorktown*, which avoided the torpedoes but suffered one bomb hit, an 800 pounder that penetrated the flat-top and exploded on the fourth deck, killing or wounding 66 men. This, however, did not affect the carrier's fighting capability and the attacking aircraft were driven off.

The *Lexington* had no such good fortune. Torpedo bombers ranged up on both of her bows in an 'anvil attack' at heights as low as 50 feet above the water. '*Lady Lex*', bigger and grander than *Yorktown* and thus less manoeuvrable, was a perfect target. One torpedo hit her port side forward, closely followed by a second strike on the same side opposite the bridge. A bomb exploded in an ammunition box on the port side of her main deck and another blasted her smokestack. She was badly damaged, but her engines were still driving her forward and there was every chance she would survive.

Admiral Takagi believed from his pilots' reports that they had sunk both US carriers and, as *Zuikaku* had not been damaged, he ordered the crippled *Shokaku* to withdraw from the battle area and make for Japan under reduced power. In fact *Yorktown*'s damage was not serious enough to endanger her and *Lexington* would have survived except for a fuel leak that went unnoticed in the general melee. An hour after the battle had ended, a sickening internal explosion shook the carrier from stem to stern. This was caused by the ignition of vapours from the ruptured fuel line and serious fires broke out, followed by more explosions. All living personnel abandoned ship soon after 5 pm and her blazing hulk was scuttled by the destroyer *Phelps* with torpedoes.

In the final analysis, US losses exceeded those of the Japanese, but the Japanese were so shaken by the surprise attack that the Port Moresby invasion fleet had been turned back towards Rabaul.

The Battle of the Coral Sea was the first strategic setback the Japanese had suffered and Port Moresby had been saved for the foreseeable future. Although the press reported it as a tremendous, morale-boosting victory, MacArthur and Curtin agreed that it would be not prudent to allay fears of an invasion because the workforce might be tempted to slow down the tempo of the war effort. Instead, MacArthur asked Washington for two aircraft carriers, a corps of three divisions and a first-line strength of 1000 planes, even though he must have known that no such forces were available. He also sent Curtin an appreciation of the situation in which he urged haste in developing Australia's 'defensive bastion'.

'The territory to be defended is vast, the means of communication are poor, the defensive forces are few in number and only partially trained,' he wrote. 'The enemy, if supported by major elements of his fleet, can exercise control of the sea lanes and consequently can strike with a preponderance of force on any chosen objective. We have present, therefore, in this theatre at the present time, all the elements that have produced disaster in the Western Pacific since the beginning of the war.'

More than anything else, the Battle of the Coral Sea swung the Pentagon firmly behind the enormous possibilities of air–sea power to the detriment of Army commanders like MacArthur, who had made no secret of his dislike for the navy or his mistrust of planes. MacArthur's own communique revived his feud with Admirals King and Nimitz when he rebuked the US Navy for missing 'an opportunity to inflict heavy losses' on the enemy's battlefleet. He neglected to mention that the only contribution his forces had made to the battle had been to endeavour to send the *Australia* to the bottom of the Coral Sea after mistaking her for a Japanese warship.

MacArthur's hostility towards the navy had been reinforced by the surrender of Corregidor. He believed King could have done a great deal more to drop provisions, weapons and ammunition from carrier-based aircraft to Wainwright's stricken troops. He pointed to the Doolittle Raid, in which carrier-based B-25 Liberator bombers had blitzed Tokyo on 18 April, as an example of the navy's ability to slip through the Japanese blockade when it suited Washington's purposes.

MacArthur had responded to the sombre news from the Philippines with a few dignified words: 'Corregidor needs no comment from me. It has sounded its own story at the mouth of its guns. It has scrolled its own epitaph on enemy tablets. But through the bloody haze of its last reverberating shot I shall always seem to see a vision of grim, gaunt, ghastly men, still unafraid.'

Unlike the gallant Wainwright, who was on his way to a Japanese prisoner-of-war camp, MacArthur had not seen the 'last reverberating shot' fired in the 18-week campaign. Despite that, in private he was scathingly critical of Wainwright for giving up the fight.

In the Bronx, Mark Muller's parents believed their son was among the captive Americans. He said: 'My foot locker had got to Manila and, according to official records, that's where I was, too. I heard that my mother and father received a message from the War Department stating I was presumed to be missing in action or a prisoner of war. I couldn't write home because censorship was in full force, so I got an Australian friend, Jim Cameron, to send them a bunch of roses through the International Florist Telegraphic Delivery Service. Apart from not being able to mention my name in the message, he could say anything within reason. So Jim's message read: "Sorry I can't send you one of Mark Twain's books from here, but these roses will have to do until I visit—Jim Cameron, Brisbane." My parents knew immediately where I was and that I was okay.'

Jim Cameron, a Post Office telephone engineer involved in work at Base 3, was one of the friends Muller had made in Brisbane. People were friendly—they loved Yanks, and they loved Mark Twain Muller. He was short, stockily built, with liquid brown eyes, black, short-cropped hair and a smile as big as a watermelon. If he'd worn a Stetson instead of his forage cap, he could have passed for Andy Devine's younger brother.

'I took a tram ride out along the river,' he said, 'and the female trammie asked me if I'd like some prawns. I said, "What are prawns?" and she said, "You know, shrimp". She dived into a seafood shop and came back with a bag of prawns and we ate them on the way to the terminus.'

A lot of people seemed intent on supplying Mark Muller with food. He said: 'I was billeted in a rented home, Rippon Lea, in Hamilton, and the next-door neighbours, Ernest and Martha Sampson, became my adopted parents. They gave me tea and freshly made scones every morning before I went to work.'

Muller had been promoted to 1st Lieutenant and his main job was to install up-to-date communications equipment at Base 3's new headquarters at Somerville House, a private girls' school in one of the few remaining respectable enclaves in the rapidly declining suburb of South Brisbane. He made friends with Lieutenant Bob Firehock, who had wound up in the cryptography section at Base 3.

Firehock said: 'From being purchasing officer, I became cryptographic officer handling all of the codes and ciphers. I never had any training; I was just given the codes and ciphers and told, "It's yours". I left Amberley and came into town and lived in Lennon's Hotel. I had a room there as my communications centre and then it was moved out to Base 3 at Somerville House. We took over the music room and established a communications centre for all our ciphering and deciphering messages.'

Shortly after the surrender of Corregidor, Firehock received an unexpected call from Mindanao.

He said: 'We got a radio message from an American officer and at first we were sceptical; we thought it might have been the Japs because a lot of them had lived in America and spoke clear American English,' he said. 'We asked him what university he went to and what was his roommate's nickname—trivia like that—and he had to send a message to us with the answers to establish the fact that he was a dinky-di American. We had quite a time establishing his identity so we could send a submarine up there to him with modern codes, equipment, money and medicine. He became leader of the guerrilla forces in the Philippines.

'As he was in Mindanao, he could send details of troop and ship movements, something like a coast watch. He could also organise pro-American troops who were not in custody, mostly Filipinos. They were organised by this officer, who promoted himself from a second lieutenant to a colonel because he figured that no one would listen to a second lieutenant. He did a lot of good work for us up there.'

On the evening of 8 May, Eddie Leonski met Pauline Thompson, a 31-year-old married woman with a wandering eye for young Americans. In a cafe, she caught Leonski's eye. 'She was waiting for an order,' he said. 'I asked if I could sit with her and she said, "All right". I told her I would rather have something stronger to drink and she told me she knew of a place.'

It was drizzling when they left the cafe and adjourned to the lounge bar of the Astoria Hotel, where an illegal after-hours drinking session was in progress. Over the next three hours, they drank gin squashes.

'She was singing in my ear,' said Leonski. 'She looked into my eyes and it sounded as though she was singing just for me.' But at one point Pauline told Leonski: 'You've got a baby face, but underneath you're vicious.' The soldier just grinned at her. When they left the Astoria at a quarter to midnight, the streets were dark and gloomy in the brownout, and they walked through the rain to Pauline's lodgings, Morningside House, at No. 13 Spring Street.

'She had a nice voice and she sang as we walked along,' said Leonski. 'I grabbed her around the neck. She stopped singing. I said, "Keep singing, keep singing". She fell down. I got mad and then tore at her. I tore her apart.'

Pauline Thompson's body, semi-naked and mutilated like Ivy McLeod's, was found on 9 May and police soon ascertained that she had been in the company of an American soldier shortly before she was murdered. This news was greeted with alarm at MacArthur's headquarters. Although the connection was only circumstantial, he ordered his staff to keep a close watch on the situation and to instruct base commanders and US provost marshals to give the Melbourne homicide squad detectives every co-operation.

The Brownout Strangler's insane rampage continued in an atmosphere of mounting hysteria. On 14 May Leonski forced his way into a young woman's home on Gatehouse Street, which bordered Camp Pell. Leonski pushed past the woman, not realising that her uncle was inside. The uncle, a Mr Jackson, told Leonski to 'get to buggery' and the soldier sauntered out of the flat. Mr Jackson reported the incident to the police.

On 18 May, Leonski drank 25 beers and half a dozen whiskies at the Parkville Hotel, not far from Camp Pell. In the street outside he bumped into Gladys Hosking, 41, secretary and librarian at Melbourne University's School of Chemistry, who was heading home to her room at 140 Park Street, Parkville. 'We walked along the street and came to her house,' said Leonski. 'I asked her to walk on with me and show me the way to the camp. She said, "All right". We came to a very dark part of the street. She stopped and said, "There's the camp over there." She had a lovely voice. I wanted that voice.

'I grabbed her by the throat. I choked her. She did not even make a sound. She was so soft. I thought, "What have I done? I will have to get away from here." I got her to a fence and pushed her underneath. I carried her a short distance and fell in the mud.'

Gladys Hosking was murdered on a grassy footpath. Her hat and umbrella were left where they fell while she was dragged under a single railing fence and onto a grassy slope near some slit trenches that had been dug as air-raid defences.

Covered in sticky yellow mud from the diggings, Leonski had almost run into the arms of Private Neil Lindsay Seymour, an Australian soldier on picket duty, who flashed a torch on him.

'Where the hell have you been, mate?' asked Seymour.

'I fell over in the mud going across the park.'

'Do you live in Camp Pell?'

'Yes, over in the street near the zoo, in Area One.'

'You're in a mess,' the Australian said.

When Gladys Hosking's body was found the next morning, Seymour reported his encounter with the muddy American to his superiors, who informed Russell Street police headquarters.

General MacArthur ordered his commanding officers to give every assistance to the civilian police, and orders were issued for all leave to be cancelled at American camps in the district, including Camp Pell. Having obtained the co-operation of the US Army command, Detective-Sergeant Sidney McGuffie visited Camp Pell with Private Seymour. The entire camp was called out on parade in driving rain while detectives, accompanied by US provost marshals, searched tents for uniforms with muddy yellow stains.

On the parade ground, Seymour walked along the ranks of men, studying each face. He walked past Eddie Leonski, hesitated, then went back for a second look. As he did so, Leonski muttered to the man standing next to him: 'Looks like the end of the line.' But Seymour failed to make a positive identification and the line-up was called off.

The following day the detectives returned to Camp Pell with Mr Jackson, the uncle of one of the women whom Leonski had molested. Once again Leonski was not identified in a line-up of every soldier in camp and he might have escaped to kill again except that, after the men had been dismissed, Jackson spotted Leonski sauntering off the parade ground towards his tent. He immediately recognised him and shouted: 'That's him—that's the man who broke into my niece's place.' Leonski was taken into custody and, during questioning by McGuffie and his colleague Detective Fred 'Bluey' Adam, confessed to the three murders. He also admitted attacks against three other women.

Inevitably, the news of Leonski's arrest damaged the image of American soldiers in the eyes of the Australian public. A small but vocal minority insisted illogically that such maniacal murders could only have been committed by an American, and the United States was suddenly projected into the Australian consciousness as a dark and dangerous place.

This hostility was made infinitely worse when it was revealed that Eddie Leonski had confessed to Private Anthony J. Gallo, his only friend at Camp Pell, that he had committed the first two murders. Gallo was the soldier whom Leonski had addressed in the line-up when he had said: 'Looks like the end of the line.' Leonski had confided his gruesome secrets to Gallo in several conversations, but the soldier had done nothing about it.

His silence had cost Gladys Hosking her life, and that was hard to forgive.

Chapter Nine

◄○►

The Dragon's Lair

THE island of New Guinea sprawled like a sleeping dragon between the Equator and the tropical north of Australia. The Portuguese explorer Jorge de Meneses had named the vast island *Ilhas dos Papuas*—Island of the Fuzzy-Hairs, from the Malay word *papuwah*—after landing on the dragon's head in the sixteenth century and encountering tribesmen with great outcrops of bushy hair.

As a matter of routine, the Portuguese name was changed to New Guinea by rival Dutch explorers who said it reminded them of Guinea in Africa. It was an Englishman, Captain John Moresby, who gave his name to the island's main port after sailing into harbour in 1873. Moresby spent several days trading bêche-de-mer and pearl shell with the villagers and, impressed by their honesty and simple lifestyle, was moved to ask in his diary: 'What have these people to gain from civilisation?'

In 1942, the island of New Guinea was divided into three sections: the western half was Dutch New Guinea, the eastern extremity of the Netherlands East Indies Empire; the eastern half of the island was split lengthways into the Territory of Papua and the Mandated Territory of New Guinea, both governed by Australia through the Australian New Guinea Administrative Unit—ANGAU.

The senior brass of the Japanese Imperial Command knew that if they could tame the dragon, they would gain forward airfields from which to launch wholesale air raids against northern Australia. But before directing their energies at New Guinea again, there was the unfinished business of the US Pacific Fleet.

Yamamoto had not envisaged the Battle of the Coral Sea when he

131

worked out his master strategy for dominance of the Pacific Ocean. His main objective all along was to force the US Navy into a final, decisive battle by striking at Midway Atoll and the Western Aleutians. With the US carriers destroyed, the Japanese would be able to occupy Fiji, Samoa and New Caledonia, thus isolating Australia by cutting the sea lanes to and from the United States. Yamamoto outlined this plan in a message dictated in the cabin aboard his new flagship *Yamato* to the naval general staff: 'In the last analysis, the success of our strategy in the Pacific will be determined by whether or not we succeed in destroying the United States fleet, particularly its carrier task force. We believe that by launching the proposed operation against Midway, we can succeed in drawing out the enemy's carrier strength and destroying it in decisive battle. If, on the other hand, the enemy should avoid our challenge, we shall still realise an important gain by advancing our defensive perimeter to Midway and the Western Aleutians without obstruction.'

Yamamoto proceeded with this plan as though the Battle of the Coral Sea had never happened. On 27 May the Japanese Midway Occupation Force of 5000 combat troops in 12 transports set out from Saipan in the Marianas escorted by two battleships and a number of cruisers and destroyers, with planes from the light carrier *Zuiho* providing air cover. Yamamoto himself commanded the main striking force from his flagship, the 60,000 ton superbattleship *Yamato*. This battlefleet comprised Vice-Admiral Nagumo's carriers *Akagi*, *Kaga*, *Soryu* and *Hiryu*, plus two battleships, each with cruiser and destroyer escorts, as well as the light carrier *Hosho*. Two additional light carriers, *Ryujo* and *Junyo*, were attached to Rear Admiral Kakuta's Second Mobile Force, which would strike at the Aleutians.

Nimitz had only three carriers, the *Yorktown*, the *Enterprise* and the *Hornet*, as well as a smaller force of cruisers and destroyers. The *Yorktown* had been repaired at Pearl Harbor in the astonishingly short time of 48 hours, but *Saratoga*, which had been damaged by a Japanese submarine in January, was still out of action. As the Midway invasion fleet approached from the west, Admiral Fletcher concentrated the three US carriers some 350 miles north-east of Midway.

The battle began after an American Catalina flown by Ensign Jack Reid sighted the enemy convoy early on 3 June. Fletcher knew from Japanese intercepts that aircraft from the carriers were scheduled to bomb the ground defences at Midway at dawn the following morning. He decided to attack the carriers from the flank while their aircraft were carrying out that bombing mission. From 8 am on 4 June aircraft from the *Enterprise* and the *Hornet* attacked the Japanese carriers. By mid-morning, most of the American torpedo bombers had been shot down without scoring a hit by squadrons of defending Zeros, but the Dauntless dive-bombers still remained. Thirty-three of them from the *Enterprise*, led by Lieutenant-Commander Wade McClusky, swooped down from 19,000 feet and attacked the carriers virtually unopposed after they caught the Zeros waiting at low altitude for more torpedo bombers. In mid-attack, the American planes were joined by *Yorktown*'s dive-bombers, led by Lieutenant-Commander Maxwell Leslie. This combined force inflicted one of the biggest defeats on the Japanese fleet of the entire war. The carriers *Akagi*, *Kaga* and *Soryu* were hit and set ablaze, all going down within 24 hours.

In retaliation, *Hiryu* launched against the *Yorktown* 46 torpedo bombers and dive-bombers escorted by 12 fighters. She was hit by three bombs and badly damaged, but, as evening closed in, dive-bombers from the *Enterprise* attacked and sank *Hiryu*.

The following day, 5 June, Yamamoto ordered his striking force and transports to withdraw. However, the disabled *Yorktown* was attacked by a Japanese submarine and sunk before she could limp to safety. Four of the six Japanese carriers that had taken part in the sneak attack on Pearl Harbor and later in the bombing of Darwin had been destroyed. In total, the Japanese lost four carriers, a heavy cruiser and 332 planes. The US lost one carrier, USS *Yorktown*, a destroyer and half as many planes.

MacArthur told a meeting of the Advisory War Council on 17 June that Australia had been saved from invasion. 'Australia was in grave danger up to the time of the Battle of the Coral Sea [but] that action and the success gained at Midway Island [have] assured the defensive position of Australia,' he said. 'From the strategical point of view, we should take the initiative and not wait for results from other theatres. Our aim should be to strike at Japanese bases in islands to the north and throw the enemy bomber line back 700 miles.'

MacArthur's plan was identical to one outlined by the Pentagon a few weeks later in its first directive governing Allied operations in the south- and south-west Pacific. MacArthur was to be responsible for seizing Lae, Salamaua and the north-east coast of New Guinea. His forces were then to be used to drive the Japanese out of their huge air and naval base at Rabaul. The US Navy would be responsible for the seizure and occupation of Tulagi, and Guadalcanal, where the Japanese were building a seaplane base.

MacArthur told Blamey: 'The task of all formations now is training for mobile offensive operations. Defensive preparations are of secondary importance. Valuable time is not to be wasted in digging and wiring. Physical fitness and intensive preparation for offensive action are our immediate objectives.'

Looking at a map of New Guinea, MacArthur asked about possible airfield sites, either in existence or that could be developed. His finger stabbed at a tiny place on the Papuan north coast called Buna, which had a mission with an airstrip capable of taking light planes. He would, he told Blamey, move engineers into the Buna area around the middle of August to enlarge the strip. In the meantime, Buna should be made secure against a Japanese landing on the northern Papuan coast.

The Australian defenders of Papua New Guinea belonged to the 49th Battalion, which was made up of young militiamen who had volunteered for tropical service. Very few of them had handled a rifle; they had been sent to garrison Port Moresby and spent months digging fortifications and wiring command posts rather than training for the offensive role that MacArthur now envisaged in meeting the Japanese threat.

The young soldiers of the 49th had had no conception of the terrors in store when their ship entered Basilisk Passage in March 1941 and approached the drowsy, ramshackle township Port Moresby in the lee of the high escarpment of Hombrum Bluff. All they could see was the line of the reef through aquamarine waters, patches of mangrove and coconut palms, strips of golden beaches, some heavily timbered hills and, 30 miles in the background swathed in clouds, the purple mass of the Owen Stanley Range.

Few armies in modern times were less prepared for active service than the 49th Battalion. Under familiar conditions in Australia they would have been hard-pressed to give a good account of themselves, but in the sweltering tropics of New Guinea they stood no chance whatsoever. They lacked training, weapons, medical supplies and even basic essentials such as mess tins, plates, pannikins, mosquito nets and waterproof ground sheets.

Instead of being readied for jungle fighting, they had been put to work as labourers on defensive projects around the capital; back-breaking manual work that entailed unloading ships, building roads and clearing jungle sites for anti-aircraft gun emplacements. Many of the young Australians were stricken with fever and all were dispirited by the tropical heat and torrential rain. After an inspection of the battalion, the chief of the general staff, Lieutenant-General Vernon Sturdee, described the 49th as 'quite the worst battalion in Australia'.

Two militia battalions, the 39th and 53rd battalions of the 30th Brigade, were hastily despatched to Port Moresby as reinforcements in January 1942. The 39th Battalion had been raised in Victoria and had received only basic training when they embarked in the old liner *Aquitania* for the trip to New Guinea with the 53rd Battalion, a poorly equipped outfit made up of New South Welshmen who had been drawn at random from other militia battalions. An official report later stated: 'The troops were of an average age of 18 and a half years, and had received no proper training. They were in the charge of inexperienced officers who appear to have had little or no control over them. They were inadequately equipped in every way; in particular, they were without much of the equipment necessary to give them any reasonable prospect of maintaining health in an area such as Port Moresby.'

The 53rd even included 100 young soldiers who had been virtually shanghaied in Sydney at the last minute to make up the numbers; they'd been given no chance to say goodbye to their families and had no idea where they were going or what might be expected of them when they got there. When the Japanese started bombing Port Moresby, they fled into the bush along with the local Papuan population.

Brigadier Selwyn Porter, a veteran of the 7th Division's campaigns in the Middle East, arrived on 17 April to take over as commander of the 30th Brigade. Porter noted that 'the brigade is not in a fit state to fight a battle' and swiftly brought in AIF sergeants, subalterns and captains to replace older officers.

After his conference with MacArthur about the possibilities of developing a strategic airfield at Buna, Blamey had ordered his commander in New Guinea, Major-General Basil Morris, to occupy the tiny settlement of Kokoda in the foothills on the northern side of the Owen Stanley Range, the mountainous barricade that ran like a spine down the middle of the island before plunging into the ocean at Milne Bay on the eastern tip of the dragon's tail. Morris chose B Company of the 39th Battalion, commanded by Captain Sam Templeton, for the impossible task of confronting the Japanese should they attempt to land on the north coast some 70 miles from Kokoda.

General Morris later admitted that these troops 'were hardly trained at all and I am quite sure that they did not look forward with any confidence to meeting the enemy'.

If New Guinea was a dragon, then the Kokoda Track was its jugular vein, a 100-mile-long artery barely three feet wide, with razor-sharp rocks that slashed boots and clothing, slippery ravines, rushing creeks and stretches of head-high kunai grass. The surrounding peaks were so lofty that they disappeared into dense cloud. The weather was boiling hot by day and freezing cold by night and it rained heavily every afternoon. The foetid swamps were a breeding ground for *Anopheles* mosquitoes carrying malaria and dengue fever, and ailments such as berri berri, scrub typhus, athlete's foot and ringworm were prevalent.

At the Port Moresby end of the track, the section scaling the cliff-face to Imita Ridge was known as the Golden Stairs, an almost vertical climb of 2000-odd steps marked out using sawn logs held in place by wooden pegs. Every foothold swam in mud that hid treacherous roots and sharp rocks. The ooze was so glutinous it sucked off laced-up boots.

Major-General Frank Kingsley Norris, director general of medical services, Australian Military Force, provided an unbeatable description of the Kokoda Track from its starting point at Ilolo, just before the Golden Stairs, to Deniki, just short of the descent into Kokoda: 'Imagine an area of approximately 100 miles long. Crumple and fold this into a series of ridges, each rising higher and higher until 7000 feet is reached, then declining in ridges to 3000 feet. Cover this thickly with jungle, short trees and tall trees, tangled with great, entwining savage vines. Through an oppression of this density, cut a little native track, two or three feet wide, up the ridges, over the spurs, round gorges and down across swiftly-flowing, happy mountain streams. Where the track clambers up the mountain sides, cut steps—big steps, little steps, steep steps—or clear the soil from the tree roots.

'Every few miles, bring the track through a small patch of sun-lit kunai grass, or an old deserted native garden, and every seven or 10 miles, build a group of dilapidated grass huts—as staging shelters—generally set in a foul, offensive clearing. Every now and then, leave beside the track dumps of discarded, putrefying food, occasional dead bodies and human foulings. In the morning, flicker the sunlight through the tall trees, flutter green and blue and purple and white butterflies lazily through the air, and hide birds of deep-throated song, or harsh cockatoos, in the foliage.

'About midday, and through the night, pour water over the forest, so that the steps become broken, and a continual yellow stream pours downwards, and the few level areas become pools and puddles of putrid black mud. In the high ridges above Myola, drip this water day and night over the track through a foetid forest grotesque with moss and glowing phosphorescent fungi. Such is the track which a prominent politician publicly described as "being almost impassable for motor vehicles", and such is the route for 10 days to be covered from Ilolo to Deniki.'

Herbert Kienzle, a planter who had been commissioned as a lieutenant in ANGAU, was given the herculean task of organising and maintaining the supply line for Australian troops along the Kokoda Track. Apart from unreliable airdrops at designated points, the only way to reach the 39th Battalion was for Papuan carriers to make the eight to 10-day trek along the Kokoda Track with backpacks. The Papuans were smallish, powerfully built men, with tattooed bodies and betel-stained teeth. They were able to walk for days at a time with little rest through the jungle swamps and over the ridge-backed mountains. Each Papuan could carry a 50-pound load on his back or, working in pairs, two could carry more than twice that amount on long poles stretched between them.

When the fighting broke out, they made the return journey to Port Moresby with stretchers carrying wounded Australian soldiers.

The callous treatment of the Australian militia battalions in New Guinea was not dissimilar to that handed out by the US Army to the Red Arrows, the men who were destined to join them in the strategically vital Battle of Papua.

Instead of going to Northern Ireland as expected, the 32nd Division had suddenly been ordered to Australia and, with just three weeks to go before embarkation, some hasty changes had to be made. The division's 107th Engineer Battalion was already on its way to Europe and had to be replaced with the 114th Engineer Combat Battalion from New England. Another 3000 troops who had barely finished basic training were added to the division as the troop trains rolled across the United States from Massachusetts to California.

The Red Arrows left San Francisco on 22 April in a nine-ship convoy escorted by the cruiser *Indianapolis*. Landing at Port Adelaide on 14 May, they were initially stationed at Camp Woodside and then moved to Camp Sandy Creek, a dry, remote region more like Arizona than the jungles of New Guinea. The division had been given no time to build up *esprit de corps* in the US and General Harding was delighted when they were invited to Adelaide to march in a Fourth of July parade. With the band playing, the Red Arrows stepped out like veterans with rifles shouldered and pennants flying. The crowd went wild when they saw that American combat troops had finally reached Australia.

Meanwhile, the Medical Department of the United States Army had quietly been assembling staff in Australia to treat the wounded from the forthcoming battles in New Guinea and other parts of the Pacific theatre. Lieutenant Floramund A. Fellmeth, the first US servicewoman to reach Australia, reported to USAFIA headquarters in Melbourne in February and, as acting chief nurse, made preparations for the arrival of female nurses, dieticians and physiotherapists. The first to arrive were more than 200 nurses of the 4th General Hospital, who were based at the Royal Melbourne Hospital next to Camp Pell.

Among the US medical staff were several Army psychiatrists whose job would be to treat American soldiers suffering from war neurosis. In June 1942, one of their duties was to assess Eddie Leonski's fitness to stand trial for three murders. Accompanied by a distinguished Melbourne practitioner, two American psychiatrists visited the prisoner at the City Watchhouse to evaluate his mental condition. The file they pieced together from those interviews, along with other sources, gives a frightening picture of a psychopath:

Leonski had been born in New Jersey on 12 December 1917, to a manic-depressive mother, Amelia, and a chronic alcoholic father, John, a Russian *émigré* whose liking for vodka outweighed any responsibilities he felt towards his young family. Eddie hated his father for his drunken rages and his physical cruelty towards his mother. Amelia had been born in Poland and was a strikingly attractive woman, with blonde hair, high Slavonic cheekbones and a good figure. In her youth, she had trained as a weightlifter and taken part in weightlifting competitions, but though she was physically strong she was no match for John Leonski when he was drunk.

John deserted the family when Eddie was six years old and Amelia moved her children to the fifth floor of a tenement at 425 East 77th Street, New York City. After her husband died of a heart attack during a massive bender, she remarried, but her second spouse turned out to be as worthless as the first. Eddie Leonski witnessed his mother suffer more drunken beatings.

He grew up loathing and fearing men like his father and stepfather. It was this conflict between aggressive male and nurturing female that caused Eddie to become confused about his own sexuality. He gradually developed some of Amelia's characteristics, particularly her voice, and started talking to her in soft, girlish tones, with each sentence ending in a giggle. He later admitted: 'I'm more or less effeminate.'

MacArthur was informed that the psychiatric evaluation showed that Leonski was not insane according to the legal definitions of the time and was therefore fit to stand trial. The Army's legal department was urged to get the trial underway as soon as possible. MacArthur had more important matters on his mind, such as moving GHQ from Melbourne to Brisbane, and thus making his way closer to the Japanese.

Chapter Ten

─◇─

Bataan, Brisbane

THERE were many things Private Norbert J. Grant would remember about 1942, but the events on two dates in particular would be locked into his memory for all time. One of those dates was the Fourth of July, because on Independence Day Private Grant lugged his army gear out of Fort Sheridan, Illinois, and headed for Australia with his comrades in the 738th Military Police Battalion.

The second fateful date would be Thanksgiving Day, but Grant had no way of knowing that when he fell in on the parade ground at San Francisco to listen to an address by his commanding officer. Colonel Kester told the assembled troops that although the Australian people were generally well-disposed toward Americans, they had a hostile attitude towards law enforcement that went back to convict times. The provosts were warned to expect special problems growing out of an army operation that was taking place in a foreign country 'with its many peculiarities'. They would work closely with civilian police forces, but police procedures differed from State to State in Australia, just as they did in the United States, and they would need tact and a strong nerve to meet these unusual conditions.

As MPs, they would be called upon to perform many difficult tasks, often under hazardous conditions, and the manner in which both officers and enlisted men met those challenges should bring credit to their units. No matter how strong the provocation, they were urged to remember the battalion's honour. Aware that many members of the 738th were white southerners, Kester stressed that the MPs were to be even-handed in their dealings with the large number of black American soldiers.

139

Alton Jensen said: 'He told us repeatedly that race was not a factor in our work and that we were to forget about it. He had called the whole battalion together just before our departure for that purpose and we were alerted to the fact that we had to treat all military personnel the same.'

The 738th boarded the *Mount Vernon*, formerly the liner *George Washington*, for the four-week voyage. Jensen said: 'Conditions were beautiful and we had three square meals a day. The 738th were on the promenade deck in bunks which were stacked one above the other. One other MP battalion was with us, the 720th, and they had the ship's ballroom and we had the outer edges around the promenade deck. It was an enclosed area and the windows had been sprayed with grey paint so that when they were closed there was no natural light. But there was also a wide open deck where we did physical exercises once a day.'

Norbert Grant discovered that the two MP battalions were the only army men on board. The rest were naval units who were going to set up a hospital in Wellington, New Zealand, and a large number of headquarters personnel from both the US Navy and US Air Force, as well as many of the fliers for the new 5th Air Force which was going to be set up in Brisbane. There were only about 1400 enlisted men on the manifest, the balance of approximately 5000 men being officers.

Grant settled down to enjoy the trip. He flicked through some of the army literature that had been compiled about Australia: 'Australians are kind, considerate and sensitive people . . . their economic development is probably 150 years behind that of the United States . . . There is one thing to get straight right off the bat: you are not in Australia to save helpless people from the savage Jap. Maybe there are fewer people in Australia than in New York City, but their soldiers in this war and the last have built up a great fighting record . . . Fraternisation with Australian women has created many problems . . .'

When the *Mount Vernon* set sail on 14 July, the newspapers of the day carried the first reports of the trial of Eddie Leonski for the murders of Ivy McLeod, Pauline Thompson and Gladys Hosking. Leonski was the first person to be tried in Australia by a military court for an offence under civil law. He was also the first citizen of a foreign country to be tried in Australia under the law of his own country. In an effort to convince the public that nothing was being covered up, the press were permitted to report the evidence, while Leonski, apparently unconcerned about his fate, sat at a table taking notes of the proceedings.

Detective Fred Adam told the court that after his arrest Leonski asked him if the civil police had anything on him. He had replied that he had been identified and that they had information concerning the yellow mud in Leonski's tent. Leonski had admitted choking Gladys Hosking and said he had washed his clothes the following morning.

Detective Sid McGuffie said Leonski told him in a cell at the City Watchhouse: 'Fancy me a murderer! I guess that girl Thompson was the hardest; she was strong and, oh boy, could she drink gin squashes.'

The Melbourne psychiatrist who had examined Leonski said he seemed to be more cheerful than might be expected of a man in his position. He displayed no real despondency and became quiet and tense only when his mother came into the conversation. He said he did not want to be declared insane because he did not want to be locked up in a mental hospital. His only concern was the effect that the revelation of his crimes would have on his mother.

Cross-examined by Leonski's defence counsel, the psychiatrist said Leonski had a psychopathic personality and was unable to adjust himself to his environment, but this did not mean that he was insane. It could be assumed that similar crimes would be committed if the accused was freed and allowed, while under the influence of drink, to be alone with a woman.

After a four-day trial, the members of the court-martial required only a 40-minute retirement to reach a verdict. Leonski was ordered to stand before the president's table. The president told him: 'Leonski, it is my duty to inform you that this court, in closed session and upon secret ballot with three-fourths of the members present concurring, found you guilty of all charges. I have to inform you also that this court, with all of its members concurring, sentences you to be hanged by the neck until you are dead.'

The execution date was set after the Commander-in-Chief of the US Armed Forces, President Franklin D. Roosevelt, endorsed the sentence. Leonski would hang at Pentridge Prison in Melbourne on 9 November.

Leonski's trial happened to coincide with a change in the disposition of many Australians towards their American visitors, particularly in Queensland. After the Battles of the Coral Sea and Midway, the sense of impending doom that had held Queenslanders in thrall had begun to ease. These abrupt changes in the fortunes of war produced a corresponding shift in the attitude of Brisbanites.

Two distinct groups with widely divergent motives—the Goodtimers and the Oldtimers—were identifiable. Goodtimers were dedicated to exploiting the Americans either for financial gain or for their own entertainment and amusement; the hero worship and the sense of excitement of the first few months might have waned, but the dollar was still king and many people, notably traders with premises close to American bases, were quietly amassing large amounts of greenbacks in biscuit tins which they secretly buried in the backyard.

The Oldtimers were traditionalists, who deplored the Americanisation of their city and firmly resisted all blandishments to have anything other than minimum contact with the Americans.

The bulk of the population, however, simply did as they had been doing all along. They accepted the situation on a day-to-day basis and got on with life as best they could, neither blaming the Americans for broken marriages and shortages or inconveniences, nor trying to take advantage of them.

Marjorie Robertson, then a 16-year-old teenager, said: 'I was a Somerville House girl and halfway through 1942 I had to leave school. I was immediately snapped up by the American Red Cross, which arrived with a flourish of wealth and took over this massive building on the corner of Creek and Adelaide streets. There was a men-only club at street level and I worked upstairs in a very big dining room. They had everything— all kinds of food, huge amounts of ice-cream, and the very latest equipment. There was a huge kitchen and all these Ascot ladies, lovely prosperous matrons like Mrs Duncan McWhirter from McWhirter's department store, were working there as volunteers.

'There were also some American women in their Red Cross uniforms, but the place was mainly run by Australians. They gave me a gorgeous, forget-me-not blue uniform, and I was terribly willing and worked as hard as I could for them. I was instantly, ravingly popular; the American servicemen yelled "Blondie!" at me. I was so young I had no idea I was a blondie!'

The pro-American lobby received a huge morale boost when General MacArthur moved his headquarters to Brisbane on 21 July 1942. Lennon's Hotel was designated as the new Bataan and MacArthur took over four identical suites on the top floor—the fourth. MacArthur and Jean occupied one, Arthur and Ah Cheu the second, and MacArthur's doctor, Captain Charles Morhouse, moved into the third. Suite No. 4 became an office for MacArthur with an extensive library. Arthur made friends with the assistant manager's son, Neil Wall, and the two boys kept a pet goat which was tethered in the caretaker's yard at the Supreme Court building across George Street from the hotel.

MacArthur ordered a long, narrow awning to be erected from the kerb to the hotel's entrance to provide a focal point for passers-by whenever he left the hotel. Crowds were encouraged to gather on the sidewalk whenever they saw USA-1—now attached to a black Bentley— at the kerb, knowing that MacArthur's tall, lean figure wasn't far away. He wore his battered field-marshal's cap, a light khaki uniform with bush jacket and dark glasses, but there were no medals on his chest, and he had thrown away his walking stick. When he replaced the bush jacket with a leather bomber jacket, he looked more like a matinee idol in one of the hell-for-leather, damn-the-torpedoes war epics being churned out by the Hollywood studios than a four-star American general.

Sergeant Bill Bentson said: 'The new headquarters was a few blocks away from Lennon's in the AMP building on Queen Street and our entrance was round the corner on Edward Street. The AMP kept the ground floor and we never used the main entrance on Queen Street. MacArthur was in room 809 at the AMP and the private phone number to his *aide-de-camp* was AMP266.'

The AMP building was a severe granite structure in the English Renaissance style with marbled Tuscan columns and pilasters, sculptured classical figures over the arched portico, and heavy bronze doors and windows. Its main architectural attraction to the American planners had been its steel and concrete construction. The roof was made of two thick layers of reinforced concrete and the walls were similarly resistant to bomb blast.

MacArthur's spacious office was furnished with a desk, a black leather couch and a conference table with chairs. The walls were lined with polished timbers and there was a solid parquet floor. Above the fireplace was a portrait of Washington, while one of Lincoln was on a wall facing the desk. Through the windows overlooking Queen Street, MacArthur had an uninterrupted view of the 'Kremlin', the Trades Hall building at the top of Edward Street. There was no telephone in his office; he rarely used the phone. His favoured means of communication was the teleprinter link that Mark Muller had set up between GHQ, Base 3 at Somerville House and other SWPA units. The advantage in using the teletype was that his messages were always on file, providing a permanent record of the clarity of his thoughts, the precision of his orders, the clear superiority of his command.

General Sutherland, Iron Duke *manqué*, was situated in an office across a reception area from MacArthur's inner sanctum. Elaine Bessemer-Clark's perfume wafted up to him via the stairwell from the first-floor lobby where she worked behind a desk just inside the front door. Elaine was able to monitor everybody's comings and goings and inform Sutherland about the visitors being received by other military occupants of the AMP's grand chambers. Visitors ranged from congressmen and war correspondents to a Chinese general, while one of the more interesting occupants was one of Churchill's military spies, Colonel G. H. Wilkinson, whose official title at GHQ was British Liaison Officer.

Wilkinson described MacArthur in one of his reports to London as 'shrewd, selfish, proud, remote, highly strung and vastly vain. He has imagination, self-confidence, physical courage and charm but no humour about himelf, no regard for truth, and is unaware of these defects. He mistakes his emotions and ambitions for principles. With moral depth he would be a great man: as it is he is a near-miss, which may be worse than a mile . . . his main ambition would be to end the war as Pan-American hero in the form of generalissimo of all Pacific theatres . . . he hates Roosevelt and dislike's Winston's control of Roosevelt's strategy . . . [he] is not basically anti-British, just pro-MacArthur.'

MacArthur's kingdom had grown in accordance with his elevated status. In June, the number of American service personnel in Australia had soared to more than 88,000 and this figure did not include the thousands of seamen in US Navy vessels who were either stationed in, or passing through, Australian ports. About a third of all the American servicemen were already concentrated in Queensland. Then, in July, MacArthur ordered his two American divisions, the 32nd and the 41st, up to Queensland from South Australia and Victoria. The 32nd moved to Camp Cable, 30 miles south of Brisbane, and the 41st went north to Rockhampton.

June, July and August were winter months in Brisbane, but the days were still warm and sunny and although the nights were chilly in the camps, Lennon's Hotel provided its VIP guests with every modern convenience, including central heating. 'Pick' Diller followed Sutherland's lead by inviting his mistress, Joy Foord, to join him in his new location.

Joy said: 'I flew to Brisbane in a very uncomfortable transport plane via Williamstown and Newcastle. I was due to report to the postal department at Somerville House the following day. On my first night, I found that my accommodation was a dirty, sleazy, rooming house in South Brisbane with no lock on the bedroom door. I was so terrified I pushed the bed against the door and stayed awake all night.

'I got a job at Somerville House for a while censoring letters and was able to move to Yale Apartments on Upper Edward Street. But I was with Pick at Lennon's much of the time, sharing a single bed which was not only taboo but also uncomfortable! Pick was my man and when you're in love you'll do anything.

'In the morning, I used to go through the fire doors outside General MacArthur's apartments, press the button opposite his front door and get into his private elevator. One morning I saw the General kissing Jean and Arthur goodbye, and I was stuck in the elevator wishing it would fall down to zero. After that, it happened every time I left Pick's suite in the morning. The General would always say, "Good morning, Joy, are you taking your constitutional?" He knew damn well what was happening, but he never said anything about our relationship. There were always two armed guards at the street entrance and, as we approached them, MacArthur would salute me and say, "Enjoy your constitutional!" before getting into his car. I think it gave him a kick to start the day that way.'

Joy Foord and Pick Diller had cocktails most evenings in Syd Huff's suite at Lennon's and were also invited to socialise with Richard Sutherland and Elaine Bessemer-Clark. Joy said: 'They asked us to drinks at General Sutherland's suite for six o'clock one evening. Pick was always very punctual and I am, too. We knocked on the door and got no answer, so we tried the door and it was open. There was no one there, but from another room a voice called out, "Make yourselves at home. We won't be long." Pick spun me around on my two legs and we went out the door. He refused to discuss it, but you know what was happening, don't you? Elaine Bessemer-Clark was slim, smart, sophisticated and beautifully dressed, and she and Sutherland were in love with each other.'

Sutherland might have been in love, but the combination of the war, the strains of the relationship and his own personal failings started to have a drastic effect on his performance as MacArthur's right-hand man. He was drinking too much, which made him argumentative, and he suffered from memory lapses. He even argued with MacArthur, angrily denying he was at fault when MacArthur pointed out a mistake he had made.

More in sorrow than in anger, MacArthur told him: 'The trouble with you, Dick, I am afraid, is you are a natural born autocrat.' Privately, though, MacArthur summed up his chief of staff as 'a brilliant officer whose own ego is ruining him. He bottlenecks all action over his own desk. The staff is scared to death of him and they all hate him.' Yet MacArthur retained him as chief of staff rather than let General Marshall in Washington and his enemies in the other services know that he had made a mistake in placing so much trust in Sutherland.

The politics at GHQ and the peccadilloes at Lennon's Hotel took a humorous turn when Jean MacArthur's name was linked to a bordello. Joy Foord said: 'Jean had turned in her car, USA-2, and the colonel in charge of the motorpool used it to visit somebody who was staying at Yale Apartments. He parked the car out of sight in a side street around the back of the building. Some American MPs checked the side street and there was USA-2 parked behind the place next door, which turned out to be a brothel. There was a lot of mirth about Jean MacArthur's car being found behind a brothel.'

When the Battle of the Coral Sea averted a seaborne invasion of Port Moresby, the Japanese decided to capture the vital strategic fortress over the Owen Stanley Range. This gruelling route over The Hump, as American pilots called the range, would bring them down to the southern coast with easy access to Port Moresby from the rear.

MacArthur had sent a group of Australian and American officers by flying-boat to Buna to make a reconnaissance of the northern Papuan coast. The survey team recommended that the most suitable site for an airfield was a flat patch of ground covered in kunai grass at Dobodura, a spot 10 miles inland from the Buna government station. Troops from the 39th Battalion and a regiment of American engineers were preparing to occupy the area when a Japanese convoy was sighted off the Papuan coast, heading in that direction. The convoy contained Colonel Yokoyama's Advance Butai, which was made up of 5900 combat, supply and base troops, as well as a workforce of 1200 native carriers from Rabaul and 2630 packhorses and mules.

The Japanese landed 1800 troops on an empty beach between Buna and Gona during the night of 21 July—the day MacArthur moved to Brisbane—and more troops and supplies were going ashore the following day when Allied aircraft from Port Moresby swooped down on them. MacArthur's communique on the action said: 'The enemy effected a landing at Gona Mission, on the north coast of Papua, a point not occupied by the Allied forces. The enemy convoy was discovered by reconnaissance and our air forces executed a series of bombing attacks throughout the day on enemy shipping, landing barges and personnel on shore. One large transport ship and one barge were sunk, and heavy casualties were inflicted on debarking troops.'

The transport in question, although burning, had in fact been run aground and the Japanese had succeeded in securing a beachhead from which they could occupy any section of the coast. After setting up base camps under the coconut trees in the narrow coastal strip between Buna and Gona, the Japanese raided hospitals, missions and plantations in the area, rounding up eight European men and women and a six-year-old boy. They were later beheaded, the boy last of all, by a Japanese lieutenant wielding a sword.

The first Japanese objective on the overland route was Kokoda, 70 miles inland from Buna at the start of the Kokoda Track in the foothills of the Owen Stanleys' northern flank. The main attraction at Kokoda was a grass airfield marked out along a narrow plateau 1200 feet above sea level, the only landing site in the entire mountain range.

Just 24 hours after landing, elements of the Advance Butai struck inland along a muddy vehicle track that wound through the dense jungle and kunai grass of the swampy lowlands as far as a suspension footbridge over the Kumusi River. The crossing point was known as Wairopi— pidgin English for the 'wire ropes' from which the bridge was constructed—and from there the track climbed up through the hills to Kokoda.

A platoon of Australians from the 39th Battalion engaged the enemy from the far side of the Kumusi after first sabotaging the footbridge and sending it crashing into the swirling torrent. Nevertheless, hundreds of Japanese marines surged across the river at various crossing points under a barrage of withering covering fire from mortars and machine guns. The young militiamen withdrew a few miles along the track in the direction of Kokoda and Captain Templeton ordered them to set up an ambush with two Lewis guns on the banks of Gorari Creek. The Japanese walked into the trap the following day and sustained 15 casualties before they could drive back the Australians with sniper fire from trees overlooking their positions along the creek.

Lacking the numbers and the firepower to stem the Japanese advance, the young Australians were forced back to the jungle wall on high ground at Oivi. Templeton was shot dead by a Japanese patrol when he left this new position in an attempt to get more men from the meagre force at Kokoda, where a grand total of 32 reinforcements had been flown in from Port Moresby.

On the night of 28 July, the Japanese stormed up the steep slope into Kokoda and, in the misty moonlight, fell upon the defenders. In a confused battle involving much hand-to-hand combat, the Japanese succeeded in seizing the tiny settlement. The enemy had mortars and Juki machine guns; the defenders only .303 rifles, grenades and a few Bren guns. The Japanese were a battle-hardened fighting force; the defenders mainly young men who were experiencing their first taste of warfare. Casualties were high on both sides and the Australian commanding officer, Lieutenant-Colonel Owen, was shot dead through the forehead as he organised a fighting withdrawal. Firing as they went, the 39th pulled back into the safety of the rubber trees in a plantation bordering the airstrip.

Dr Geoffrey Vernon, the only medical officer with the 39th, described the retreat: 'Among the many impressions of that exciting night, none stands out more clearly than the weirdness of the natural conditions— the thick white mist dimming the moonlight, the mysterious veiling of trees, houses and men, the drip of moisture from the foliage, and at the last, the almost complete silence as if the rubber groves of Kokoda were sleeping as usual in the depths of night . . .'

The Australians regrouped at Deniki, a camp on a hill a few miles further down the Kokoda Track, but there was no sign of the enemy. Having no idea that the Australian force consisted of just a few hundred exhausted, wet, hungry and frightened young men, the Japanese themselves were waiting in Kokoda for reinforcements and fresh supplies to reach them from the coast before pushing further along the track.

In Brisbane, MacArthur was telling war correspondents that Australia could be saved in Papua and only in Papua. He said: 'We must attack, attack, attack.' The remnants of the 39th at Deniki were ordered to mount a counter-attack on Kokoda on 8 August, but even when they secured a foothold on one side of the airstrip, a relief plane from Moresby circled overhead and refused to risk a landing because of the proximity of Japanese forces. Short of food and ammunition, the Australians were inevitably driven back down the Kokoda Track again.

Lieutenant Lance Watts said: 'Our Citizen Military Force boys had to fight a rearguard action along the track and MacArthur was always ridiculing them, saying it was a small party of Japs. He didn't know what the poor buggers had to put up with and he didn't believe our fellows when they told him.'

Some footsore reinforcements had reached Deniki along the track from Port Moresby and supplies had been trickling in on the backs of Lieutenant Kienzle's carrier force. Dr Vernon described the harshness of the carriers' lives: 'Many carriers were without a single blanket, rice was practically the only food issue, meat was withheld for two or three weeks and tobacco scarce; the regulation governing the reduction of loads to 40 pounds was often ignored and excessive weights and distances imposed on the carriers as if they were merely pack animals.'

Kienzle had spent the previous few days reconnoitring the territory adjacent to the track to find a new dropping site. The 'dry lake' that he discovered at Myola proved to be one of the Australians' most valuable assets of the entire campaign . . . 'a large patch of open country right on top of the main range of the Owen Stanleys. It was just the very thing I had been looking and praying for to assist us in beating the Japanese. The "dry lake" is a patch of open ground measuring roughly about one and a quarter miles long by one-third of a mile wide, a creek running through the middle, a tributary of the Efogi, and swampy, each side covered with a sharp reed and the higher ground with short tufts of grass.'

Evacuating the wounded from Deniki involved a nightmare journey that required four Papuans for each stretcher case. As tropical damp soon rotted the canvas on army stretchers, the Papuans made replacements by lashing a double blanket between two poles with lawyer vine. At nightfall on the track, the Papuans built almost rainproof shelters for the wounded from saplings and palm leaves, and then slept beside the patients to minister to their needs during the night. One Australian captain said: 'They tended the men on stretchers with the devotion of a mother and the care of a nurse.'

Those who could still walk, however painfully, made the journey on foot to allow their more seriously wounded mates to be carried. Chester

Wilmot, an Australian war correspondent, reported after climbing the Kokoda Track: 'Some have been hit in the foot and they can't even get a boot on, but they're walking back over root and rock and through mud in bare feet, protected only by their bandages. Here's a steep pinch and a wounded digger's trying to climb it. You need both hands and both feet, but he's been hit in the arm and thigh.

'Two of his cobbers are helping him along. One goes ahead, hauling himself up by root and branch. The wounded digger clings to the belt of the man in front with his second hand while his other cobber gets underneath and pushes him up. I say to this fellow he ought to be a stretcher case, but he replies, "I can get along. There's blokes here lots worse than me and if we don't walk they'll never get out."'

There was an interested new spectator to the debacle that was unfolding in New Guinea in the short, energetic shape of General George C. Kenney, who had just replaced George Brett as head of the Allied air forces. Kenney flew over the mountainous terrain in a B-17, and what he saw convinced him that the air force had a major role, if not *the* major role, to play in deciding the outcome of the battle for Papua.

General Brett had lingered on at GHQ long after MacArthur had frozen him out. When a member of General George Marshall's staff, Colonel Sam Anderson, returned to Washington from a fact-finding mission in Brisbane, Marshall asked him whether or not he should relieve Brett of his command. Anderson replied: 'Yes, Sir. As long as General MacArthur and General Brett are the commanders in the south-west Pacific, there is going to be no co-operation between the ground and the air, and I don't think you are going to relieve General MacArthur.'

Asked by Marshall for his opinion, MacArthur effectively shot Brett down: 'He is naturally inclined to more or less harmless intrigue and has a bent, due perhaps to his delightful personality, for social entertainment and the easy way of life. I would rate his service during the last three months under my command as only average.'

Brett was unceremoniously booted out, but went home in style. Piloted by Frank Kurtz, he flew to Washington in a specially converted B-17 called a swoose (part swan, part goose) in 47 hours—the fastest time ever—thus getting his name into the record books.

Brett described MacArthur as 'a brilliant, temperamental egoist; a handsome man, who can be as charming as anyone who ever lived, or harshly indifferent to the needs and desires of those around. His religion is deeply part of his nature. Everything about Douglas MacArthur is on the grand scale; his virtues and triumphs and shortcomings.'

George Kenney had spent several days at the Pentagon being briefed for his new assignment before flying to Brisbane at a more leisurely pace. As short in stature and abrupt in manner as Brett was tall and congenial, Kenney was a loose cannon who wasn't afraid to take pot-shots at his superiors and, in the past, several of them had been aimed at MacArthur.

A World War I fighter pilot with two enemy 'kills' to his credit, Kenney had converted his reckless combat skills and great energies into an aggressive directness in urging the General Staff to set up an air force that was entirely independent of both the army and navy. Heretical though this was according to the canon law of the US armed forces, the spectacular successes of the Japanese in the air had dramatically proved Kenney's case for him.

He arrived in Brisbane on 28 July, moved into Lennon's Hotel and reported to GHQ the following morning. The blonde receptionist at the entrance to the AMP building fixed him with a dazzling smile and her Chanel No. 5 followed him up in the elevator to Brett's office on the fourth floor, where Beryl Stevenson was working.

'Kenney came first to Brett's office with Bill Benn, his aide, and then went up to see MacArthur, but Brett did not go with him,' said Beryl. 'The relationship was very strained. I hadn't realised until Kenney arrived that Brett hadn't seen or spoken to MacArthur for eight weeks. Kenney was absolutely a revolution and I hadn't seen this kind of action before. He arrived in the morning and that evening flew to New Guinea, astonishing everybody. I didn't realise how hopeless the command was until Kenney took over.

'At that point, my brother in 10 Squadron over in England was missing in action and my family was in a state of stress. I had a lot of calls from my parents saying I'd done enough and should come home, so I thought this might be the time when Kenney was replacing Brett.

'However, on the first day that he took control, 4 August 1942, Kenney walked into his office, dominated by a huge globe with maps around the wall, and I suddenly heard him speaking on the intercom. He was committing the whole of the Allied air force on the bloody intercom! I'd been brought up with West Point and Sandhurst generals who always covered their backs with five carbon copies, one on pink, one on blue, one on green and so forth, to distribute to their different section commanders. And here was this strange little man committing the whole of the air force on the intercom! I tore in with my notebook and took down what he was saying.'

When Kenney finished issuing his instructions, he replaced the handset and looked inquiringly at his new secretary, who said: 'General, would you like me to confirm that in writing?'

Kenney studied her nonchalantly.

'Mrs Stevenson, I was talking to my A-3,' he said quietly. 'If he doesn't do exactly as I tell him, I'll just get me a new A-3.'

Beryl said: 'The war was transformed by George Kenney. For the first time, here was an airman who knew what he was about. In my book— and in MacArthur's book, if he was quite honest—all the bright ideas came from Kenney. Sending troops, machineguns, bulldozers, everything they needed, up to New Guinea in US planes. One simple fact was knowing how many airplanes there were in Australia. Many of the planes didn't have protection for themselves, and we were losing planes because they weren't properly equipped, but that didn't last long after Kenney arrived. He transformed MacArthur's whole attitude towards the air and that was an achievement in itself.'

Kenney's first obstacle was General Sutherland, who believed he knew how to run an air force better than anyone. When Sutherland tried to interfere with his command, Kenney brushed him aside and won the right to report directly to MacArthur. He proceeded to set up the 5th Air Force as a US command independent of all outside controls, and to re-form the 43rd Bombardment Group, which had practically ceased to exist because so many aircraft had been lost or damaged.

Kenney said of Sutherland: 'He was an arrogant, opinionated, and very ambitious guy. I don't think Sutherland was ever loyal to MacArthur. He pretended that he was and I think MacArthur thought he was, but I wouldn't trust him.'

Four weeks after General Kenney's arrival, Lieutenant-General Robert L. Eichelberger, an altogether different type, was appointed corps commander of the 32nd and 41st divisions. At 56 years of age, 6 foot 4 inches tall, lean and rangy, Eichelberger was a former classmate of General Harding at West Point, where he had recently completed a term as superintendent.

Eichelberger had expected to land with I Corps in North Africa, but he and his staff had suddenly been switched to Australia and he accepted the change with an old soldier's resignation. Army life had never been quite what he had anticipated. Instead of serving in France during World War I, as he had expected, he had ended up in Siberia as assistant chief of staff to the American Expeditionary Force fighting on the side of the White Russians against the Bolsheviks.

When Eichelberger reported to MacArthur's suite at Lennon's, the first thing MacArthur told him was that he was to have as little contact as possible with Blamey and the other Australian generals. As Blamey was head of Allied Land Forces and had just moved his advanced headquarters to the new University of Queensland buildings in Brisbane,

Eichelberger realised *this* would undoubtedly create problems, but once again raised no objection.

Instead, he set up I Corps in Rockhampton, where the 41st Division was based, 500 miles away from the divisive interference of MacArthur's GHQ. Eichelberger neither liked nor trusted Richard Sutherland, but had a grudging respect for his skills in handling MacArthur. He said: 'He knew how to work on General MacArthur like Paderewski playing the piano. He could bring out in MacArthur any latent jealousy and envy in his nature. Sutherland had a strange control over MacArthur. He knew all of MacArthur's little failures, weaknesses and foibles, and he could manoeuvre him and play on these characteristics like an expert plucking the strings of a fine violin.'

If Sutherland was a master of intrigue, MacArthur's intelligence chief, Brigadier-General Charles Willoughby, was positively lethal. Prussian-born, boorish and single-minded, Willoughby was devoted to MacArthur for saving his skin by getting him out of Corregidor. He approached his job like a dishonest accountant who fiddled the figures to give substance to MacArthur's fantasies. Viewing the world through a pince-nez which dangled from his neck on a black silk cord, Willoughby had a reputation for having the most perfect hindsight of any officer in the US Army. Sutherland despised the intelligence chief, but he was a member of the Bataan Gang and MacArthur needed the facts and figures supplied by his network of coastwatchers and informants, even if his interpretation of the available data was liable to be wildly inaccurate.

The other gang member who was indispensable to MacArthur was Colonel LeGrande Diller, who gloried in the power that MacArthur gave him over famous war correspondents from some of the biggest organisations in the news business, including *Time* magazine, CBS and the *New York Times*. 'Colonel Diller was MacArthur's imagemaker and he acted like a buffer between the correspondents and General MacArthur,' said Mark Muller. 'No one got past him to see the general unless Diller decided it was okay.'

Although Diller's friends called him Pick, he was known to reporters whose stories he massacred with a blue pencil as 'Killer Diller' and he operated on one simple, inflexible principle: all stories must agree with MacArthur's communiques. Any journalist who refused to comply with this rule went onto a blacklist and any military censor who gave dispensation to a reporter to file a story containing even the mildest criticism of MacArthur was either immediately reprimanded or marked down for future punishment.

Diller candidly described his job as 'seeing that General MacArthur got credit for everything in the Pacific'. He performed this onerous task with great efficiency.

According to Frank Kelley of the New York *Herald Tribune* and Cornelius Ryan of the London *Daily Telegraph* in their book *Star-Spangled Mikado*, 'with the help of sycophantic correspondents who scrambled for small favours, and aided by a ruthless system of censorship which was political as well as military, the Public Relations Office of MacArthur's headquarters built MacArthur into a demigod.'

Censorship under MacArthur was strictly controlled by the Public Relations Office, they wrote. This was not only a contradiction of functions, but it violated accepted War Department practice. One side was supposed to put out the news and help correspondents get it. The other was the watchdog of military security. In MacArthur's command reporters hardly knew who was the censor and who was a publicity agent. The principal rule of censorship was: do not contradict the official communique—even when it is wrong.

The inaccurate communiques were many, the authors said, but the correspondents could do nothing—unless they wanted to get out, go home and tell the story there. Nothing was more useless to a newspaper than a correspondent whose credentials had been lifted. In the Pacific, Diller said the correspondents were a bunch of 'two-bit palookas and sportswriters'. Some of those 'palookas' had been all over the world as correspondents for leading newspapers and agencies. They had been shot at and bombed long before the war came to the Pacific.

As the war moved into a dangerous new phase in which MacArthur's grand strategy was to be tested for the first time, Diller's propaganda methods were applied with crushing force.

Chapter Eleven

-‹o›-

Kokoda

NORBERT J. Grant landed in Australia on 14 August 1942, heading for Brisbane. In Sydney, the port of debarkation, the 738th Battalion was immediately split up. Headquarters and medics along with Companies B and C went by train to South Brisbane, while Company D remained in Sydney and Company A headed off by train and truck to Darwin.

The Brisbane units were quartered at Ascot Racecourse for a week, then moved 15 miles south-west to Camp Columbia which sprawled across hundreds of acres of virgin bushland at Wacol. The 738th Battalion was given a large chunk of territory complete with mosquitoes, snakes and ant-hills. Companies B and C each had two big wooden huts for barracks. The officers had one, and there was one each for the mess hall, medics, headquarters detachment and motor pool personnel.

'We were not permitted to trim any of the bush and grass, or make any permanent changes because we'd been told we were moving to a new camp in a convent at Whinstanes in December,' said Alton Jensen. 'Our small drill and training area was down near the railroad tracks at Wacol, and we hiked along the road past the station and into the woods. A couple of times we were taken to an Australian rifle range for some target shooting.'

B and C companies were assigned to their duties at a number of locations within a 50-mile radius of Camp Columbia. There was the main provost base in South Brisbane, GHQ in the city centre, the 108th General Hospital at Gatton, the airbase at Amberley and army camps at Wacol, Darra and Redbank. One detachment was sent down to the

154

south coast, where they drilled with Australian lifeguards in preparation for the amphibious landings to come.

There were various one or two-week assignments in which MPs acted as train guards for shipments of military equipment to northern Queensland, or guarded dignitaries such as visiting US congressmen and the President's wife, Mrs Eleanor Roosevelt. MPs were also on permanent duty outside Lennon's Hotel and the AMP building. Alton Jensen said: 'We saw MacArthur almost every day. Some of our unit had to watch over MacArthur and his son as they went walking in the park.'

B Company undertook patrol work in Ipswich, Toowoomba and Gatton and was placed in charge of security at Brett's Wharf, Hamilton, where they encountered the recalcitrant Australian wharfie. Alton Jensen said: 'When teatime came for the Australians, all work stopped at the wharves. Much needed material was left hanging in baskets up in the air. They'd just leave it there until teatime was over, then they'd drop it down and go on with the work. We weren't used to that as far as the military was concerned because, in the States at that time, the military had top priority over everything. The work had to be done and no strikes or layovers of that nature were permitted. It was a problem for us, but, apart from that, I had wonderful rapport with Australians and so did most of our units.'

C Company took over the city patrol along with the 814th Military Police Battalion. Norbert Grant's detachment worked at the main provost centre, which was situated in front of the Base 3 communications and logistics complex at Somerville House in Vulture Street, South Brisbane. 'The provosts had the Town Hall, with a jail downstairs,' said Bill Bentson. 'MPs would bring guys there until they could send them out to the stockade at Eagle Farm. Soldiers doing jail time were sent to a prison farm called Round Mountain out in the boondocks near Beaudesert.'

Alton Jensen admitted: 'We were what you might call untrained, yet we got very good results.'

Around this time, American diplomats were dismayed to find that there were severe problems with the local population over the influx of American troops. Nelson Johnson wrote in August: 'Brisbaners are being pushed around on their streets, in their favourite eating places and out of their homes. Naturally they are uncomfortable, irritable and inhospitable in their relations with their invading hosts [sic].'

Marjorie Robertson, who lived in East Brisbane, said: 'The city was jam-packed with Americans strutting around in fancy clothes. Walking down Queen Street in 1942, I would say there were nine men to every woman, and six or seven of the men would be Americans. The trams were always crowded and we were packed in like sardines. There were always loads of Americans on them; they used to catch trams just for the sake of mixing with the populace and seeing what went on a bit further out.

'The Americans gave presents to the girls and won them over, which was extraordinarily annoying for the Australians. But my mother encouraged me to invite Americans home and we always had oodles of people for dinner. My brother was away with the Royal Australian Air Force and my mother's contribution to the war was to give anyone else's son a bit of ordinary home comfort. I went out with several Americans. I was very innocent and very good, and I had a wonderful time with them. We went to the pictures and I took them to my church functions.'

Alton Jensen said: 'The people were kind to us and there were a lot of fathers and mothers who had eligible daughters and were anxious to get them married off. One of the attractions was that the Americans had so much more money to spend, but most of them treated Australian girls very nicely. I was invited to several homes where, despite all the rationing, these mothers had prepared wonderful meals. They always asked us to eat with them and then we'd take the daughters out for the afternoon.

'I formed an attachment with one girl from Morningside whom I met at church—that was the primary way of meeting girls; the best ones anyhow—but I didn't get married myself. A lot of matchmaking went on in our company and I had to file the papers for one of our men who got married to an Australian girl whose father was a sergeant in the civil police. The women were very nice but the men were a little rough. One of the bigger problems with Australian soldiers was in the pubs, where they thought we were taking the beer away from them.'

Acts of petty meanness by individual American servicemen sometimes caused great distress. Pamela Davenport was a young girl living on the south side in Ipswich Road, Moorooka, on a route to American camps at Rocklea, Wacol, Redbank, Darra, Amberley and further afield at Beaudesert. 'The American soldiers irrevocably blotted their copybooks for me when they took my beloved dog Tony as a mascot,' she said.

According to some of Pamela's neighbours, who witnessed the incident, an American army truck pulled up, a soldier picked up the dog from the footpath, and the truck drove away. Pamela said: 'I was distraught. My parents phoned all the camps and the neighbours were up in arms. Over a week later, Tony came home—his paws raw, his body gravel-rashed, and he was thin and exhausted. He must have jumped from the truck and found his way home. After that, the

Americans were as much the enemy in my eyes as the Japanese.'

When Pamela's parents forbade her from taking her dog for walks in case of further trouble, 'I blamed the American soldiers for this change in my lifestyle, though in hindsight it was the war itself and not just the arrival of the Americans which changed our lives forever. We had come of age and it was not a happy experience.'

Molly Mann and Bethia Foott, two young Australian women who followed their husbands into the war zone in August, wrote: 'We pictured Brisbane as a quiet, lotus-eating city, whose even tempo was punctuated by bursts of gaiety when people from the country invaded it for the races, wool sales, or Exhibition Week. Instead of this imagined, tranquil scene, we found we had come to what was almost a garrison town. Soldiers, sailors and airmen were everywhere. Concrete air-raid shelters stretched as far as the eye could see down the centre of the narrow streets.

'Water pipes, laid hurriedly down in all the gutters, reminded us of the dangers of fire in a city built so largely of wood. Buttresses of sandbags outlined the doors of all the public buildings whose windows were either boarded up or reinforced with wire-netting. Noting the troop trains carrying their cargoes of men and guns, tanks and nets northwards, and the convoys of three-ton trucks and lorries that thundered in a long procession from the docks to the distant camps, we realised we had left the safety of the southern states for a city which had been evacuated by hundreds of women and children, and which was being run under wartime conditions.'

Some diggers were openly hostile towards Australian girls who went out with Americans. Joy Foord said: 'Pick and I were walking one night past the American Red Cross on Adelaide Street when three drunken Australian servicemen slapped me and called him an effing Yank. Pick said, "This is where I lose my rank." He was only a small person and he took off his coat, and I thought he would be killed. The sentries outside the Red Cross saw what was happening and came running down, and the Australians ran away. The animosity between the Australian and American soldiers was very strong and a lot of Americans wouldn't take it.'

After the female question, the main source of contention between Australian and American troops was the availability of luxury items at the American Postal Exchange (PX) stores. As a friendly gesture, the Australian government had granted the Americans excise exemption on cigarettes, a privilege that meant a pack of 20 cigarettes cost American soldiers just sixpence at a PX canteen, and they were allowed to buy two packs a day, while Australian troops paid seven pence ha-penny for just 10 cigarettes. Canberra bureaucrats had persuaded the government not to make a similar concession to their own soldiers on the grounds that it would cost £4000 a week.

The powers-that-be also allowed the Americans to use Australian canteen facilities, but Australians were banned from American PXs, where the shelves bulged with cigarettes, cigars, chocolates, candy bars, biscuits, tinned cream and a full range of hard-to-get toiletries. As an Australian private earned only £9.15s for a 30-day month, compared with £17 for an American, the Australian had only about half the spending power of his American rival. *Truth* newspaper commented: 'Our six-bob-a-day boys reckon there is something cock-eyed with a law that calls upon them to pay through the neck for smokes while the visitors who get better pay and also enjoy an advantageous exchange rate can secure similar goods at next-door-to-nothing charges.'

Marjorie Robertson said: 'The Australian servicemen were very, very bitter about the opulence of the American PX compared with what they could get themselves.'

Australian soldiers picketed MacArthur's headquarters over this blatant favouritism. News of the demonstration was suppressed by the censors, but on 15 August MacArthur changed the rules to permit Australian soldiers to enter the American PX to buy one pack of cigarettes a day per man. To make this possible with existing stocks, the American allowance of two packs a day was cut in half.

The Brisbane PX was situated on the ground floor of the red-brick Primary Building on the corner of Adelaide and Creek streets. It was soon inundated with Australian troops lining up to buy popular American brands like Lucky Strike, Camel and Chesterfield at the give-away price of sixpence a packet. However, many Australians decided that one pack a day was not nearly enough and lined up several times to get more than their fair share. This created endless arguments between the diggers and the American military policemen who were in charge of crowd control at the PX. The Australians also bought large quantities of chocolates and other items, which they sold to civilians at a profit, an illegal form of profiteering.

Alton Jensen said: 'I was involved in a raid by the Military Police on Australian and American soldiers who were tied into a scam on cigarettes. They were stealing cartons of cigarettes from the docks and storing them in a warehouse in an industrial part of the city. We found out where it was and I was taken out in a jeep in a raiding party of 15 or 20 from B, C and Headquarters and the 814th Battalion. This was about 10.30 at night and we were armed with pistols, with orders to shoot if necessary. But most of the culprits were warned about the raid and only three—two Americans and one Australian—were captured.'

By August, there were 99,000 Americans stationed in Australia and two-thirds of them were camped around Brisbane, which meant that increasing numbers of Americans were also using the PX. Many of them regarded the Australians as unwelcome intruders and harsh words and the occasional fisticuffs were exchanged. Alton Jensen said: 'Cigarettes were a big problem. The Australians were chalked on the back of their uniforms so that if they came in the front door again they would know they had had their quotient of cigarettes.'

One frequent visitor to the American PX was Ed Webster, who still wore his gunner's uniform, even though he was no longer in the army; it was the only way he could get served in the American PX or the Australian canteen 50 yards further along Adelaide Street.

'Webster had been discharged as medically unfit because he had trouble with his leg,' said Lieutenant Ron Shea. 'He was removed from the unit and placed in a staging camp until discharge proceedings had been concluded. There was a staging camp at the Exhibition Ground and another at Kalinga and another at Ascot Racecourse. He would have been out of the army by August 1942.'

Webster was living with his wife, Alice, and his son, John, receiving treatment for his leg and trying to get something going in the way of a job. He was 31 years of age and it was time for him to become a husband and father, but times were tough. He'd lost the gauntness, though, and filled out on Alice's home cooking.

Webster had several grounds for complaint about the state of affairs he had found in Brisbane upon his return, and finding suitable work was one of them. He had two campaign decorations, but neither he nor any other Australian soldier had anything specifically to show they had fought in Syria. More Australians had taken part in the Syrian campaign than any other nationality, and the performance of troops from the 7th Division had been particularly impressive. However, the campaign received hardly any publicity because Churchill ruled that it would be wrong to celebrate a victory over France, a former ally. As the Australian government had to seek permission from London before it could strike a campaign medal, Syria remained 'the forgotten campaign'.

When word of the Churchill veto passed around the bars where Ed Webster drank, he cursed Churchill and the British to anybody who would listen. At home, he told Alice what the diggers had said when they came back from World War I: 'You can't eat glory. It doesn't put meat and potatoes on your plate.' It was a familiar complaint to anyone who had lived through the Depression, and now history was repeating itself.

However, Webster's former comrades in the 2/2nd Anti-Tank Regiment had more important things to worry about than battle honours. The 7th Division was being regrouped in the Brisbane area for their next overseas posting, and it didn't take a military genius to work out where they would be going. Lieutenant Lance Watts: 'They were getting the 7th Div. together to go up to New Guinea, and all our units were moved to Woodford. The Yanks had taken over all the best camps and we were pushed to the backblocks.'

Webster reflected it was a good thing nobody could send *him* to New-bloody-Guinea. It never crossed his mind that he might be in danger in Brisbane.

Time and Pick Diller had smoothed the wrinkles in the MacArthurian legend until it was one of the most seamless in America's pantheon. Yet during the southern winter of 1942, unauthorised words like 'tired and drawn', 'emotional', and 'depressed' started to creep into whispered descriptions of the Commander-in-Chief. The reason for his staff's concern was that MacArthur, whom they wanted to believe was infallible, at least militarily, was making serious misjudgements about the enemy.

For one thing, he had completely misread the intention behind the Japanese landings at Buna and Gona after listening to Charles Willoughby. The intelligence supremo informed him that the Japanese were probably only interested in building an airfield and securing the ground around it. As this reflected MacArthur's own strategic plan for the area, he had no reason to doubt Willoughby's assessment. But Willoughby, who had no wish to contradict his benefactor, had in fact tailored his comments to suit MacArthur's prognosis.

One of Willoughby's reports stated: 'An overland advance in strength is discounted in view of logistic difficulties, poor communications and difficult terrain.' MacArthur refused to believe that a new Japanese offensive was in progress also because Willoughby's estimates put the Japanese force at only a fifth of its true strength. As Eichelberger sourly noted, Willoughby was 'always positive in his views and usually wrong'.

Once the Japanese had secured Kokoda, they immediately took full advantage of the airstrip to fly in supplies and reinforcements. Major-General Tomitaro Horii, a short, podgy, bespectacled figure, joined his troops and rode around Kokoda on a white stallion. From Kokoda, the track wound down through thick bush and up sharp ridges, reaching a height of 6500 feet before plunging through muddy jungle to the coast.

With any form of motorised transport out of the question, Japanese troops would have had to negotiate the full length of the track on foot, albeit with light-weight backpacks and light weapons, while native carriers and packhorses hauled the heavier equipment, including Juki heavy machineguns and a mountain gun. At the vanguard of the Japanese column were teams of Korean and Formosan labourers, who widened the narrow track with machetes. In jungle-green uniforms with leaves camouflaging their steel helmets, the Japanese pushed towards Port Moresby as fast as they could force back Australia's 39th Militia Battalion. General Morris had belatedly sent the 53rd Battalion and the headquarters of the 30th Brigade, commanded by Brigadier Selwyn Porter, along the Kokoda Track to reinforce the 39th, but the situation remained perilous. Both the Australian and American high commands knew that if Moresby fell, MacArthur's plan to fight the Battle for Australia in Papua would collapse at a stroke. This was not a risk MacArthur was prepared to take, and he ordered the veteran 7th Division, who had been holding the so-called Brisbane Line, to stop the enemy's advance in New Guinea.

While these troops were in transit, MacArthur received a US Naval intelligence report alerting him to Japanese plans for a landing at Milne Bay. He split the division in half before it reached Port Moresby, sending the 2/9th, 2/10th and 2/12th battalions of the 18th Brigade to reinforce the defences at Milne Bay, while the 2/14th and 2/16th battalions of the 21st Brigade carried on to Port Moresby.

As Allied land forces commander, General Blamey placed both brigades under the command of Lieutenant-General Sydney Rowell, who was ordered to retake Kokoda and push the Japanese back across the Owen Stanleys to Buna and Gona. Rowell, a dashingly handsome and not inhuman man, commented grimly to Osmar White, the Australian war correspondent: 'We need a victory in the Pacific, and a lot of poor bastards have got to get killed to provide it.'

Rowell had been Blamey's chief of staff in the Middle East, an experience which had endowed him with a consummate loathing of his commanding officer. He had vowed never to serve in the field under Blamey again because 'we are now not tuned to the same wavelength and are never again likely to be'. He referred disparagingly to Blamey as 'the Lord' because of his egotism, or as 'the little man', referring to his moral, as well as physical, stature. In particular, Rowell despised Blamey's 'debauched' lifestyle.

From the outset, Rowell's biggest problem in Papua was logistical, and he was relying on air drops from Dakota 'biscuit bombers' onto the dried-up lake that Kienzle had discovered at Myola to supply his troops in the field. When he drove past Seven Mile Airdrome near Port Moresby on the evening of 16 August, he noticed that a row of Dakota transport planes had been lined up wingtip to wingtip beside a line of B-17s. He alerted Kenney's new commander of the US Air Force in New Guinea, Brigadier-General Ennis Whitehead, to the potential danger in the event of an air raid. 'There are too many aircraft stacked at the end of the runway,' said Rowell. 'Few things are more capable of demoralising an army than seeing their aircraft smashed on the ground.' Whitehead took the point and promised to shift the planes, but they stayed where they were while the Fortresses were refuelled and bombed up for a mission the following day and the Dakotas were loaded with supplies to be dropped at Myola.

The aircraft were still conveniently parked in the same positions when Japanese bombers, escorted by Zero fighters, appeared over Hombrom Bluff at 10 am and attacked the airfield. Five Dakotas, the only planes immediately available to supply the troops on the Kokoda Track, were destroyed or damaged along with eight Flying Fortresses.

The infantrymen of the 2/14th and the 2/16th were not equipped to deal with the rigours of the Kokoda Track. They had spent the past three months in the scrub country of south-east Queensland after fighting in the Western Desert, hardly suitable training for jungle warfare. They had only their desert clothing of khaki shorts and short-sleeved shirts, and their bare arms and legs were an open invitation to mosquitoes, leaches and deadly ticks. Their webbing had been bleached white by the African sun, making them easy targets for Japanese snipers to pick out against the green jungle background.

Blamey, who had never been anywhere near the Kokoda Track, insisted that khaki was the ideal colour for jungle fighting because of tests that had been carried out by the British Army in India. His own preferred mode of dress was a khaki shirt, bush jacket and a pair of short trousers with long socks, which gave him the appearance of an overgrown boy scout.

Rowell commented: 'The only real way to train for jungle operations is to train in actual jungle. The 7th Division had trained for three months in southern Queensland, but even there, conditions bore no relation to the jungle and rainforest of the Owen Stanley Range. Unless troops live under conditions in which they have to fight, they will be dominated by their environment.'

When the commander of the 21st Brigade, Brigadier Arnold Potts, reached Isurava on 23 August, his two battalions were strung out along the mountain track for miles behind him. He was dismayed to discover that his reserve of rations at the base camp was one quarter of what was supposed to have been dropped by the biscuit bombers. Rowell inquired into the deficiency only to find that the missing rations had indeed been despatched from Port Moresby and jettisoned from aircraft into the enveloping mists of the Owen Stanleys.

Many of the pilots were civilians who were employed by the army on a contract basis and they lacked the discipline of servicemen. Whenever bad weather obscured the dropping site at Myola, they figured it was better to offload supplies somewhere in the region rather than return to base with them and face a grilling from land commanders who had very little appreciation of the atrocious flying conditions.

Sergeant Bill Benston thought he had solved the air-drop problem when he was having breakfast one morning at the Shingle Inn on Edward Street. 'They'd imported a waffle iron from the United States and I was in there eating genuine American-style waffles with ice-cream when I noticed ice-cream canisters being unloaded from the back of a truck outside the restaurant. They were big, padded, airproof containers and the delivery man was dropping them onto a cushion on the sidewalk. I figured these canisters would be ideal for dropping supplies to the troops on the Kokoda Track. We tested the idea with air drops at Archerfield, and the canisters proved excellent for most goods, although there were some breakages among the medical supplies. But the Army shelved the idea because they preferred to continue experimenting with the use of parachutes.'

Having driven the Australians back to Isurava, Colonel Yokoyama waited for General Horii and the bulk of the Japanese force to join him. By the third week in August, Horii had 13,500 Japanese troops at his disposal, including five elite battalions of the Nankai Shitai (South Seas Force), who had been responsible for the invasion of Rabaul and the subsequent slaughter of many of its Australian defenders.

Some members of the 2/22nd Battalion who had escaped from Rabaul prior to the surrender were among the battered remnants of the 39th Battalion already on the Kokoda Track. The 2/14th and 2/16th linked up with them at Isurava and, on 27 August, found themselves facing *bansai* suicide attacks by a vastly numerically superior enemy. These attacks were repulsed, often in desperate hand-to-hand combat, but outflanking movements by the Japanese over the next few days forced the Australians to make a fighting withdrawal to Ioribaiwa.

MacArthur received news of the retreat with undisguised fury. He sent off blistering messages to Blamey, making it plain that he thought the Australian troops were reluctant to engage the enemy and accusing Australians in general of defeatism. He wearily confided to a friend in America: 'To make something out of nothing seems to be my military fate in the twilight of my service. I have led one lost cause and am trying desperately not to have it two.'

Or three, counting the grisly symmetry that was taking shape in the environs of Milne Bay. Buna and Gona were situated about halfway along the coast between the Japanese enclaves at Lae and Salamaua, and the Allied base at Milne Bay at the island's eastern extremity. At Milne Bay, Australian and American forces had been secretly building an airfield with three landing strips since June; one of these strips had been completed and the other two were well advanced. The Japanese had found out about this project and decided to capture Milne Bay by amphibious landing and thus protect the flank of the overland attack. An advance party of Australian troops, consisting of the 7th Militia Brigade's 9th, 25th and 61st Battalions, all Queensland units, had arrived at Milne Bay on 11 July to prepare for just such an eventuality.

With three battalions of the 18th Brigade added to the 7th Militia Brigade, the Australian force at Milne Bay totalled 8824 infantry and artillery men. There were also 1365 American servicemen in engineer and artillery units, but no US combat troops. Milne Force, as it was called, was placed under the command of Major-General Cyril Clowes, a taciturn pipe-smoker known among the officer class as Silent Cyril. For air support, he had two squadrons of Kittyhawks, flown by pilots of the Royal Australian Air Force.

The Japanese knew little about the size of the garrison when they landed 1250 members of the Special Naval Landing Force—the Japanese marines—on the northern shore of Milne Bay on the night of 25 August with written orders to 'strike the white soldiers without remorse'. They landed virtually unopposed, but owing to a navigational error came ashore at the wrong spot, some distance to the east of the Australian base and its vital airstrips. The Japanese hastily rounded up Papuans living in a village near the beachhead, secured the area with patrols and unloaded their barges. They also captured members of D Company, 61st Battalion, who were returning to base in a lugger that unfortunately chugged past the Japanese landing site. The Japanese tied these men to coconut trees with wire and, after interrogation, bayoneted them to death. Papuan women were raped and mutilated, and a small Papuan boy was incinerated by flame-thrower for 'target practice'.

When the first shafts of pearly light pierced the jungle mist the following day, Kittyhawks took off from the completed airstrip at Milne Bay and strafed Japanese barges and supplies at the beachhead. Serious damage was inflicted, but the main Japanese force had already advanced through swampy jungle towards one of the Allied positions, KB Mission, where members of the 61st Battalion were dug in.

Allied defences had been prepared in a number of places clustered around the foot of the bay, but it was impossible for Clowes to judge where the Japanese might strike or indeed even how many of them had come ashore. Clowes held his perimeter during 26 August to ascertain whether more enemy troops might be landed on the southern shore. Although no such landing occurred, the Japanese attacked KB Mission with frontal assaults and flanking movements under cover of darkness that night, forcing the 61st to pull back.

The following day the 2/10th Battalion was sent to KB Mission to counter-attack. They engaged the enemy during the nights of 27 and 28 August, but were driven back with 43 men killed and 26 wounded, most of them hit by fire from Japanese tanks and artillery.

In Brisbane, MacArthur described the situation as 'serious' and told Blamey that Clowes must 'at once clear the north shore of Milne Bay, without delay'. In a message to General Marshall in Washington, MacArthur intimated that the Australians would be to blame if the Japanese invasion was successful. He said: 'This is the first test of Australian troops under my command. The Australians claim that the commander is excellent and rate half his troops as good. The other half from the 7th Australian Division they rate excellent. With good troops under first-class leadership I would view the situation with confidence unless enemy reinforcements are landed but, as I have previously indicated, I am not yet convinced of the efficiency of the Australian troops and do not attempt to forecast results.'

While MacArthur was covering his own back, Clowes had quietly and methodically brought the situation at Milne Bay under control. Even an injection of 1200 reinforcements failed to help the Japanese make much headway during the cover of night, while during the day they had to dodge constant attacks from RAAF fighters which strafed them 'until their gun barrels were lopsided'.

The Japanese regrouped and launched their most ferocious assault on the moonlit night of 30 August, advancing as far as one of the unfinished airstrips, where the 25th Battalion was dug in. The enemy made suicidal charges across open ground in unsuccessful attempts to seize the airstrip and were cut down by machinegun fire. When the Japanese broke off contact after one desperate final assault, the Australians chased them back into the jungle.

The strident, drum-beating communique that MacArthur issued late on 31 August gave no indication of his earlier lack of faith in the Australians: 'The Milne Bay area is rapidly being cleared of the enemy. Australian combat troops, ably commanded by Major-General Clowes and brilliantly supported by American and Australian air units, have thrown the enemy back into the narrow confines of the peninsula north of the bay. Enemy losses have been heavy. Some remnants of his forces probably were saved from destruction by evacuation by naval war craft under cover of darkness. All his heavy supplies and equipment, including tanks, were lost.

'This operation represents another phase in the pattern of the enemy's plans to capture Port Moresby. His latest effort was to turn the right flank by a surprise attack at Milne Bay. The move was anticipated, however, and prepared for with great care. With complete secrecy the position was occupied by our forces and converted into a strong point. The enemy fell into the trap with disastrous results for him.'

Brisbanites cheered up when they read this report in the *Courier-Mail* on 1 September, and the communique was published in newspapers throughout Australia. However, William Dunstan, general manager of the powerful Melbourne *Herald*, stated: 'Correspondents in Brisbane hold the strong feeling that communiques deliberately falsify the position. The changes from acute pessimism in reports of Milne Bay to riotous optimism bear out this point. It all boils down to the fact that MacArthur has ruled that all reports are subject to his communiques.'

That same morning, 1 September, Clowes sent troops from the 2/12th Battalion to drive more deeply into enemy-held territory. Seventy Japanese were killed in a swift advance on the north shore and reinforcements from the 2/9th were due to arrive the following morning to press home this advantage when another intelligence report landed on MacArthur's desk at GHQ. He immediately cabled Clowes: 'Expect attack Jap ground forces on Milne aerodromes from the west and north-west supported by destroyer fire from bay. Take immediate stations.'

This information was woefully inaccurate and caused a crucial delay while troops retreated to guard the airfield and waited for an attack that never came. As a result, the 2/9th did not arrive on the north shore until late the following afternoon. Even though MacArthur had been responsible for the lost time, he continued to push Blamey for quick results. Blamey's response was to pull Clowes out of Milne Bay and send him on extended leave.

'Silent Cyril' broke his silence years later to say: 'The "flap" messages were decodes of "most secret" Jap signals, but whether they were correctly interpreted or otherwise, the fact remains that they were of little use to us and served merely to hinder and hamper the development of our counter-attack which, otherwise, I feel would have reached its conclusion days earlier than it actually did.'

When the 2/9th went forward, they encountered a narrow strip of jungle terrain with patches of open ground flanked by the sea on one side with the mountains on the other. The ground inland towards the mountains was riddled with creeks along which foul-smelling kunai grass and dense foliage provided good defensive positions for Japanese snipers and machine gunners. As Allied communications were poor, torrential rain was beating down most of the time, and there were no reliable maps, progress was understandably slow and dangerous.

However, the Allied advance was marked by individual acts of heroism, most notably that of Corporal John French of the 2/9th who attacked three Japanese machine-gun posts single-handed. After wiping out two of the posts, he came back to his men for another grenade and attacked the third, silencing that as well, but when his men caught up with him they found that he had been shot dead during his final attack. French, described as 'a usually quiet, smiling, young soldier', had accounted for nine enemy dead and was awarded a posthumous Victoria Cross.

For their attack on the main Japanese base, the Australians had the benefit of Kittyhawk fighter and Hudson bomber support, and heavy casualties were also inflicted on the enemy by artillery and mortar barrages. After heavy fighting, the 2/9th stormed the base to find only Japanese dead; the Japanese command in Rabaul had called off the invasion overnight and survivors of the Special Naval Landing Force had been evacuated by warship just as MacArthur had predicted.

Japanese reinforcements were being diverted to Guadalcanal, which had become the scene of the first full-scale offensive against Japan of the war after Nimitz ordered the 1st Marine Division to seize Guadalcanal and Tulagi. The marines had quickly captured the airfield at Guadalcanal and driven out the Japanese defenders from Tulagi. The Japanese were throwing everything they had at the marines, and the Moresby invasion and its Milne Bay component had become mere sideshows in comparison.

By 6 September, Milne Bay was safely in Allied hands again and Japan had suffered her first defeat of the war in an engagement on land. In Brisbane, MacArthur's staff congratulated him on a brilliant military triumph and the champagne flowed at Lennon's. With breathtaking duplicity, MacArthur's cabled report to General Marshall that same day was completely at variance with his bullish press communique for public consumption.

He wrote: 'The Australians have proven themselves unable to match the enemy in jungle fighting. Aggressive leadership is lacking. The enemy's defeat at Milne Bay must not be accepted as a measure of relative fighting capacity of the troops involved. The decisive factor was the complete surprise obtained over him by our preliminary concentration of superior forces.'

MacArthur was deliberately misrepresenting the facts because he believed that Marshall would use a defeat in Papua to discredit him. His stratagem was merely a variation on what would become a familiar theme of shifting the blame onto the Australians. His concern then, of course, was the Japanese advance along the Kokoda Track.

In his memoirs, *Reminiscences*, MacArthur sought to perpetuate the myth of his own infallibility with two massive distortions of the truth. He claimed he had 'moved headquarters forward to Brisbane and then to Port Moresby' in anticipation of the Japanese attack along the Kokoda Track. He wrote: 'If I could secure Moresby, I would force the enemy to fight on ground of my selection—across the barrier of the Owen Stanley Range.'

The truth was that MacArthur had not even set foot in New Guinea at that stage of the Kokoda campaign, let alone moved his headquarters from Brisbane to Port Moresby. It was an even more blatant falsehood to suggest that it was he who had decided the fighting ground when in fact all his moves had been dictated by a Japanese advance which his own intelligence chief had said was impossible.

Chapter Twelve

◄◄o►

Hotter than Harlem

THE South Brisbane Town Hall was a fine colonial red-brick building at the foot of the Base 3 citadel. With a commanding view of the river and the city, it was an ideal bastion for the keepers of military law and order. Its undisputed lord and master in September 1942 was the chief provost marshal, Lieutenant-Colonel Harry H. Vaughan, whose Army number, 0-7962, attested to long and faithful service in the US Army.

Vaughan had been born in Virginia on 24 July 1888, and had graduated in civil engineering at Virginia Polytechnic Institute. He had joined the Army in 1911, gone on active service on 24 April 1917, and after World War I, joined the regular army on a captain's commission.

In Brisbane, Vaughan lived in the style of a colonial gentleman with other senior officers at Montpelier, a rambling three-storey timber dwelling situated behind a high brick wall on Wickham Terrace overlooking the city centre. Mark Muller said: 'I served on many courts martial with Colonel Vaughan dealing with charges against American soldiers. He was a cigar-smoking, rough, tough individual and a great friend of Harry S. Truman—they'd been in the Army together and he later became Truman's military aide.'

Joy Foord got to know Vaughan socially. She said: 'Some of the secretaries were permitted to take their meals in the officers' mess and the receptionist at Base 3 got Colonel Vaughan to sign a pass for me. But the first time I went into the mess, he was there and he demanded to know who had given me permission to eat there. I said, 'You did, Sir!' He realised he'd made a fool of himself and I thought he might

169

withdraw my pass. Instead, he contacted me to see if I would like a ride home in his staff car because Yale Apartments were close to his quarters at Montpelier. He invited me in for a drink and, while I was there, a call came through from Harry Truman in the States and he took it in the other room. They were very close friends.'

By the time Norbert Grant arrived at Vaughan's station, South Brisbane was not only in the military front-line, but also straddled the colour line. Vaughan said MP units were breaking up 20 fights a night at that time and many of them were between white and black Americans. In September 1942, thousands of black troops were carrying out vital military work within a 20-mile radius of MacArthur's headquarters and racial friction was showering sparks that threatened to ignite an explosive mixture of black expectations and white supremacy.

The situation was rich in irony. Shortly after MacArthur's arrival in Australia, General Marshall asked him for his comments about Afro-American troops. MacArthur assured George Marshall: 'I will do everything possible to prevent friction or resentment on the part of the Australian government and people at the presence of American coloured troops.' But racial violence erupted soon afterwards when 450 Afro-American troops set up camp on the outskirts of Mount Isa. Most of them were given leave on the morning of their arrival and went into town. According to Mount Isa police, three of the soldiers hired a cab and attempted to rob the driver. When police went looking for the suspects, they found hundreds of black soldiers wearing identical uniforms.

At 10 o'clock that night, four policemen approached a group of Afro-Americans who were using obscene language outside the Star Theatre after being turned away from a concert. The police asked the soldiers to refrain from using bad language, but they persisted, so Constable Corner hit one of them over the head with his revolver and then fired a shot in the air. He then retreated inside the police station, while the black troops gathered outside, demanding that he be handed over to them.

A brawl broke out between the three remaining police officers and about 25 black soldiers, with civilians and Australian soldiers going to the aid of the police. One policeman was stabbed twice in the back and an Australian soldier suffered a wound to his hand while warding off a knife. Several of the combatants on both sides were seriously injured. The Afro-American troops were swiftly despatched to Camooweal, still in Queensland but many miles from Mount Isa.

There were 7285 Afro-American soldiers in Australia at that time, mostly in Brisbane and other parts of Queensland, out of a total of approximately 90,000 American servicemen. When there had been a preponderance of black troops in the camps between Brisbane and Ipswich, they had enjoyed leave in friendly country towns such as Ipswich and Redbank. But once white American troops started to pour into the area, there were brawls whenever blacks found whites in 'their' territory.

One clash was so serious that civilian police asked Vaughan to draw a colour line which banned black troops from Ipswich and white troops from Redbank. However, a new influx of white troops a few months later meant that Redbank also had a majority of white troops—1500 at one camp compared with only 150 blacks—and they started pouring into Redbank despite the ban. According to one police chief who studied the problem, 'These two factions will not blend and sooner or later some of the personnel of both factions will receive serious injury.' At Wacol, 150 black soldiers from the 28th Chemical Company fought with white American troops because 'their territory was being invaded'.

Effectively barred from any reasonable social amenities close to camp, black troops took the train into South Brisbane to spend their leave in hotel bars and clubs in an area bordered by the river on one side and the railway line on the other. In this maze of dilapidated streets, factories, wharves, warehouses and alleys, prostitutes, mainly Aboriginal girls but some white, plied their trade in bars and seedy hotel bedrooms. There were illegal card games, off-course bookmaking, jazz music, overproof rum, drugs and syphilis.

Any black soldier who strayed north of the river was liable to receive summary justice at the hands of Vaughan's military police. Pauline Eglinton's flat was above a doctor's surgery high up on Wickham Terrace in an exclusive residential area with a view of Anzac Square, where the eternal flame burned in remembrance of the glorious dead. 'I heard a shot during the night,' said Pauline. 'A Negro soldier had come across Victoria Bridge and was shot just near the flame at Anzac Square. My flat was in direct line, so I heard the shot very clearly.'

Ivan Bradshaw, a soldier who was attached to a workshop unit that repaired vehicles for the Australian 3rd Division, said: 'The American provos didn't hesitate to shoot. It wasn't a big deal if someone did get shot, especially an American Negro. The American provos would shoot them as quick as look at them. They were pretty ruthless, really. There were a lot of dark fellows among the American troops. I used to meet them on the wharves and at Clapham Junction railway station on the south side, where they used to transfer goods from the New South Wales line to the Queensland line. We picked up stuff there and I'd strike the black Americans there because they did most of that sort of work. At the railway station, they'd be up there tap-dancing on the steel trucks.

They were a happy lot, they were, really happy, but they weren't allowed on the north side of the river at all.'

Frank Higgins said: 'The Negroes, whom I personally found to be very decent and well-spoken men, were treated harshly by their own army—one was shot for simply crossing Victoria Bridge.' However, Alton Jensen claimed: 'The friction I encountered in Brisbane was mostly from our own coloured troops who were out to get the MPs. They were in the Quartermaster Battalion with large trucks and they would try to drive our jeeps and motorcycles off the road.'

Major-General Patrick J. Hurley wrote to a friend in the United States: 'I have never seen the racial problem brought home so forcibly as it is over here in Queensland.' Another visitor who commented on the situation was then Congressman Lyndon B. Johnson of Texas. Johnson visited the Pacific war zone and he expended a few words, and no more, on the race issue in his diary: 'Negro problem—no hard liquor an order'.

Even though white soldiers were based in northern and western areas of the city, they often crossed the Victoria Bridge to visit the Trocadero, which was just over the bridge in Melbourne Street, South Brisbane. White Americans, many of them armed with knives, swarmed into the area every night, except Sundays, and when they met up with black troops it was hotter than Harlem.

That was the situation on the South Brisbane colour line on the evening of 11 September 1942, when Norbert Grant and his comrades in C Company, armed with batons and service revolvers, were told to go out there and keep the peace.

James 'Jimmy' Nettles from Philadelphia was in a bar in Stanley Street on the ghetto side of the Town Hall guardhouse. He was jammed in a corner of the bar, looking dreamily through the whorls of smoke that floated up from the Lucky Strike between his lips.

Jimmy was 18 years of age and dressed in the uniform of a private in the 28th Chemical Company, the unit which had been involved in the Wacol brawl. The 28th's duties included the decontamination and sterilisation of military areas in the event of chemical warfare; even the training was dirty, dangerous work, and Jimmy Nettles hated it.

In his first three months in Queensland, he spent as much time as he possibly could away from Wacol in the hotels at Redbank, where he made several friends, including Joe Anderson, a private in the AIF's 2/103rd General Transport Company. He'd meet up with Joe, and maybe Joe's girlfriend, and they'd go drinking together.

Jimmy told Joe that he'd had a hard time convincing himself he ought to enlist in the US Army, but he'd done it for the money and the chance to travel. As soon as he'd got to boot camp, however, the white sergeant was down on him and had Jimmy eating his own 'arguments and justifications' about it being all right for a coloured man to join up. 'Coloured' was the word he always used in referring to his race; he considered 'black' to be an insult. Jimmy showed Joe one of the things he'd written in his diary: 'Segregation doesn't express itself any place as loudly as in the Army.'

On the trip to Australia, Jimmy told Joe, all the coloured soldiers had been put in the hold and the white guys were up on deck, playing guitars and singing as though they were on a cruise. It was disgusting, he said, putting the coloured boys down in the hold like it was a slave ship. Joe Anderson agreed it was disgusting, but that was America for you and this was Australia, and Jimmy Nettles would be all right as long as he kept out of the way of white Americans, particularly southerners.

Jimmy showed Joe some of the new things he'd written about 'the hospitable treatment of coloured soldiers by the white Australian native . . . visits to white homes . . . escorting girls to dances'.

When more and more white Americans started coming into Redbank, Jimmy took the train to South Brisbane or hitched a ride in one of the quartermaster's trucks. He would book into Gibson's boarding house on Grey Street and go out looking for a good time. He would go roller skating at the Blue Moon, or to a dance, but mostly he would go drinking. His room at the boarding house was cramped and airless, and even in winter it was suffocating under the iron roof when the sun was out and freezing when it wasn't.

On 11 September 1942, Jimmy had been drinking in the bars along Stanley Street. He was short and slightly built, and for self-protection he was carrying a three-bladed jack-knife.

Joe Anderson had no idea Jimmy Nettles had come up to Brisbane. He had been to the pictures with his girlfriend on Queen Street and they had crossed the Victoria Bridge, heading for the station in the rush-hour crowd, when his girlfriend said: 'Isn't that Jimmy from Redbank over there?'

Jimmy's bar crawl had brought him as far as the bridge and he was deciding whether to chance his luck and go over to the white side. When he told Joe what he had in mind, Joe said he shouldn't do that; there were plenty of bars where they were and it was better to drink in them. It was 4.30 pm and Joe had also had a few drinks during the course of the day. In a bar, Jimmy showed Joe the knife he had bought and Joe's girlfriend said he was looking for trouble and he would surely find it. Joe and his girlfriend had an argument about that, and she went off to the station to get the train on her own.

Jimmy wanted some more drinks, and then go to the dance and find some girls, but Joe said they ought to eat something first. They went to the Tip Top Cafe, a greasy spoon on Stanley Street, but Jimmy didn't do much in the way of eating. He fell over as he left the cafe and Joe had to help him to his feet. When they entered the Adelaide Hotel on the corner of Stanley and Russell streets they attracted attention.

Edna Haldane, a widow who was drinking in the lounge of the Adelaide, said: 'I saw this American Negro soldier and an Australian soldier and they were both arguing between themselves. The Negro soldier drew a knife and said, "I'll kill every fucking Australian in the place". I heard the Australian soldier say to the Negro soldier, "Go on, let it go!" The licensee, Mrs Jeffrey, walked into the street to see if she could get a military policeman, but she came back into the bar and said she could not see anyone. She asked some more American Negro soldiers who were also in the lounge if they would put out the American Negro with the knife. There were three of them and they walked up to the American Negro who had the knife and told him to get out of the hotel.

'Mrs Jeffrey eventually got the Negro with the knife and the Australian soldier to go out into Stanley Street and then she closed the bar. I followed this Negro American soldier and the Australian soldier as they ran down Stanley Street with their arms around each other's necks. Both these men were intoxicated.'

Jimmy and Joe came to the Palace Hotel on the corner of Stanley and Melbourne streets and opposite the Trocadero. A group of white American sailors were standing outside the hotel and Jimmy bumped into one of them. Maybe it was an accident, maybe it was just the drink, but either way the sailor got riled up and shouted at him: 'Where're you going, you black bastard?' Jimmy's head filled up with hate. He said later: 'The many insults heaped upon us coloured soldiers seemed to swell up and explode.'

The sailor, John E. Robinson of the SS *William Ellery* said: 'I had my back to the wall facing the street and suddenly someone grabbed me by the shoulder and swung me around. Then this coloured American soldier who had swung me around walked past me. After passing me, he turned around and started cursing and I noticed he had a knife in his hand.'

Other people were milling around and Edna Haldane saw Joe Anderson drag Jimmy away and heard him say, 'Forget it, Jimmy. Let's go!' but Jimmy could only hear the tumult in his head. Breaking away from Joe, he dashed back and two of the sailors, John C. Grimes and John T. Hail, went for him. Jimmy stabbed both of them.

John C. Grimes said: 'There were four of us together from the same ship, namely Hail, Baldwin and Robinson. We were standing on the sidewalk looking for a taxicab and I noticed an Australian soldier and an American coloured soldier both in uniform coming up the sidewalk. The coloured soldier almost knocked my friend Robinson down and Robinson said something to him. I turned around to see what was happening and the Negro kicked me in the stomach. I struck back at him with my fist. When I noticed the coloured soldier first, he had a knife in his hand with the blade open. After I hit him, he went to work on me with the knife. I tried to get out of his way, but he cut me in the back of the neck and on each shoulder.'

John T. Hail said: 'When I seen the knife in his hand, I said, "Let's go!" and then this Negro soldier started after us with the knife and he punched Grimes and knocked him off balance and stabbed him in the back and then he stabbed me in the stomach.'

Sergeant Archer Brown of the Queensland Police Force, who was in charge of traffic duty in the area, saw the fracas outside the Palace Hotel. He said: 'I observed a number of persons on the footpath, which included white American sailors and soldiers, AIF soldiers, American Negro soldiers, and civilians.' Brown was used to trouble from the troops and often worked with US provosts in breaking up brawls. The provosts went straight in with their batons and beat everybody up.

Brown said: 'From where I was standing, I observed an American Negro soldier attack an American sailor. I saw the sailor fall to the ground, which caused me to walk hurriedly across Melbourne Street to the scene; there, I broke up the brawl. An AIF soldier in uniform said to me, "Leave him to me, cop", meaning the Negro soldier—Jimmy Nettles—"I'll take him away and look after him". I said, "Yes, take him away. I don't want any further trouble here". I saw them walk off in the direction of Stanley Street. I then turned to walk over to where the American sailors were standing when I observed Nettles running back along the footpath to the place where the brawl had previously started.

'He shouted out loudly, "Where is he?" and immediately attacked the second American sailor, who was standing with three others, one of whom screamed out, "Look out! He's got a knife!" which caused people to scatter in all directions. Nettles then attacked the second American sailor by stabbing him in the back of his shoulders. While Nettles was attacking this sailor, I grappled with Nettles with a view to effect[ing] his arrest.'

Joe Anderson was shouting, 'Let 'em have it, Jimmy, stick the bastards.'

Edna Haldane said: 'Sergeant Brown tried to take the knife away from the Negro soldier and they both fell to the ground. The police sergeant managed to get the knife away from the Negro and it dropped to the street, the Negro wriggled over and got the knife again and then he stabbed Sergeant Brown in the right arm and Sergeant Brown fell to the ground. When he got to his feet again, the Australian soldier punched him in the face. After this Negro soldier had stabbed Sergeant Brown, he ran up to a civilian who was standing in the street and struck him in the back with the knife.'

The civilian, James E. Mannix, said: 'As he ran past me, he stabbed at my back. I did not see anything in the Negro's hand as he had his fist closed. I put my hand around my back and found out that my jacket was ripped down the back.'

At 5.45 pm, Sergeant William J. O'Brien was on duty at the Town Hall guardhouse when a call came in telling him that a coloured American soldier was stabbing everyone in sight on Stanley Street. He and three other American provosts jumped into a command vehicle and headed down there.

Edna Haldane and another of the onlookers, Herbert Cave, followed Jimmy and Joe and saw them duck down the lane beside Delaney's Hotel. Edna saw Jimmy hand the knife to Joe and heard him say, 'Here, take this. They won't find it on me and they won't have anything on me.'

Police reinforcements arrived in the shape of Constable Frank White, and Haldane told him which way Jimmy and Joe had gone. White cut through the lane into Grey Street and saw his quarry. They weren't expecting to be followed and White caught up with them and said he wanted to talk to Jimmy about some stabbing incidents outside the Palace Hotel on Stanley Street a few minutes earlier. Joe Anderson barred the policeman's path, but he made a grab for Jimmy and caught hold of his shirt. Joe shouted: 'Go for him, Jim. He can't beat you. I'll stick with you.'

Jimmy broke free and ran while Joe tried to block the policeman, but he was too drunk to hold him for long. There was blood on Jimmy's khaki shirt and his hair was sticky with the stuff when he went back to Gibson's boarding house to pack his belongings and get out of South Brisbane. Edna Haldane and Herbert Cave saw where he went and told Constable White, who entered the boarding house and found Jimmy in his room. Jimmy said: 'I'll kill you, Australian policeman, if you try to take me.' Then he made a break for the door and the two men grappled with each other down the hallway and out onto the street.

White pulled his police revolver and Jimmy saw it. An Australian policeman was going to shoot him! The fear took all the fight out of him and he collapsed on the footpath with the policeman's knee in his back.

While he got the handcuffs out, White handed his gun to an onlooker, who took this as a sign that he was intended to shoot Jimmy the way he'd seen it done in the movies. He sighted the gun like he was John Wayne and it would have been all over there and then for Jimmy except White shouted at him: 'Don't shoot, you fool!' The man lowered the gun and wondered what he'd done wrong. Jimmy was handcuffed and searched, but there was no knife on him.

Sergeant O'Brien, the head of the US provost patrol, finally caught up with Jimmy on Grey Street. He said: 'We saw a crowd and I jumped out of the car and saw an American Negro soldier on the ground being handcuffed. I took charge of him and put him in our car and sat alongside him. While I was talking to an Australian police officer, the Negro took my gun from my holster and pointed it at me. I immediately grabbed his hand and twisted the gun out of it. He tried violently to get out of the car while we were moving and he kicked and spat at me. Later at the CIB watchhouse while he was still handcuffed he struck me with both hands.'

Jimmy was charged with three counts of causing grievous bodily harm to sailors Grimes and Hail and to Sergeant Brown. The following day he limped into Brisbane Magistrates Court in the same bloodstained shirt. The prosecutor, Detective Sergeant C. E. Risch, said the US authorities had requested that Jimmy should be handed over to them to face trial by court-martial. The magistrate, Mr W. P. Wilson, asked Jimmy if he had anything to say. He said: 'I didn't do it, but they're going to do what they're going to do, so I can't see why you keep on talking about it.' The magistrate discharged Jimmy into the custody of the US Army. He had a wry grin on his face when he was led away by members of the US Provost Corps.

Joe Anderson appeared before Brisbane Police Court, charged with inciting James Nettles to resist arrest by Constable Frank White, resisting arrest himself and with assaulting Sergeant Archer Brown. He was fined £5 on each of the first two charges and committed for trial on the more serious charge of assault.

At Joe's trial in the Supreme Court, the prosecutor asked him: 'You are a little sympathetic towards Negroes?'

'No.'

'If you saw Jimmy attacked, wouldn't you go to his assistance?'

'No.'

'Did you know that Jimmy had a knife?'

'No.'

The jury found Joe Anderson guilty as charged. Mr Justice Philp told him: 'This knife fashion is quite foreign to Australian and British ideas.

If I thought you'd known he had a knife, the sentence would be two years. But as there is no evidence that you knew, you will serve six months with hard labour.'

Jimmy Nettles appeared before a US Army court martial. In his defence, he told the nine white officers hearing his case about the abuse he'd suffered since he had joined the army, about the discrimination on the trip over, about his head exploding when the sailor called him a 'black bastard'. He said he'd been well treated by white folk in Brisbane and did not have any deep-rooted hatred of whites, only the ones who abused him about his colour.

He was sentenced to 10 years' hard labour in a Californian stockade. He was also dishonourably discharged from the US Army and ordered to forfeit all pay and allowances due to him.

Major-General Horii had forced Brigadier Potts and his men to pull out of Isurava on 1 September. It seemed that the Japanese were unstoppable, but an order issued by Horii's headquarters that day showed the Japanese had logistical problems that were almost identical to those of the Australians.

'Although the loss of time caused by the difficulties of the terrain, and delays brought about by enemy action were foreseen, we are concerned at the small quantity of ammunition and provisions which remains,' the order said. 'All unit commanders and others in authority, of whatever rank, must exercise the most painstaking control and supervision, so that every bullet accounts for an enemy, and every grain of rice furthers the task of the Shitai. Full use must be made of captured ammunition and provisions. Although some provisions were captured in the Isurava area, a reduced scale of rations must be observed. It will be less than the present ration.'

With no fresh supplies due to reach his troops for eight days, Horii reduced the daily rice ration to about one and a half pints per man, barely subsistence level. They were expected to get the rest of their nourishment by raiding native gardens or capturing Australian supplies.

The Japanese attacked the Australians on the Kokoda Track with 1000 fresh troops before dawn on 8 September. After working around the Australian flanks, the Japanese cut the track between 21st Brigade Headquarters and its forward units at Mission Ridge. Despite its precarious position, the 2/16th Battalion attacked with great valour towards brigade headquarters and, in some of the heaviest fighting seen so far, some platoons managed to crash through the enemy line and reach headquarters. The carnage was so great that this section of the track became known as Butcher's Hill. Osmar White wrote in one despatch from the front: 'They were in the last stages of exhaustion but somehow they kept going. I am convinced for all time of the dignity and nobility of common men. They never gave up the fight. They never admitted defeat. They never asked for help.'

The Japanese occupied Iorabaiwa on 15 September after the Australians pulled back to Imita Ridge 26 miles from Port Moresby. But although the enemy were winning this fight hands down according to the armchair theorists on the AMP's eighth floor, they were in fact in serious trouble. General Horii was running well behind the schedule set by the Japanese high command in Rabaul for reaching Port Moresby. He had equipped his men with rations for only 11 days' fighting, believing he could rely on captured Allied stores to feed them, but very little had been left behind. Whenever the Australians retreated from a position they spoiled any food they could not take with them. The result was that Horii's men remained hungry, and those who had eaten contaminated food developed dysentery and diarrhoea. Some of them were eating grass and roots, even wood.

Outnumbered five to one, the Australians were also suffering from malaria and dysentery, but with the coast route wide open behind them they regrouped on the knife-edged crest of Imita Ridge to prepare for a new offensive. Sutherland, who had left New Guinea without seeing any of the fighting on the ground, had returned to Brisbane and reported to MacArthur that the Australians were being 'out-generalled' and 'out-manoeuvred'. These, at least, were the damning phrases that MacArthur used in conversation with Curtin, adding for good measure that the Australians greatly outnumbered the Japanese (which was the opposite of the truth), and that they had withdrawn to Imita Ridge because of a 'lack of efficiency'.

George Kenney was also responsible for misinforming MacArthur. He reported that Rowell was preparing to leave his precious airfields undefended and the air force commander threatened to pull his planes back to northern Queensland unless American troops were sent to Papua to guard them. Visibly shaken, MacArthur ordered Curtin to despatch Blamey to New Guinea to take personal charge of the campaign or, as he put it, 'energise the situation'.

Blamey had only recently flown back from a quick trip to Port Moresby, after which he had assured the Australian public in a radio broadcast that everything was going well up there. In advance of his return, he wrote to Rowell, expressing confidence in his command and saying he hoped they could work together. However, Rowell suspected Blamey's motives and doubted his sincerity, and was noticeably uncommunicative after Blamey arrived back in Port Moresby on

23 September. Five days later, Blamey ordered Rowell into his presence and summarily dismissed him.

Blamey's report of the dismissal read: 'On my arrival here, I informed General Rowell of my instructions from the Prime Minister and the Commander-in-Chief, South-West Pacific Area. He proved most difficult and recalcitrant, considering himself very unjustly used. I permitted him to state his case with great frankness. It was mainly a statement of grievances primarily against myself. The atmosphere is now completely strained. Although I have exercised great patience, it is quite obvious that Rowell has taken my coming here as personal against himself. He would be a serious disruptive influence if retained here. Moreover, I am not satisfied that the necessary energy, foresight and drive is being put into certain activities. Rowell is competent, but of a temperament that harbours imaginary grievances. He has had very limited experience of command.'

Blamey never explained what he meant by 'certain activities' and Rowell's grievances against his commander-in-chief were far from imaginary. Blamey replaced Rowell with Lieutenant-General Edmund Herring, but it would not have changed the Australian position one bit if he had personally offered to fight Horii in hand-to-hand combat.

At night from the twin peaks dominating Iorabaiwa Ridge, the Japanese could see searchlights piercing the skies over Port Moresby and during the day they could actually make out the vast expanse of the sea, but that was as close as they got to the coast. Horii's orders to his troops on 20 September failed to acknowledge that his campaign was in any difficulty whatsoever. He said: 'More than a month has elapsed since the Shitai departed from Rabaul, following the gallant Yokoyama Advance Butai. We have crushed strong positions at Isurava, Iora, the Gap, Efogi, etc., advanced swiftly and after a fierce battle destroyed the Australians' final resistance at Iorabaiwa. We now hold securely this high hill, the most important point for the advance towards Port Moresby.

'Each Tai has marched over mountains and through deep valleys, conquered great heights, and pursued the Australians for more than 20 days. We have waded through deep rivers, scaled breath-taking cliffs, uncomplainingly carried heavy burdens of guns and ammunition, overcome shortage of provisions, and thereby triumphed over the reputedly impregnable Owen Stanley Range. The reason why we have halted is to regain our fighting strength before striking a decisive blow at Port Moresby. Fortify your morale, and make your preparations complete, so that the Shitai is strong for our next operation.'

The true situation was that the Japanese supply lines had been ripped to pieces by Kenney's fighters for weeks and many native carriers had deserted the Japanese and fled into the jungle. The rebuilt Wairopi Bridge had been breached again by a bomb blast, making it difficult to move supplies across the Kumusi River. As a result, Horii's men were disease-ridden, exhausted, demoralised and starving. At 9 o'clock on the morning of 25 September, three days before Rowell was fired from his command, Horii announced to his officers that the Japanese command had ordered him to make a fighting retreat back to the Gona–Sanananda–Buna beachhead. Japanese reverses at Guadalcanal meant there was no likelihood of reinforcements; everything was being gambled on the winner-take-all battle against the US Marines.

Horii's disbelieving men obediently turned around and began to pull back over the Owen Stanleys. Pursuing them back along the trail, the Australians found the remains of Horii's white horse in the bed of Efogi Creek.

The time had come for MacArthur to pitch the first American combat troops into the fighting. For this honour, he chose the ill-prepared Red Arrows of the 32nd Division. After he had moved the Red Arrows from South Australia to Queensland in July, they had received only rudimentary training in jungle warfare and had taken part in a couple of amphibious landings in churning surf along the southern Queensland coast. According to General Eichelberger, who was in charge of training, this was not nearly enough to tackle the job in hand.

Eichelberger had read MacArthur's estimates of the 32nd Division's capabilities, but held an entirely different personal opinion: 'Our own inspections had convinced my staff and me that the American troops were in no sense ready for jungle warfare. I told Generals MacArthur and Sutherland that I thought the 32nd Division was not sufficiently trained to meet the Japanese veterans on equal terms. The senior officers of the division were, of course, well aware of these deficiencies which stemmed principally from three causes: First, the large number of inexperienced replacements who had to be absorbed and brought up to the level of physical condition, technical knowledge, and pride of unit of the division's older members; second, the lack of suitable terrain for jungle training; and third, the most important as it turned out, lack of time.'

Eichelberger knew that his main problem was not MacArthur but Sutherland, whom he described as 'a natural climber trying to advance his own interests at the expense of the other fellows. He told me personally with great pride of how he had managed to get rid of Eisenhower and become MacArthur's chief of staff . . . Sutherland was a smoothie and I had to be something of one myself in dealing with him'.

When I Corps drew up a plan for the taking of Buna and Gona which involved rebasing Eichelberger's headquarters in Papua, Sutherland used his powers of veto to alter the plan and keep Eichelberger in Queensland. MacArthur, seeing only the revised plan, demanded to know why Eichelberger planned to direct the fighting from the safety of Rockhampton.

Playing the 'smoothie', Eichelberger replied that it was Sutherland's idea to change the plan to get him fired so that he could take over command of I Corps himself. MacArthur's response was to promote Eichelberger to brigadier-general, thus outranking Sutherland. Significantly, though, he did not overrule the Sutherland veto keeping Eichelberger in Queensland, an omission that was to have dire consequences for the Buna campaign.

MacArthur visited the Red Arrows at Camp Cable, and gave them a send-off they would remember with a shudder: 'The last time I saw your outfit was on the battlefield in France. It had just completed one of the finest actions that the World War saw. I wasn't a member of it, but I took a peculiar pride in it because in that time half of it came from my beloved section of the country.

'General Haan was one of the best friends I ever had and one of the finest soldiers I ever co-operated with, and his outfit was one of the best—I am going to modify that and say it *is* one of the best; because I have every confidence that in this war, in the fight in which we are going to be very shortly engaged, you will carry out in full the old traditions.

'I have been through your camp today in a very sketchy sort of way, and I found much to praise and practically nothing to criticise. I have been particularly pleased at the reports that have continually reached me about your behaviour and conduct. You have won the hearts of the Australians.'

MacArthur paused melodramatically before reaching the main point of his address: 'The Japanese soldier is no easy enemy. He is a hard fighter, and one who fights courageously and intelligently. He gives no quarter. He asks for no quarter. Never let the Jap attack you. Make it a fundamental rule, whatever your position might be, to be prepared for an attack. When the Japanese soldier has a co-ordinated plan of attack, he works smoothly. When he is attacked—when he doesn't know what is coming—it isn't the same. The Japanese soldier has an extaordinary capacity to fight to the end. He never stops. All I ask of you men is that when you go into action each of you shall kill one Japanese. If you do that, you will win.

'It won't be very long now, probably, before you are in action. It is

possible that I won't see a great many of you again; but I want you to
know wherever you go, it will be my hope and prayer that Almighty
God will be there with you to the end.'

The 32nd Division received its orders to embark for New Guinea on
13 September. When Kenney heard about the mobilisation, he
approached MacArthur with a radically new concept: let the 5th Air
Force fly the troops in. Kenney's argument was that in the time it would
take to send them there by ship, the Australian units might 'be behind
the barbed wire at Port Moresby with no air support'.

MacArthur asked him how many men would be lost in an airlift from
Australia to New Guinea. 'I told him that we hadn't lost a pound of
freight yet on that route, and that the airplanes didn't know the difference
between 180 pounds of freight and 180 pounds of infantryman,' said
Kenney. 'The general said he hated to hear his doughboys compared to
freight, but for me to fly a company up there and we would see how
long it took and how the scheme worked out. It was decided that we
would start at daybreak on the morning of 15 September with a company
from the 126th Infantry of the 32nd Division. I figured I'd have them
all up there by that evening, and then I'd see if the general would let
me fly the rest in.'

Harding agreed to allow the 126th to become the first US regiment
to become airborne, and chose Company E, 126th Infantry, as the first
unit to take off from Amberley airfield. Having learned from the 7th
Division's mistakes, their khaki uniforms had been sprayed with green
camouflage dye, but there was not time to allow the uniforms to dry, so
they dried on the men's backs on the flight north.

Kenney's airlift was a bold move, but it had one critical defect: the
troops had to leave behind all but one of their howitzers, about two-
thirds of their 81-millimetre mortars, and a battalion of field artillery.
Going into battle without artillery support was a suicidal gamble for an
infantry battalion, but they had no choice in the matter and it would
cost them dearly.

Kenney, however, was enjoying himself: 'On the 15th, at first light,
230 doughboys of the 126th Infantry, with small arms and packs, loaded
on board a mixed collection of Douglas and Lockheed transports at
Amberley. At six that evening, Whitehead radioed me that they had all
landed at Port Moresby. I rushed upstairs to General MacArthur's office
to give him the good news and asked him to let me haul the rest of the
regiment. He congratulated me most enthusiastically, but told me that
he had already ordered the rest of the regiment shipped by boat and that
the loading had already begun.'

Nevertheless, MacArthur agreed to let Kenney fly the next regiment, the 128th, to New Guinea and the air force commander rustled up every available plane, including 12 transport planes from Australian civil airlines and bombers that had been withdrawn from service for repairs.

MacArthur's plan was to pursue the Japanese over the Owen Stanleys with two forces. The Australians would follow them the way they had come—back over the Kokoda Track, then down through the coastal swamps to Buna and Gona. The 2nd Battalion of the 126th Infantry, 32nd Division, would take a more direct route to Buna over the Kapa Kapa Trail, which cut across the spine of the Owen Stanleys at 9000 feet. The Americans, using the shorter route, would come out of the mountains in front of the Japanese while the Australians harassed them from the rear. The Allied forces would then join up for the assault on Buna and other Japanese entrenchments extending 15 miles along the coast to Gona, and drive the enemy into the sea.

General Harding was so confident of success that he committed his optimism to print in a memo to Sutherland. 'I think it quite possible that we might find it easy pickings, with only a shell of sacrifice troops left to defend [Buna] and Kokoda,' he wrote. 'This may be a bum guess, but even if it proves to be incorrect I don't think it would be too much trouble to take Buna with the forces we can put against it.'

It was a bum guess all right, and it would destroy Harding's military career.

Chapter Thirteen

❖

Thunder Down Under

THE girls were wearing ballgowns and calling everyone 'Honey' in the better class of 'tolerated house' in Albert Street. Outside the cheaper brothels, hundreds of servicemen sweated in the hot, humid nights along the corrugated iron fences to take their turn for £1-a-time sex with prostitutes who had flocked to Brisbane to take advantage of the 'khaki gold rush'.

The law stipulated that girls working in 'tolerated houses' must have regular medical check-ups and any woman found to be suffering from a sexually transmitted disease could be detained in a 'lock hospital' for compulsory treatment. Hundreds of troops had contracted venereal disease and their officers suspected that many of them had knowingly done so to avoid going to New Guinea. 'VD has become a major problem for the military authorities,' said the Health Minister, Mr E. D. 'Ned' Hanlon. 'The whole of the medical and hospital resources of Queensland will be placed at the disposal of the army people.'

Sir Raphael Cilento, the director general of health, reported to Parliament: 'The professional prostitute has naturally been more in evidence during the past year corresponding with the increase of armed forces personnel. During the past 12 months, 611 were examined in Brisbane corresponding with 477 in the previous year. Of these, 41 were found to be infected and isolated.'

But those 41 professionals were not regarded by the health supremo as a major health problem. Cilento singled out 'the enthusiastic amateur and the goodtime girl' as the chief sources of male infection. He said: 'A number of girls infecting the soldiers have been found to be both

185

unco-operative and unreliable in respect of regular treatment and abstention from promiscuous sexual intercourse. As a result, many woman have been transferred to the [Wattlebrae] Infectious Diseases Hospital and to the Venereal Isolation Hospital.' Dr Cilento said amateurs were five or six times more dangerous than professional prostitutes; one of these women, who was reported to the authorities by an infected soldier, had spread venereal disease to 11 other men before she was forcibly placed in hospital.

Rosemary Fielding, a nurse at Wattlebrae hospital, said: 'Some of the girls there had gonorrhoea. Some were prostitutes and others had husbands away in the army and they'd fallen from grace. They'd get out of the window and still meet Yanks in the bushes at the back of the hospital."

Brisbane's leading Catholic cleric, Archbishop James Duhig, an inveterate gambler himself, was both saddened and scandalised by the loose behaviour of some of his female parishioners. He commented 'I have heard it said that the cheapest thing in Australia is the girls.'

Pick-ups in hotel lounges, usually adults, many of them married, were known as 'lounge lizzies', while young promiscuous girls who congregated around dancehalls were called 'cuddle bunnies'.

Donald Friend, an offical war artist with the AIF, watched the activities of a group of 'cuddle bunnies' at a dance: 'They call this place now "The American Village" and the name is justified; the Aussies are very much in the minority. At the Town Hall there was a dance for servicemen. There were about 2000 there—and I saw eight Australian soldiers. And the girls! It was quite incredible. One has read so much about juveniles going on the streets, being found in brothels with sailors etc., but it took the females at the Town Hall to make me realise how widespread it is. I really think the majority of them were under 18 years old, and a few were no more than 12, 14 and 15. Painted up in the reckless Queensland style.

'The dancing was another innovation. The band was good, Yankee and very hot. I remember how Queensland danced a little while ago: waltzes, two-steps, the Pride of Erin and all those Victorian affairs. Now they jitterbug at terrific speed ... kicking, belly-wobbling, bum-popping, tapping, whirling insanely like people possessed by devils. All the time during these chaotic activities, the girls' faces were expressionless, mesmerised, thin shallow eyes glazed, thin lips which seemed to express at the same time the softness of childhood and the viciousness of accomplished whoredom—set and straight. They seemed drugged, while their bodies (bedwracked, easy) pulsed erotic contortions to the rhythm.'

One Brisbane official told American historian Hammond Moore in all seriousness that a trainload of hookers, known as the 'Curtin Special', had been recruited in Sydney for active service in Brisbane: 'The Prime Minister, or one of his aides, turned to the Sydney underworld for help. They contacted Thommo's two-up school, a veteran gaming establishment in Surry Hills, and asked if anyone could provide whores for Brisbane. These federal authorities were, in fact, very explicit. Could anyone fill a train with warm, active females eager to assist the national war effort by relieving pressures building up in Brisbane? In short order, Sydney filled the train. This was all done very quietly and in a most efficient manner. The whores got their fare to Brisbane and were paid relatively low weekly wages once they went to work. The whole purpose was to achieve maximum turnover and solve a crisis which was causing concern at the very top levels of federal government.'

That story was apocryphal, but like most of the rumours flying around Brisbane at the time it got a ready hearing. In reality, most of the combat troops in Queensland were anxiously waiting to be sent to New Guinea to fight and that anxiety combined with heightened sexual tension and widespread drinking was to undermine discipline and morale on a massive scale. Gambling, sly-grogging and prostitution abounded. Dr Cilento's report about the incidence of VD was already outdated when he presented it to Parliament. Gavin Long, Australia's official World War II historian, said the city had become 'barbarous' in a few short months.

Within the space of one week in October, a knife fight between an American serviceman and three Australian soldiers left one Australian dead and two wounded; an American soldier was arrested after slashing a US medical orderly in a fight at the Coronation Hotel, South Brisbane; an Australian soldier was shot by an American military policeman during a brawl in a fish-and-chip shop in Townsville; and an American soldier was charged with stabbing three other US soldiers and a young Brisbane woman.

The woman, Miss Ruby Johnson, said she was attacked in Edward Street near Central Station at 7.30 pm. 'A soldier rushed at me and he seemed to punch me in the breast,' she said at the US Army court martial of Private Florentine Munoz. 'I pushed him away but he came at me again; he got me around the neck and threw me to the ground. Two soldiers pulled me away and two ladies helped me off the ground.'

For no apparent reason, Munoz had also stabbed three fellow Americans, Private William O. Curry, Corporal Norman F. Frederickson and Corporal Hubert Larson. Munoz said he had drunk beer and whisky in various hotels during the afternoon and, between 4 pm and 5 pm, went to Stewart's Criterion Hotel, where he had four or five rums and about the same number of wines. He told the court the next thing he remembered was waking up in the guardhouse the following morning. Munoz was found guilty and sentenced to five years' hard labour.

The antipathy between Australian and American forces reached its lowest level when an Australian soldier was killed and two others wounded after an argument broke out with some Americans in Centenary Park, Fortitude Valley. Several eye-witnesses claimed the three Australians had made offensive remarks about the American practice of wearing ties with their uniforms. This had provoked a fight and one of the Americans, Edward C. Balsar, 27, had fought himself clear with a knife, leaving all three Australians lying on the ground covered in blood. One of them, Raymond W. Tatchell, died from a deep stab wound in the chest before he reached hospital. Balsar was charge with wilful murder and handed over to the US Military Police.

The official history of the 814th Military Police Battalion said the cause of the argument was 'a disagreement over the relative personal appearance of Australian and American soldiers in general'.

Truth commented on the spate of stabbings: 'The unlawful use of weapons has increased out of all proportion to the incidence of such offences during peacetime. There have been a number of serious woundings, and a number of fatalities, and to describe the public mind as "uneasy" is merely to gloss over the actual feeling of a populace quite unused to regard murder with equanimity, and grievous bodily harm as some sort of playtime recreation.'

Sex crimes soared. An American soldier was jailed for 20 years on sex charges after being found with a girl of nine under his bed. A Brisbane doctor said: 'One of the girls in grade three at my old school, aged no more than eight, was a prostitute. The girl's mother and her older sister were also prostitutes who serviced the soldiers.' A Methodist minister described Brisbane as being worse than Sodom and Gomorrah, and even some of the city's finest establishments were brought into disrepute. Gavin Long noted that 'the Bellevue and Lennon's were just brothels' and that many United States senior officers 'had brought women from Melbourne and installed them in houses and flats around Brisbane'.

In its inimitable style, *Truth* reported a divorce case involving an American serviceman and a married Australian woman:

> More than a century has passed since a sentimental civilisation decided that a ducking stool was a bit too tough, even for 'scarlet' women, but so fashionable has defiance of conventions become these days that Judge Ross Philp hinted in the Divorce Court that reintroduction of this ancient form of punishment might be

necessary. It was the conduct of Helen Craig McKenzie which prompted the judge's terse observations. Helen had been the principal figure in a hectic party at a block of flats, allegedly run by 'Yanks'. She had triumphed in a fight with another woman for an American lover, in front of whom she had then undressed and got into bed under the scandalised eyes of her sailor husband.

The lady was all unaware that her James and a private 'demon', one Samuel Walker, were standing outside her lighted and wide-open bedroom window and, like a pair of ostriches, she and her Yank went to ground with their heads beneath the sheets when the watchers revealed their presence. [James] McKenzie told Judge Philp they were very happy in their wedded bliss until last October when, he said, he returned from a trip and found his wife 'very strange'. McKenzie added that his wife left him after a certain incident that marked his next homecoming from the sea and in August he engaged the services of a private inquiry agent, Samuel Walker. On 13 August, they went to flats called Burnside, Hastings Street, New Farm. They looked in a bedroom there and McKenzie saw some of his property and suitcases. Next night they kept watch.

'I saw several Americans going and coming to the place, and there seemed to be a big party in progress,' said the husband. 'There was a lot of music and singing, and bottles being thrown out of the doors. Walker and I watched through the window of the bedroom where I had seen my property. About 11.30 pm I saw my wife enter the bedroom with an American sailor. They were arguing and I heard him say he'd be her boyfriend the next night. I heard my wife say she'd slap some other woman's fucking face. She pushed the American sailor on to the bed and took his boots off. Then she went out of the room and there was a row with another woman you could have heard half a mile away.'

His Honour: Apparently the prize was the American sailor?— Yes, that was about it.

'I heard loud noises which appeared to come from brawling women. Then she came back to the bedroom and got undressed in front of the American. She put on a pair of pink pyjamas and got into bed with the American and put the light out.'

Mr Justice Philp said when he granted McKenzie his freedom on the grounds of his wife's adultery with an unknown man: 'All this is a sad state of affairs and leads us to believe that we might introduce the ducking stool again.'

It wasn't that local girls like Helen McKenzie were any more desirable to Americans than the wives or sweethearts back home. Ivan Bradshaw said: 'One Yank who'd hooked up with an Australian girl got a letter from his girlfriend asking what have Australian girls got that American girls haven't got? He wrote back saying, "Nothing—only they've got it here.".'

Fed up after several rebuffs from Brisbane girls, Bradshaw and his mates, who were all Victorians, had tried a different tactic to get dates. 'A girl called Beryl Smith worked in our canteen and we used to chat her up and tell her hospitality was bad in Queensland; nobody ever invited us home. So she invited three or four of us to her home at Ashgrove and asked a couple of girlfriends to come along and meet us. I married one of them, Gloria Valentine, and my best mate married another.'

The intrepid newshounds of *Truth* ventured onto the Queen Street front-line and reported that in one 45-minute period on a single block they had counted 93 American servicemen in the company of 126 girls, while 52 members of the Australian services were spotted with just 26 girls. 'Later in the evening, during interval in a talkie theatre, we counted 19 proprietorial American arms stretched out at chairback height and taking in most of the territory occupied by 26 feminine Australian backs,' gushed the reporters. 'In approximately the same area, eight of our blokes were noted, five of them escorting girls.'

The demoralisation among many Australian troops was painfully apparent. English writer Christopher Thorne said: 'I could never be accused of being what Australians call a "wowser" but I am frankly shocked at the drunkenness I've seen among the Aussies. In Brisbane, Aussies in uniform reel through the streets all day and all night. They aren't happy drunks. They're just sodden, with their baggy, shoddy uniforms hanging sack-like from them. Their uniforms are enough to give them an inferiority complex, compared with the Americans. And of course the American troops get all the pretty girls and they have more money, and the American canteens are cleaner and better equipped, and the Americans have snap and drive and are eager for a scrap. The Aussies who came home after being mauled in Egypt and Singapore can only brood and drink.'

Ivan Bradshaw maintained that it was poor pay and lack of care on the part of the Australian authorities that had depressed the average digger, whereas the US Army made every effort to ensure that its men got the best food and conditions that money could buy. Bradshaw had come to Brisbane with the 46th Battalion of the 3rd Division, but transferred to a workshop unit as a mechanic to get a better life.

He said: 'I was on five bob a day to start with and then it went up to six bob and eventually seven bob. In the infantry, you got nothing extra—there were so many of you that you couldn't get any luxuries at all. You got your issue of clothes and that was it. If you got a hole in your socks, you had to mend them yourself with a little sewing kit. You got leave once a fortnight.

'In the workshop, we could go on leave whenever we wanted. There was a truck going into town every night and if you missed it they'd get someone to drive you in. If you tore a shirt, you'd get a new one. In the infantry if you lost your hat you'd have to pay for another one. We went into a few of the cafes in town and we'd put our hats down and after eating a meal say we were going outside and we'd be back for our hats, but we'd never go back. We'd not pay at all because it was easy to get another hat.'

This attitude was engendered largely by the profiteering of cafe owners and hoteliers who 'Ned Kellied' the richer Americans by charging them well above listed prices for everything. Americans paid between £5 and £10 for a bottle of whisky and around £3 10s for a dozen bottles of beer, while an Australian expected to pay only about £1 for these goods, at least on the open market. The *Philadelphia Record* described the Australian behaviour at the time as particularly ungracious because American troops 'probably helped to save the continent from invasion by the Japanese'. The newspaper reminded Australians that they might have to make sacrifices and swallow their pride in the cause of harmony.

Many Australian soldiers found that sort of advice galling. Drinkers who were told there was no more beer or that the bar was closed or the kitchen was shut would see Americans being served. This shabby treatment made the diggers as angry with their own people as with the Americans, many of whom had been only too willing to share goods in friendlier times. That mood had changed and some Australian soldiers started to demand money from Americans in the street. Begging with the threat of violence became one of the most repugnant features of Brisbane life.

An official American army bulletin to its troops warned: 'Don't flash your roll of greenbacks unless you want to make enemies for yourself and your country.'

An incident on a train carrying ammunition to Townsville started a spate of 'crazy Yank' stories which spread like wildfire. When the train pulled into Inkerman station, the only people on board were three Australian guards, the conductor, Corporal Peter Jamieson, and two passengers—an Australian corporal, Cecil W. Irwin, and an American corporal, Fred T. Simons.

Simons, who was based in Townsville, was on two weeks' leave from his unit and had been to Sydney, where he had blown most of his money on a good time. He had set off for Townsville, but was having trouble getting there. At Mackay, he spent a night in the police cells for being drunk and, reaching Bowen further up the coast, had wandered around the town broke and hungry before boarding the ammunition train.

According to an official police report in the Queensland Archives, Corporal Jamieson claimed that Simons appeared to be in a depressed state. He had picked up the conductor's .455 Webley revolver, which had been left on a carriage seat, and tried to push him from the train, firing a shot at him in the process. The shot missed, but the Australian, Irwin, was shot and fatally wounded by Simons when he rushed to the conductor's aid.

As it happened, another train conveying Australian soldiers had pulled into Inkerman ahead of the ammunition train and Corporal Jamieson told these soldiers there was a man at large with a gun. A number of Australian soldiers chased after Simons who was making a getaway down the tracks. He was shot and killed as he fled.

Although news of this shooting was suppressed, there were too many eyewitnesses for it to remain a secret for long. Soon, stirring rumours about Wild West-style gunfights between Australian and American troops were doing the rounds of the bars. A few days later in Brisbane, a mob of up to 20 men attacked two American submariners when they rejected demands for money. Members of the USN's Shore Patrol who tried to intervene were also beaten up. The significance of this attack was that it was the first time a mob had rounded on MPs in this violent fashion.

A War Department analysis of comments in American soldiers' letters home drew the following conclusion: 'The [Australian] people, the army and the government are apathetic towards the war and depend entirely on America to hold their continent. Plane production is slow, food supply adequate but limited, communications system inadequate. No definite effort is made to conserve gasoline, transportation facilities and other vital necessities. Waste and general indifference to the war effort is prevalent.

'Labour unions have the country at their mercy . . . enforcing strictly their peacetime rules and working conditions, which extremely curtail all production and supply activities. Strikes are particularly widesperad among the coal miners and stevedores. An indecisive Government is completely controlled by labour, resulting in much red tape, waste and delay in the war effort. Indecision of the government is reflected in the army. It gets its orders from a wrangling parliament and is mediocre in efficiency and training.'

In one report, Major-General J. M. A. Durrant, commander of Australian troops in Queensland, summarised causes of 'growing ill-feeling' against Americans as: 'Resentment at the first claim on accommodation, foodstuffs and luxuries which, rightly or wrongly, they believe is accorded to US personnel because their spending power is so much greater than Australians.'

In a reference to the sexual adroitness of American servicemen, the Australian Provost Marshal in Queensland criticised 'the conduct of a large section of women folk who permit themselves to be literally "mauled about" in public irrespective of the time and place'. Many of the fights between the two armies were started by this type of behaviour.

All the goodwill towards the American trailblazers of the *Pensacola* Convoy had evaporated in just 10 months. Hostility had grown to such frightening levels that Mason Turner, US Consul in Brisbane, was obliged to take official action. He advised the State Department on 7 November of the development of a 'considerable dislike of Americans' in some Queensland circles. Conditions in Brisbane were noticeably deteriorating, he said, and American nurses had complained of being harassed as they walked down the streets or travelled on trams. Turner blamed the failure of the Australian Army 'to maintain and enforce discipline in certain minority rowdy elements'. He claimed that in parts of northern Queensland matters had 'reached such a pass that Australians and Americans would rather kill each other than the Japanese'.

The American Military Attache in Melbourne, Colone K. F. Baldwin, noted in October 1942 a 'distinct trend away from the friendly relationship which existed when General MacArthur first arrived in Australia'. Baldwin wrote to influential army figures in the US that the people of Adelaide were upset at the 'excessive drinking and indiscreet attitude towards Australian women' of the 32nd Division and had been glad when it moved to Queensland. Baldwin said the complaint was unjust because 'drunkenness is five times as common in the Australian Army and our soldiers are much more courteous and polished'.

Baldwin noted 'much confusion' at Australian army headquarters over the discerned attitude among Australian troops in New Guinea that 'the war will last four or five years and they should not kill themselves by overworking in one or two months'. As for the Battle of Mine Bay, he remarked that the Japanese had been driven out by the American Air Force 'despite the fact that the Australian commander with superior forces was rapidly withdrawing'.

The official Australian War history does not make even a passing reference to American Air Force intervention at Milne Bay.

Things had sunk to this low point virtually on the eve of the historic moment when MacArthur was about to put American combat troops into action in New Guinea with Australians for the first time.

MacArthur was supremely confident that he could take Buna and Gona in no time at all, then push ahead with his promised return to the Philippines. He had been persuaded by George Kenney to make a flying visit to New Guinea, his first, in early October. En route, the B-17 stopped for refuelling in Townsville, a vital strategic port in North Queensland which had been even more widely affected by wartime occupation than Brisbane.

Herbert C. Jaffa, a 21-year-old enlisted man serving in a US signal unit in Townsville (later a professor at New York University), recalled the anti-climatic effect that MacArthur's visit had on the local population: 'To them, the general had become a 'southerner', living in high style in Melbourne and Brisbane, with a large retinue who went to parties, rode around in limousines, and lived in luxurious hotels. Living as they did with increasing privation and anxiety, people were angry that MacArthur as well as some of their own leaders in Canberra, seemed to know nothing about them or Townsville or what was happening to their city, and no one seemed to care.'

When MacArthur arrived in Port Moresby, he was greeted by the biggest security operation in the territory's history. The writer George Johnston, an Australian war correspondent, noted in his diary: 'Roads from the Seven Mile drome lined with American troops standing at attention and a top-cover of fighters overhead, and his car escorted by an armoured car with guns manned and pointed everywhere!'

The following day MacArthur drove by jeep to Owers Corner near the start of the Kokoda Track with Generals Blamey and Herring to address members of the 16th Brigade under the command of Brigadier J. E. Lloyd. MacArthur said, 'Lloyd, by some act of God, your brigade has been chosen for this job. The eyes of the western world are upon you. I have every confidence in you and your men. Good luck and don't stop.' Before he flew back to Brisbane, MacArthur was photographed smoking a cigar and chatting to Australian troops, who dutifully smiled for the camera.

Now it was the Red Arrows' turn to come to grips with the horrors of the Owen Stanley Range. The 2nd Battalion of the 126th Infantry, 32nd Division, set off on 9 October to climb the Kapa Kapa Trail, steeper and wider than the Kokoda Track and some distance to the east of it. Walking in single file through knee-deep mud, the men were forced to chop their way along the thickly overgrown track, then climb mountains thousands of feet high, edging their way along the cliff faces dripping with slime.

Lieutenant Paul R. Lutjens of Big Rapids, Michigan, a platoon leader with Company E, which was leading the expedition, gave a vividly surreal account of a place called Ghost Mountain: 'It was the eeriest place I ever saw. The trees were covered with moss a half foot thick. We would walk along a hogback, straddling the trail, with a sheer drop of thousands of feet two feet either side of us. We kept hearing water running down somewhere, but we couldn't find any. We could thrust a stick six feet down in the spongy stuff we were walking on without hitting anything real solid. It was ungodly cold. There wasn't a sign of life. Not a bird. Not a fly. Not a sound. It was the strangest feeling I ever had. If we stopped, we froze. If we moved, we sweated.'

The young infantrymen did not reach Jaure at the headwaters of the Kumusi River on the Buna side of the mountains until the last days of October, and that was only the halfway point.

Ironically, an Afro-American, Private Roy Hicks, of Georgia, had already beaten the Red Arrows into action. Hicks, an engineer who was working with a supply unit in Port Moresby, attached himself to an Australian gun crew as a volunteer. Donning an Australian uniform and carrying a rifle and a grenade, he had gone forward along the Kokoda Track with an Australian patrol. When they ran into three Japanese, the Australians shot two of them with their rifles and Hicks wounded the third with his grenade. He claimed the distinction of being the first US ground soldier to go into combat against the Japanese in New Guinea.

Although the Australians encountered tough resistance at Templeton's Crossing and Eora Creek, MacArthur's distant voice could be heard rumbling in the background with ceaseless complaints about 'light casualties' and 'slow progress'. This pressure led Blamey and Herring to relieve the popular Major-General A. S. 'Tubby' Allen as commander of the 7th Division, replacing him with George Vasey. Not even Vasey's ebullience could prevent dissension in the ranks over Tubby Allen's dismissal, and a general feeling of unease crept along the track. To the fighting man, it seemed that he was being bayoneted in the front and stabbed in the back.

At Templeton's Crossing, voices shouted at the Australians in immaculate English: 'Cease fire!' 'Retreat, Dig!' 'We're surrounded!' The Australians recognised this as a Japanese trick and immediately reverted to signalling one another in Arabic words they had learned in the Middle East. Drenched under the jungle canopy in the freezing Kokoda night, the men of the 7th Division knew they could trust no one but themselves; that even their own commanders could not be relied upon in the face of an enemy rearguard that was committed to fight to the death. It was the camaraderie moulded in the battles of the previous year that got the 7th through the desperate days of October 1942.

When the Australians retook Templeton's Crossing, they discovered the Japanese were even more barbaric than they had previously feared. The mutilated bodies of two Australians were uncovered and the captured diary of one Japanese officer starkly stated: 'Because of the food shortage, some companies have been eating the flesh of Australian soldiers. The taste is said to be good.'

Chapter Fourteen

Thanksgiving Day

November 1942

THE Australians recaptured Kokoda on 2 November and gained their first airstrip of the Papuan campaign. Planes from Moresby could then land with fresh supplies and evacuate the sick and wounded.

The Australian 16th Brigade chased Horii's retreating Shitai down through the deep valley that acts as a watercourse for the Kumusi River from the Owen Stanleys across a flat plain before it spreads into marshland and swamps as it approaches the sea at Holnicote Bay. November had seen the start of the monsoon season and although blinding rain pelted down every afternoon, the Australians caught up with the Japanese rearguard at Oivi, broke through their defences and made contact with Horii's main force two days later. On 6 November, the new commander, George Vasey, ordered the 25th Brigade to cut the enemy's line of communication to Wairopi on the Kumusi, thus trapping the Japanese between the two AIF brigades.

In a battle that lasted three days, more than 600 Japanese were killed and many broke ranks and fled into the countryside. The bulk of the Shitai, including Horii himself, attempted to cross the Kumusi some miles downstream from Wairopi. Horii and several of his officers were drowned when their makeshift craft capsized and threw them into the swirling floodwaters. However, many Japanese managed to get safely across the river and dragged themselves to the beachheads at Buna and Gona, where Japanese marines had been making elaborate preparations for a defiant last stand.

General MacArthur had moved his advance headquarters to New

Guinea on 6 November, deposing Blamey in the same manner as Blamey had superseded Sydney Rowell. With the battles for Buna and Gona due to begin in 10 days' time, MacArthur set up shop in Government House in Port Moresby and went into a huddle with Willoughby. Adding up his numbers, Willoughby informed MacArthur that the enemy at Buna and Gona consisted of a few thousand sick, starving Japanese clinging forlornly to the water's edge; with one push, they'd be gone. This was a fatal miscalculation of both the enemy's strength and determination to avoid the disgrace of defeat.

In fact there were more than 4000 Japanese firmly entrenched at Gona and about 2500 at Buna, with 1000 fresh reinforcements arriving from Rabaul. Kenney's fighters could do nothing to stop Japanese destroyers sneaking close to shore at night and landing men and supplies in barges.

The Japanese were dug in along a shallow arc extending for 12 miles along the coast and clustered in four defensive groups around Gona, Sanananda Point, Buna and Cape Endaiadere. The defences consisted of concrete and steel pillboxes, as well as bunkers and trenches with interlocking fields of machine-gun and rifle fire. The bunkers were made of steel oil drums filled with sand and covered with coconut logs, earth and vegetation.

The Japanese had also tunnelled under the vast, spreading roots of banyan trees and strangler figs to set up machine-gun nests. From the air, these deadly enclaves were indistinguishable from the landscape, which meant that photographic reconnaissance revealed very little about the defences.

MacArthur's strategy called for the Allies to seize the beachheads to enable them to take the offensive against the heart of Japanese strength in the south-west Pacific. Capturing the north coast would give the Allies their first secure airfields to use against enemy defences protecting Rabaul, 400 miles to the north-east. These airfields would not only extend the range and bomb load of Kenney's planes, but also eliminate the climb through dangerous turbulence over the Owen Stanleys which Kenney called 'a barrier almost as bad as the mountains themselves'. Port facilities would also be developed in the run-up to seaborne attacks on the Japanese bases at Lae and Salamaua, about 200 miles up the coast from Buna.

Three days after MacArthur's arrival at Port Moresby, Mark Muller flew into the heat, red dust, steaming jungle, disease and intrigue of New Guinea with orders to install teletype communications between the advanced GHQ at Government House and the main bases to be used in the campaign. The teletype equipment and field wire travelled with him in a B-17 bomber from Amberley Airfield.

'As we landed on the dusty runway, the humidity and heat hit me like a blast furnace,' he said. 'My life revolved around C rations, heat and work in the field. We had to sleep on the ground because there were no quarters for us at Government House, and out in the field we wound up sleeping in jeeps. As long as we were at GHQ itself we could scrounge some food, but once we were away from there it was very rough.

'I spent many days at Seven Mile and Seventeen Mile airdromes and came in contact with the young fighter pilots. They lived in tents on the edge of the dusty airstrips and their food was all C rations. During the day the pilots would fly their missions and return before dark since there were no landing lights on the field. Every night about 11 o'clock as punctual as could be a lone Japanese plane would appear and fly over Seven Mile drome, drop several bombs and depart. We used to call him 'Bed Check Charlie' and laughed at his poor aim; most of the time his bombs landed in the jungle. The ack-ack guns would fire for the next 15 minutes and still not hit him in the blackness of the night. Occasionally a stray searchlight would play upon him, but he was beyond the range of our fire.'

Lieutenant Helen Hoffman, a tall, slender, brown-eyed brunette from Texas, was one of the nurses treating the sick at the 105th Field Hospital at Seven Mile Airdrome. Helen said: 'I came over on the USS *Lurline* direct to Brisbane from Fort Mason, San Francisco, in July 1942. I was with the 108th General Hospital at Gatton and then we moved to Camp Columbia. We were just six nurses and a doctor and they attached us to bigger hospitals whenever the need arose.

'When the fighting broke out in New Guinea, we took a hospital ship from Brisbane to Townsville and then flew to Milne Bay. We set up a field hospital to treat the wounded and then the big hospitals came in and we stayed with them until we were needed elsewhere. After Milne Bay, we moved to Seven Mile in readiness for the battle of Buna.'

At Pentridge Prison in Melbourne on 9 November, Eddie Leonski was hanged. The night before his execution he was heard singing popular songs in his cell and, with true gallows humour, even joked about being invited to a 'necktie party'. *Truth* reported: 'Leonski came onto the scaffold from the adjoining room and a black cap was placed over his eyes while his legs and hands were shackled. Everything was carried out by USA Army authorities, the only exception being the ususal hangman pulled the handle which sent Leonski to his death. After the execution, the body was removed on a stretcher to an ambulance which left the prison.' There was no entry of Leonski's name or his execution in the prison's execution book. As far as the Australian legal system was concerned, he had ceased to exist.

Although the Leonski case did not itself foment anti-American demonstrations, it was grist for the Japanese propaganda machine, which was ever anxious to stir up trouble between Australians and Americans. On the day of Leonski's execution, for example, Japanese broadcasts referred to clashes between Australian and American troops and drew attention to 'the trouble and expense' caused by the presence of American troops in Australia.

According to an Australian intelligence report at the time, '"America's interest in Australia is only strategic" is a catch-phrase both in Tokyo and Batavia, and Australians are warned that in the event of an Allied victory they will find themselves "bound head and feet to the dollar imperialism of the United States".'

On the eve of the battles for Buna and Gona, no one was more concerned about strategic matters than MacArthur. He called on the 32nd Division's commander, Major-General Harding, and told him: 'Harding, you will be on your way in a matter of hours. You will make history. You will lead the first offensive against the Japanese. Here and now I begin a campaign of movement where speed and tactical surprise and superior strategy will demonstrate again how generalship can win with lightning strategic strokes against potentially overwhelming forces.

'With less than one infantry division and a handful of airplanes we are starting on the road to Tokyo. We shall redeem the disgrace of Pearl Harbor. We shall drive the Japanese to their knees and we shall do it by master strategy.'

The plan of attack was for the 7000 officers and men of the 32nd Division already in the combat area to attack in concert with the depleted Australian 7th Division, who had come over the Owen Stanleys. At first light on 17 November, the Red Arrows would move against Buna and Cape Endaiadere from the south-east, while the Australians attacked Gona and Sanananda slightly to the north. The boundary line between the divisions would be marked by the Girua River, which filled the swamps behind both villages before spilling out into the sea at Buna.

Harding very nearly didn't make it to his headquarters. At 6.45 pm on 16 November, the general, several of his staff and some US soldiers were moving along the coast in a small fleet of luggers and a barge that constituted the main link in the 32nd's supply chain from Porlock Harbour on Oro Bay to American troops in the Buna area. Don Caswell, an American war corespondent with United Press International, described what he saw that day from Horaki, a base camp near Cape Sudest: 'Throughout the afternoon Allied bombers could be seen shuttling backwards and forwards on bombing missions. They appeared to have the sky to themselves and the absence of Japanese aircraft lulled them into a sense of false security.

'This illusion was shattered just before sunset. Down the coast came the reverberating roar of radial engines and 23 specks quickly resolved themselves into bull-nosed Zero fighters. There was a rush for cover in the bush as two of them came in from the sea and headed for the camp. Apparently they did not see us for they swung away and attacked two trawlers off a point about a mile away. They were joined by seven others and made a concentrated attack on the ship. Incendiary and tracer bullets swept the decks and soon both ships were ablaze. The Zeros then strafed the men in the lifeboats and in the water before scurrying off out to sea. Other Japanese planes bombed and strafed other trawlers beyond our range of vision as well as shore positions.

'The attack on the two trawlers near us lasted 20 minutes and the larger ship burned and exploded throughout the night. Survivors from both ships struggled into camp. Most of them were nearly naked. A general [Harding] who was aboard one of the trawlers swam half a mile to the shore, dodging bullets from the attacking Zeros. He had grabbed a rifle when he jumped into a dinghy from the burning trawler and lay on his back blazing away at the enemy machines. When this did not get results he dived overboard and swam ashore.'

Twenty-four Americans were killed and 100 wounded in the air raid, and valuable cargoes of mortars, ammunition, rations and radio supplies, as well as a portable hospital, were lost into the sea. Many of these supplies had been in the barge, a Japanese landing craft which had been captured by the Australians at Milne Bay in August. Harding was badly shaken by the near miss on his life and the loss of his men and he was further disturbed by the disruption to his supply system. He never really recovered from that initial blow.

According to Major David B. Parker, US Corps of Engineers liaison officer, who witnessed the attack from Horaki: 'Nearly all hands on the boats showed up well in this, their first attack, firing back at the planes with small arms and in no case giving way to panic. However, some of the men, especially the crews, who went below to escape machine-gun fire, were subsequently burned to death. They would have had a much better chance to survive by staying on deck and then jumping overboard.

'Little or no attention had been paid to the possibility of air attack on our advancing troops; no anti-aircraft guns had been sited or arranged for, and no protective cover constructed. Within an hour every man in our camp area had succeeded in digging himself a slit trench, using entrenching shovels, heavy knives, bayonets, mess kits, helmets and bare hands.'

The following day Harding decided to postpone the Allied assault in view of the lost supplies and there was another setback to overcome. Soldiers of the 128th Infantry who had flow into a hastily improvised airstrip at Wanigela Mission on Collingwood Bay, 65 miles from Buna, were having great difficulty getting into position. When they tried to march along trails west from Wanigela to Pongani, about 25 miles from Buna, torrential rain had swollen the Girua River and the water level in the swamps had risen sharply. They took to dry land and fought their way through the kunai grass, but eventually had to divert to Porlock Harbour and be ferried to Pongani in boats.

The main assault was eventually launched on 19 November, with the Australian 7th Division attacking Gona and an under-strength 32nd Division pitted against Buna. Both the diggers and the Red Arrows went in looking forward to an easy victory; both attacks were unmitigated failures.

On the American front the 1st Battalion of the 128th made first contact with the enemy on the outskirts of Duropa Plantation, just inland from Cape Endaiadere. The Americans were advancing in single file on either side of a jungle path running parallel with the beach when they encountered heavy machine-gun and rifle fire from hidden positions. It had rained heavily overnight and the downpour continued during the day, drenching the troops and their equipment. Even though visibility remained fair, the Japanese positions were difficult to pinpoint. Well camouflaged and sited to take advantage of natural alleyways through the undergrowth, they provided their machine-gunners with excellent fields of fire.

The Red Arrows were allowed to advance to within five feet of a post before the Japanese opened fire. Sometimes, they allowed a patrol to pass them completely, then opened up on the rear elements. The Americans attempted to press ahead in squads and, when that failed, small patrols were sent forward and managed to make short advances.

The US Army's *Victory in Papua* said: 'Yielding a dozen or so yards when strongly pressed, the Japanese covering troops fell back that evening to new positions about 300 yards from the original point of contact. Out of rations, and with a greater part of its ammunition used up, the 1st Battalion ended the day a badly shaken outfit. The troops had entered the battle joking and laughing, and sure of an easy victory. Now they were dazed and taken aback by the mauling they had received at the hands of the Japanese.'

According to Don Caswell, the Americans noted with alarm that the few Japanese dead left on the battlefield were well clothed and well equipped, and appeared to be members of a marine force from Formosa.

The 3rd Battalion of the 128th fared no better. After wading chest deep through swamps and gaining a narrow causeway, they came under withering machine-gun fire and could go no further than the edge of the woods just south of the Buna strip. The Americans discovered during this opening exchange with the enemy that many of their machine-gun cartridges were of the wrong type, and a large percentage of their hand grenades failed to explode.

The Australians also encountered fierce resistance at Gona with the 2/31st losing 32 men, including four company commanders, in their first assault on the Japanese positions.

Progress on the following day, 20 November, was no better, despite MacArthur sending a message to Blamey ordering that his forces must be 'driven through to objectives, regardless of losses'. The 1st Battalion advanced about 200 yards towards Cape Endaiadere under cover of an Allied mortar barrage, but the 3rd Battalion, out of rations and short of ammunition, got nowhere. That evening, rations and ammunition reached both American battalions, but most of the Australians' supplies were dropped without parachutes and 50 per cent disappeared into swamps or patches of jungle from which they were irretrievable.

On 21 November, the Australian 2/33rd advanced directly on Gona and the 2/31st moved round to its right to come in from the east. The 2/31st charged the Japanese posts, cheering as they went, and 65 men lost their lives before their commander ordered a withdrawal. On 23 November, the 2/25th attacked from the east, but gained little ground. In five days' fighting, the brigade had lost 204 men in battle for small territorial gains and was then only 736 strong.

On 24 November, Gona was bombed by the 5th Air Force and the following day the Australians attacked from the south-west with the support of four field guns, firing from Soputa. The American 1st Battalion, 126th Infantry, after an exhausting march from Pongani, arrived to reinforce the 1st Battalion of the 128th, but instead were placed under the control of Major-General Vasey, commander of the Australian 7th Division. This move greatly disturbed General Harding, who asked General Herring to reconsider, saying it would lead to confusion, resentment and misunderstanding. Herring replied curtly that the decision would stand and he expected Harding to say no more about it.

Mark Muller had advanced to within 25 miles of Buna with his communications team. He said: 'I was flown over the Owen Stanleys and went to work at Pongani. The fighting was going on and I was working in the kunai grass getting the communications in. We ran field wire lines from the intelligence people at the front-lines back through several links to a teletype machine in Government House.'

MacArthur was distraught when he read the reports coming down Muller's line and laid the blame for the failure of his battle plan on his troops' fighting abilities. For two days heavy rain had prevented Kenney's planes from flying in supplies or attacking the Japanese positions and some of MacArthur's staff advised him to withdraw his forces before even heavier losses were incurred. MacArthur's response was to send Harding an uncompromising six-word message: 'Take Buna today at all costs.'

Kenney promised his planes would be able to support the attack, but when Harding's men went in at Cape Endaiadere, they were bombed by American planes that had mistaken them for Japanese. Most of the B-25s however, could not find the target, which might have been a blessing because one made a direct hit on Companies B and C of the 128th Infantry, killing six, wounding 12, and 'seriously affecting the will to fight of the whole battalion'.

This was just the first of many such losses to friendly fire; the official history of the 32nd Division stated: 'The repeated failures to deliver effective tactical support to the ground forces—and often to erroneously attack them—has to be charged to air-crew inexperience, the nature of the country, and particularly to lack of air–ground communication.'

A week after the beginning of hostilities, the Americans were held up on all their fronts at Buna and the Australians were not doing any better at Gona or Sanananda Point. Harding's headquarters were at the Dobudura airstrip, about eight miles from the Buna front-line, which Herring considered to be too far to the rear to give the American commander any clear picture of what was happening on the coast. After receiving an adverse report from Herring, Blamey saw MacArthur on the afternoon of 25 November and alerted him to the failure of Harding's command. As a result, MacArthur sent Lieutenant-Colonel David Larr on a fact-finding mission to the front. Larr did not go as far as that, but he saw the wounded coming back and that was enough evidence for him to report to MacArthur that the 32nd lacked fighting spirit.

MacArthur then ordered General Eichelberger to come up from Rockhampton to take charge of the situation and he sent Sutherland to see Harding. Sutherland got no closer to the beachhead than Larr, but he informed MacArthur from what he had been told that the Japanese had only 'hasty fortifications' on the beaches. He had been too worried about his own safety to make a closer inspection, which would have made it obvious that without supporting artillery bombardment, further assaults against the Japanese redoubts would be suicidal.

The artillery at the disposal of the 32nd Division during the entire campaign was never more than eight Australian guns of various light calibres and just one 105-millimetre American howitzer. The other 47 howitzers had been left behind in Australia because Sutherland himself had decreed that it would be impossible to ship the ammunition for them to New Guinea. Even the howitzer they had brought with them was useless for want of ammunition. However, Sutherland's report to MacArthur confirmed his view that the troops were frightened, even cowardly, in the face of a weakened enemy. He decided to replace Harding with Eichelberger.

The most illuminating observations about the real state of affairs at Buna were contained in the report of Major David Parker, who was in the area from 14 to 25 November. He wrote: 'Our inital contact with the enemy after the main assault constituted a considerable shock to our troops, who had to revise completely their conception of the enemy's strength in firepower, accuracy, camouflage, defensive plan and, above all, in his determination to fight. The enemy camouflage of machine-gun, outposts and sniper positions was perfect. Time and again our troops advanced to suicidal range, or passed completely by, concealed machine-gun nests and snipers.

'When our troops were pinned down by fire, it was nearly impossible to determine whence the fire was coming. The enemy used natural foliage and local materials extensively for this effect. Enemy soldiers used headnets and their uniforms were dyed to blend with the scenery.

'It was obvious that our troops were poorly trained in almost every aspect of jungle warfare; they learned rapidly, but the lessons were bitter and because of inferior junior leadership resiliency was greatly reduced. It was obvious in many instances to riflemen in the line that their leaders were frightened and reluctant to lead their men into fire.

'More than one man was heard to remark that he wished his officers were more like the Australian officers, who were believed to lead their men into enemy fire. It is believed that even a small amount of psychological conditioning by some senior officer who knew his ground would have had great effect in strengthening the junior leaders. It has been noted that the Jap junior leadership is superb.'

Unfortunately, Parker did not compile his report—marked 'Most Secret' and copied to the War Department in Washington—until after he had returned to Brisbane on 1 December.

Meantime, the Red Arrows of the 2nd Battalion, 126th Infantry, had ended their marathon 42-day trek over the Kapa Kapa Trail, on 20 November. They were ordered to rest for a week and received food, medicine, ammunition and replacements for their rotting uniforms and sodden leather boots. After Thanksgiving, they would move down the Kumusi River to come together with the Australians for an attack on Gona.

The seasons had rolled around and the jacarandas were blooming once again in Brisbane. To many of the Americans, Thanksgiving in spring merely accentuated their sense of alienation; made them keenly aware that they were a long way from America; that many of them would never see home again. With the first anniversary of Pearl Harbor coming up in 11 days' time, it was a particularly poignant time to be an American serviceman away from home.

Nothing exemplified this feeling more than the hit song of the moment, Bing Crosby's *White Christmas*. When a pressing of the record was flown across the Pacific to Eagle Farm airfield in Brisbane, US service crews crowded around an old phonograph. 'The guys all stopped work and sat around and listened, tears in their eyes,' said a Brisbane girl whose father worked at the airfield. 'Here they were in the tropics and I suppose talking about a white Christmas brought back so many visions of home.'

Captain William Porter's love for the fair Estelle had not waned despite numerous separations in the intervening months. Estelle said, 'He'd go off in the *Tulsa* and come back, and once when he came back all his eyebrows had been blown off and his ship was back in dry-dock being serviced again. When I asked him what had happened to his eyebrows, he just sort of brushed it off, but I later found out he'd been in one of the big naval battles against the Japanese.'

The *Tulsa* was moored at South Brisbane wharves in late November when Porter rang Estelle for a date. She had celebrated her 16th birthday on 5 November and he had a present for her. Estelle was spending a few days at the home of her aunt, Mrs Marjorie Meehan, who lived in the suburb of Greenslopes on the city's south side. When she invited Porter over to lunch with the family on Thursday 26 November, he said. 'That's Thanksgiving Day—can I bring Thanksgiving dinner?'

'I nearly said, "What's that? but I held my tongue,' said Estelle. 'I don't think I'd ever heard of Thanksgiving Day.'

Traditionally it was a day for rejoicing and reconciliation, but before Thanksgiving Day 1942 was over, the gulf between Australian and American in Brisbane would have become an unbridgeable chasm. The ill-feeling between the wartime Allies had gone past the point of reconciliation and an explosion of some kind had become inevitable. Fate's only role was to nominate the exact location where the showdown would take place.

In Port Moresby, General MacArthur's Thanksgiving guest was the American World War I fighter pilot Eddie Rickenbacker, who had arrived in a B-17 at Seven Mile Airdrome that morning. MacArthur drove out to meet him. 'God, Eddie, I'm glad to see you!' he said and invited Rickenbacker to stay at 'my shack', as he called Government House, and celebrate Thanksgiving with him.

Long before the Papuan campaign had turned into a shambles, the Secretary of War, Henry Stimson, had experienced a mounting sense of agitation over MacArthur's attempts at self-glorification. Secretly, he had despatched Rickenbacker as his personal envoy to Brisbane to deliver a severe reprimand.

However, the 7th Air Force plane in which Rickenbacker was flying to Queensland had run out of fuel owing to navigational errors and had crash-landed in the Coral Sea. Rickenbacker and several other survivors spent 24 days in rubber boats before being rescued. In fact the search had been called off and only a personal approach from Rickenbacker's wife to Roosevelt had reactivated it. Close to death, Rickenbacker and the other survivors had been pulled from the sea and flown to safety.

Still gaunt and haggard after his ordeal, Rickenbacker had carried on with his mission and flown to Port Moresby. After the turkey had been eaten and good Dutch cigars fired up, he disclosed the true purpose of his visit. Stimson, he told MacArthur, wanted him to stop seeking personal glory, to end his whining about the lack of manpower and supplies reaching SWPA, and to cease his hysterical tirades against the navy.

MacArthur took the dressing-down as well as might be expected of a four-star general. He knew he was in a vulnerable position while the outcome at Buna and Gona hung in the balance and it was imperative for him to appear to be in control not only of the situation but also of himself. MacArthur calmly told Rickenbacker that everything in the Papua campaign was going according to plan and that he could drive the Japanese out of Papua whenever he liked.

'I could take them within 48 hours, but in so doing I would lose a minimum of five American boys for every Jap casualty,' he said. Instead, he intended to play a waiting game and starve and blast the Japanese into submission, thus saving American lives.

Rickenbacker nodded appreciatively. The fantasy that MacArthur wove for his guest would have been an eminently sensible course of action for him to have taken, but it was actually the last thing he had in mind. He wanted an immediate victory and he was determined to get it no matter what the cost. Rickenbacker, however, could be relied on to report back to Stimson that MacArthur was taking good care of America's young, inexperienced soldiers.

There was a moment of unexpected drama in the middle of this scene when Mark Muller stumbled into Government House. He said: 'I was bitten by a tick in the kunai grass and developed a very high fever. I was so delirious and out of it that I don't remember getting back to Port Moresby. When I got to Government House, MacArthur's physician, Major Charles Morhouse, took my temperature and admitted me to hospital. I was running a temperature of 104 degrees and the doctor had written 'fever of unknown origin' on my sick note.

'We arrived at the 105th Field Hospital at Seven Mile Airdrome and I was placed in a large tent that served as a ward. There were five such wards and most were filled by men who had malaria or dengue fever. Nearly all of them were from the 32nd Division and were veterans of the Buna campaign. Many of the men with dengue fever died within 48 hours, but I was fed aspirin, sulpha pills and fruit juices, and my fever started to subside after 48 hours. I was one of the lucky ones—I had dengue fever, malaria and dysentery, yet I survived with medicine and the help of one of the nurses who attended me. She had a soft, drawling voice and a calm, easy manner.'

In Brisbane, Thanksgiving Day dawned warm, sunny and humid. Purple blossom spilled over the city reaches of the river, and the gardens were a riot of crimson, gold and green; in such a setting, the war seemed a long way off.

Estelle said: 'Bill Porter arrived at Aunty Marjie's house in Greenslopes in a staff car with a huge turkey and our eyes nearly fell out; none of us had ever seen a turkey like that before. The turkey was already cooked and it was beautiful; we had turkey and cranberry sauce. My Uncle Darcy was there with his wife, Marcia, and my cousin Marjorie, whom I called Bubbles. Uncle Darcy was a Communist and he'd started smiling again since Russia had entered the war. He was always up to date with the latest news from Stalingrad.

'After lunch, Bill set up a movie projector in the lounge and we saw home movies for the first time. We saw his father the general with all his medals, his family home—one of those Scarlett O'Hara mansions, with servants—and his little boy running around kicking autumn leaves. We were very impressed with Bill's background, but he wasn't showing the movie to impress us—he was just sharing it with us.'

Ed Webster had been in Greenslopes that morning, having his leg treated at the military hospital, where he was registered as a day patient. As Alice had just returned home to Millmerran, Webster had time on his hands and he caught a tram into the city centre to go drinking with his mates in the public bar of the Gresham Hotel on Adelaide Street.

One block away in his paint-spattered office at the *Courier-Mail* building, Ian Gall, the paper's cartoonist, was putting the finishing touches to a pen-and-ink sketch for the following day's paper. He had chosen a Thanksgiving theme which showed an American serviceman shaking hands with an Australian soldier. Pointing to a sign advertising a Thanksgiving dinner, the American says: 'Thanksgiving? This, Dig, is our way of celebrating a good harvest—and we'll fight on together till we celebrate the greater harvest, victory!' Gall, a portly figure with a twinkle in his eyes, presented his work to the editor, T. C. Bray, and then adjourned to the office pub for a few drinks.

Everything in the city was quiet and orderly. Most Americans were peaceably occupied having Thanksgiving dinner in people's homes, hotel dining rooms or service canteens. The American Red Cross had carved 250 turkeys in advance for Thanksgiving dinners at their dining room opposite the PX in Adelaide Street and were doing a brisk trade.

The only sour note was that a fight had broken out just before noon between an Australian and an American in Albert Street. An American MP had tried to break it up and, in doing so, hit the Australian over the head with his baton. A general free-for-all had broken out and tempers were running high when those involved in the melee adjourned to the bars. There was rough talk against 'provo bastards' of whom the gun-toting, baton-happy Americans were considered to be the worst offenders. The war photographer Damien Parer said: 'Those American MPs, the bloody bastards, they always hit first and talked afterwards.'

Ian Gall's cartoon depicting Allied unity of purpose had barely reached the process department, where it would be etched onto a zinc alloy plate for printing, when many of the bars shut down at 6 pm, an hour before the permitted closing time, and hundreds of soldiers were turned onto the streets. Brisbane remained under a night-time brownout, but it was a warm, clear night and still light. Some of the troops headed for the Australian Army's wet canteen on Adelaide Street for more beer.

At 6.30 pm Private Norbert Grant was seated on a bench in Memorial Park in front of the South Brisbane Town Hall. The park was an island of greenery with a view across the river to the gardens at the point of the peninsula. Trams clanged up Stanley Street parallel to the wharves where the *Tulsa* was moored and continued past a group of noisy drinkers at the Ship Inn. These sounds did not distract Grant; he was reading a book in the late-afternoon sunlight that spilled into the park from the west and bathed the big weeping fig tree beside the Town Hall's clock tower with a warm, golden glow. He was off duty and looking forward to a quiet night.

Over in the city on the other side of the river, Private James Stein of the US Army's 404th Signal Company accepted an invitation from an Australian soldier to have a Thanksgiving drink in the Australian canteen on Adelaide Street. Short of build and inoffensive of manner, Stein was not expecting any trouble. Americans were often invited into the canteen to make cigarette deals with the Australians.

American MPs were patrolling Adelaide Street, but Stein had a leave pass in his pocket and was not worried about being challenged. He later admitted, however, that he had partaken of more than a few drinks when he made a beeline for the door of the canteen at 6.45 pm and collided with Ed Webster and four of his mates who were on the way in. For a moment, it seemed that Stein might get a punch in the face for his troubles. Webster was bigger than him and he'd had a bellyful of Yanks, but he barely had time to make his feelings known to Stein before they had company in the shape of two US provost marshals who had seen the incident.

Private Anthony O'Sullivan of the US 814th Military Police Company pushed Webster and the other Australians aside and demanded to see Stein's leave pass. O'Sullivan was with a fellow MP, Michel, and both men were armed with batons and sidearms. As Stein fumbled in his pockets for his pass, his shirt became unbuttoned and O'Sullivan ordered him to do it up. The gruffness of the command and the general air of intimidation changed the atmosphere in a moment. Suddenly, Stein was the little guy being bullied by the law, the underdog with whom Webster had identified all his life. The Australians turned their aggression on O'Sullivan:

'Leave our mate alone.'

'Give him back his pass.'

'Provo bastards!'

A few dozen extras, attracted by the noise, came out of the canteen to see what was happening. One of the MPs struck one of the Australians with his baton and, in the melee that followed, someone thumped O'Sullivan in the mouth and he was kicked to the ground. When the MP struggled to his feet, several Australians chased him and Michel down Adelaide Street, striking them about the head with their webbing belts.

The American PX was only 50 yards from the Australian canteen with its main entrance on Creek Street and another door around the corner on Adelaide Street. The PX building was across Creek Street from the Gresham Hotel and diagonally opposite the American Red Cross canteen where American servicemen were tucking into roast turkey, pumpkin pie and plum pudding, blissfully unaware of the disturbance outside in the street.

Other MPs at the PX, however, saw what was happening and charged into the fray with batons flailing. A couple of them dragged O'Sullivan semi-conscious inside the PX, while a dangerous stand-off developed around the PX door. The Australians demanded that the Americans produce the MP who had hit one of their number; the MPs told them to get lost.

At that point, the number of troublemakers was relatively small and the MPs were able to keep the Australians at bay. But by the time First-Lieutenant Lester Duffin of the US 814th MP Company arrived soon after 7.15 pm, he found about 100 Australian soldiers struggling to break through a semi-circular cordon of his men. He said: 'They were shouting for the Yankee bastards to come out or they would come in.'

Duffin used the telephone inside the PX to call up reinforcements.

When the light faded in Memorial Park, Norbert Grant had stopped reading and gone back to the provost station in the Town Hall. He was there when Duffin's summons came in, and the sergeant in charge of the watch handed him a riot gun and told him to get over to the PX 'because,' said Grant, 'there was a riot and our boys were getting hurt'.

Grant jumped into a light weapons carrier with another MP, a corporal, and they took off down Vulture Street, heading for Victoria Bridge. On the way he checked the gun he had been given; it was a 12-gauge Stevens shotgun, a familiar weapon. Grant worked the pump action, putting a cartridge in the breech, just in case.

Alton Jensen of B Company 738th MP Battalion happened to be in the city centre after celebrating Thanksgiving with some buddies. He said: 'I was going back to camp and I was at Central Station when I heard kind of a furore down at the PX. I dashed down to Creek Street, which was just a block away, and witnessed the riot. There were no American soldiers there because it was Thanksgiving Day and all Americans who didn't have anything official to do had the day off. I didn't mix with the troops because I could see that our military police were there and I didn't want to get involved with C Company's duties. It was getting dark in the early evening and I stayed and watched what happened.'

At 7.20 pm, Sergeant Bill Bentson saw the disturbance when he came out of the enlisted men's quarters at the Rich Building at the corner of Adelaide and Wharf streets. Bentson had no intention of mixing it with a bunch of angry Australian soldiers. Not only was he on his way to work, but he was dating an Australian girl, Joan Staines, who had seen the *Pensacola* Convoy from the deck of the *Koopa* in Moreton Bay. They had met at a dance in the City Hall and were making plans to marry.

Bentson said: 'I'd had Thanksgiving dinner at the barracks and had to go back on duty—we usually worked in the evening too—so I started out along Adelaide Street and I saw Australian troops down by the PX about a block away. There was a lot of noise and a big ruckus going on, but there didn't seem to be any American soldiers involved, only American MPs. I didn't want to get involved because I had to get to work at the AMP building, so I just kept going.'

One of the first civilian police officers on the scene was Inspector Charles Price, who arrived to find a rapidly growing crowd of soldiers and a few civilians hooting and shouting.

'Pull the bloody place down.'

'Come out and fight, you bastards.'

'You bastards are yellow; you used the baton on our mates but you ran away at Milne Bay.'

The crowd had grown to about 200 Australian soldiers, some trying to break into the US canteen. Plate-glass windows criss-crossed with anti-blast masking tape were hit by pieces of wood flung by the crowd. Parking signs were ripped up and used as battering rams. Truck tyres were deflated to cause obstructions, and vehicles and trams were halted the length of Adelaide Street. Rocks, sticks and the uprooted parking signs began raining down on the PX, breaking the windows and the skull of Private Joseph Hoffman, one of the American MPs guarding the door. He was struck squarely in the face with half a brick. Another eight US military policemen were injured.

With Australian Army MPs and civilian police strangely reluctant to become involved in controlling the crowd—much to the chagrin of the besieged Americans—the crowd around the PX door continued to swell in numbers. Some estimates put it at between two and four thousand, but even 500 men would have filled that intersection to bursting point. Reinforcements of armed American MPs began arriving in answer to frantic calls for assistance. Each new detachment started a renewed chorus of jeers and threats, and there was more shoving around the PX door.

Then a fire brigade tender that had managed to get through the blocked traffic from the main firehouse on Edward Street turned up in response to an alarm call. There was no fire, but a police officer had decided that a fire hose might quell the disturbance. He ordered the fireman to turn their hose on the mob. The head fireman, Chief Officer Jack Stephens, an ex-drill instructor at Aldershot Army Barracks in England, snapped: 'My men are here to fight fires, not to quell riots.'

One of the firemen, Edward Earley, said: 'Without further ado [Chief Stephens] ordered us back to the station and gave the police officer a dressing-down for daring to instruct his firemen to obey his dictates. I dare not think what would have happened to us had we complied.'

On the balcony of the Gresham Hotel, Captain Robert M. White, an American liaison officer, had a grandstand view of the riot along with several war correspondents. 'Civilian police were lined across the door backed by US military policemen,' he said. 'Every so often green-clad soldiers milled in front of the door and rushed it, and I could see night-sticks fly and there would be much fighting.'

Forgotten by the mob, Private Stein—without his leave pass and therefore technically AWOL—wandered through the confusion into the PX. He saw an embattled line of MPs, batons drawn, and heard the mob howling for American blood. He accosted a harassed sergeant and asked if his missing pass might be extracted from the pocket of the semi-conscious O'Sullivan. Stein said: 'He told me to forget about it and I stood in line with the other fellows and helped them out.'

So the man who inadvertently started the Battle of Brisbane became one of the custodians of law and order.

Around 8 pm Captain White felt things were quietening down outside the PX. Then he heard a grumble go up from the crowed. Peering into the gathering darkness, White saw that an American light weapons carrier had pulled up across the road. He said: 'I noticed a ruffle run though the crowd between the vehicle and the PX and then, out of the crowd, broke two American MPs who stood with their backs to the PX about 10 yards from the entrance. One had a riot gun which, to my mind, had caused the grumble.'

Ed Webster was one of the Australians closest to Norbert Grant, the MP with the shotgun, who was waving the weapon to and fro outside the Adelaide Street entrance to the PX. Webster said to him:

'What are you going to do with that gun?'

'Get back!'

'Put that fucking gun away,'

'If you come any closer, I'll have to shoot.'

Grant said he worked his way through the crowd, telling them to break it up and move away. 'Suddenly they all came for me and I had my back to the wall of the PX and I menaced them with the gun and told them to break it up, and one of the Australian soldiers came close to me, so I jabbed him with it. Then as I was standing against the wall they grabbed the front of the gun and this other Australian had a hold of me by the neck and tried to strangle me, and this was when the first shot went off.'

It was Ed Webster who seized Grant's shotgun by the barrel; when the gun fired, Webster took the blast in the chest and went down. Sumultaneously, the provost corporal standing beside Grant knocked out the second Australian, who had 'a Japanese stranglehold' on Grant, with the butt of his service revolver.

One witness, a detective constable, said: 'The men were shouting, "Put that fucking gun away". Twelve to 15 men rushed the MPs and about two minutes later I heard shots and saw two gun flashes. I saw one man stagger away from the pavement and another lying on his back on the ground.'

An American Army sergeant, who was on leave, said: 'I think the attention of the crowd was centred on Grant because he had the gun. A soldier walked out in front of him and said, "What do you think you are going to do with that gun?" Grant said, "Stay away or I will shoot," or words to that effect. The man seized the barrel of the gun and I heard a shot.'

In fact three shots were fired from Grant's riot gun, making a total of 27 buckshot pellets that had ripped into Webster and the crowd. Seven other men, six soldiers and one civilian, had also been wounded, according to medical records assembled that night. Private Christopher Henkel had pellet wounds in his right cheek and left forearm; Private Ian K. Tieman, 19, had a puncture wound on the right side of the chest; Private Frank Corrie, 25, got a pellet in his left thigh; Private Richard Ledson, 35, suffered a compound fracture to his left ankle, and gunshot wounds in his left thigh and left hand; Private Walter Maidment, 18, had a pellet embedded in his right leg; Private Edward French, 37, suffered a laceration to the head as did Private Ronald Cameron, 30. The civilian, Joseph Hanlon, 38 received a gunshot wound in his right leg.

Alton Jensen said, 'I heard the shots. There was an extra amount of shouting and then an extra amount of milling around and more people were trying to get into the PX. But I didn't see anyone go down—it was just a big mess. It quietened down when extra police came in with more weapons and the crowd started to disperse. C Company had sent out the riot squad and the riot squad had shotguns. One of the Australians had grabbed hold of one gun. Company C people told me that there was this wrestling around and then the weapon discharged—it was accidental.'

First Lieutenant Duffin said: 'We got all our men inside and managed to hold the main doors of the canteen leading into Creek Street. I heard some shots and then saw Grant being assisted into the canteen. He had severe head injuries and looked as though he had received a severe beating.'

There was a brief lull in the rioting as the wounded Australians were carried away from the Adelaide Street entrance. This gave Major H. A. Cummins, Assistant Adjutant-General of the Queensland Line of Communication Area, an opportunity to take command outside the PX. He summoned a group of helmeted Australian Army pickets, who were armed with unloaded .303 rifles, to disperse the mob.

The use of a shotgun on Australian troops had enraged the rioters and they urged the pickets to join them. One policeman said that a majority of the pickets, who had been hastily drawn from signals personnel, had 'doubled back, mingled with the rabble, passed their rifles over to anyone who would take them and changed their helmets for hats or went bareheaded after secreting their steel helmets'. He heard rioters urge the pickets: 'Shoot the bastards, or give us your guns and we'll use them.'

The Police Commissioner, Cec Carroll, who had arrived to take charge of civilian police, moved into action himself and disarmed one Australian soldier who had been given a picket's rifle. At the subsequent Army Court of Inquiry, Captain L. W. Barnes, the senior Australian provost present when the fighting broke out, explained that he had ordered 'five or six' MPs to remove their armbands and move into the crowd 'to see if they could influence them to keep quite', even though Captain H. T. Gibbs, the Queensland Area Deputy Assistant Adjutant-General, claimed to have seen possibly 20 MPs thus undressed.

Major Cummins told the inquiry that he believed that if the MPs had moved among the crowd undisguised 'they would have been kicked to death'. He claimed that police had actually wrenched rifles from members of the picket in the mistaken belief that they were rioters. Furthermore, civilian police had been much thicker on the ground than MPs but had failed to take positive action to quell the riot.

Ambulances took the wounded Australian soldiers to Brisbane General Hospital. Ed Webster suffered a huge loss of blood and died on the operating table. Privates Ledson and Tieman were both seriously ill in intensive care. In addition to those cut down by Grant's riot gun, a further eight Australians were treated for injuries caused by baton blows.

None of Webster's former comrades in the 2/2nd Anti-Tank Regiment were involved in the brawl. Lieutenant Lance Watts of the 2nd Anti-Tank Regiment said: 'We were out at Strathpine that particular night, so we weren't in that one. The injured were from the 2/9th Battalion of the 7th Division. When one of the Yankee provos drew a gun, they just went for him—you can't do that with our blokes. The 9th was going to turn out—the whole battalion—and there would have been strife then.

'The 9th had been to the Middle East and they had a very big history in the desert. When the British withdrew at Giarabub, the 9th was still out there and they fought their way back into Tripoli. They'd also fought well up in New Guinea; they were at Milne Bay and went in to help the CMF crew, the 61st Battalion, and were one of the main stumbling blocks for the Japs. They [the American MPs] picked on the wrong mob; it was the silliest thing they ever did.'

Order was gradually restored in Adelaide Street, but raiding parties of Australians went searching for Americans and there were brawls whenever they found them. One Australian who 'could not help being in the middle of it', wrote in his diary that 'the riot was the Aussies and some Yanks against the Yanks' MPs. All told it was a disgraceful exhibition. I blame the Americans' lack of tact, on their Thanksgiving Day too'.

Another diarist, Brigadier-General Clovis E. Byers, Eichelberger's chief of staff in Rockhampton, placed the fault at the top with MacArthur. He noted that the supreme commander's main function was to see to 'his own house in Brisbane' rather than trying to provide general direction for operations in New Guinea.

The official war historian Dudley McCarthy said: 'It is probably a fair generalisation to say that in the United States, the display of batons and firearms in the hands of police is an effective way of quelling a riot, whereas in Australia it is an effective way of starting one.'

Censorship forbade any mention of nationality in press reports of the riot. Bill Bentson said: 'They didn't want the Japanese to know that the Aussies were fighting the Americans. It would have been catastrophic for the war effort.' Another reason was that police feared that publicity would incite further outbreaks of violence. However, Pick Diller was in New Guinea and the *Courier-Mail* was permitted by officials on duty at the censor's office to carry a single-column story on Page 3 of the following morning's paper under the heading '1 Man Killed, 8 Injured In City Riot'. Although any mention of Americans was deleted, the article inadvertently appeared next to a photograph of one of the most famous Americans of the period, Mrs John Jacob Astor, in an advertisement for beauty products: *'Mrs Jacob Astor, one of the present leaders of the family which has dominated American society for generations, has for years observed the Pond's beauty ritual . . .'*

In the absence of Diller, the voice raised loudest against publication of any story was that of Commissioner Carroll, who seized the opportunity to stomp noisily into the political arena. He said: 'I made it my business to get in touch with the censorship office and asked for total prohibition of publicity of the unfortunate incident and, failing this, that the publication be confined to reference to a brawl between soldiers in which some soldiers were injured and one subsequently died. It is obvious from the type of article published that my efforts did not meet with the success which, to my mind, is so desirable at the present time.'

The reason given by the censor for allowing publication was that many people had witnessed the riot and it would be unsafe to allow word-of-mouth to spread unsubstantiated rumours. He was right. Throughout that night and the following morning, the bush telegraph worked all over Brisbane and surrounding districts, disseminating news of the shootings. Despite the censor's prudence, however, the riot was elevated to the status of a 'massacre' somewhere along the line: American marines had opened fire with tommy guns on unarmed Australian troops; diggers had broken into an armoury and fought back with rifles; the bodies of the dead had been laid out on the steps of the General Post Office; an American had driven a Harley-Davidson through the crowd; trams had been overturned.

Bill Bentson said: 'There were no marines because the marines didn't arrive in Brisbane until December when they got out of Guadalcanal; there were no tommy guns and no Harley-Davidsons, and none of the many people I've discussed this with saw any overturned trams.'

Lieutenant Bob Firehock said: 'I lived on Upper Edward Street and we drove right by it all when I went home from the AMP building. I didn't see anything much, although there was a lot of noise and I heard of windows being smashed, fisticuffs and shots being fired.

'The Battle of Brisbane was a tragedy that should never have happened.'

Chapter Fifteen

-◦-

Worse than War

December 1942

MARJORIE Robertson knew nothing about the riot when she reported for work as usual at the American Red Cross in Adelaide Street at 9 o'clock the following morning. 'The place was still vibrating with shock,' she said. 'There were MPs everywhere and a sort of traumatised feeling. People were scuttling guiltily to where they had to go.

'I was young and I was simply going to the American Red Cross to work, so I just walked through it serenely. The PX was smashed. It was all hushed up at the time, but I walked by it the next morning and saw the damage. There was very strict censorship and you weren't supposed to know things like this and, even if you did know, you weren't supposed to pass them on. But even after all the trouble of the night before there was a wonderful feeling of kindness and welcome at the American Red Cross that day.'

An hour after Marjorie arrived for work, Commissioner Carroll presided over an emergency meeting in his office at police headquarters. Present were Australian and US service representatives, three civilian members of the State Publicity Censor's Office and two senior police officers. Indicating a copy of that day's *Courier-Mail* on his desk, Carroll claimed the paper's reporting of the riot had been inaccurate and that the editor's decision to publish was an affront to the authority of his office.

The offending article said:

> *Six servicemen were shot, one fatally, a civilian was wounded by a bullet, and two other soldiers were injured when servicemen rioted at the corner of*

Creek and Adelaide streets last night. The disturbance began when military police attempted to take a soldier in charge. Other soldiers are alleged to have interfered, and they claimed that one of their number was struck with a baton. Soldiers tried to force an entry into a canteen. The shooting occurred when soldiers rushed military police carrying riot guns while they were on duty outside a canteen. One soldier, wounded in the chest, died in a military hospital.

The newspaper then published the identities of the men who had been shot, with the exception of the name of Edward Webster.

At the meeting, Carroll muttered some dire threats against the newspaper and suggested that the article 'should be contradicted by giving a summary of the facts of last night's occurrence'. Colonel Donaldson, the American Base 3 representative, had just flown back from New Guinea and was unfamiliar with the details of the riot, but he was not prepared to go along with the commissioner's 'bull-at-a-gate' approach and attempt to interfere with the freedom of the press. Surely, he argued, the most urgent point was to prevent a repetition of the violence. The heart of the problem seemed to be that there was a greater measure of discipline among American troops in Brisbane than among Australians.

Major Cummins, who had been in the thick of the riot, told the commissioner he would take immediate action to have adequate forces available that day, including commissioned AIF officers to control and, if necessary, arrest any unruly members of the Australian forces. As quite a number of arrests could be expected, he asked that civil police should be ordered to assist with the handling of military prisoners.

Cummins said there were only 110 Australian provosts in the Brisbane metropolitan area compared with 800 men in the US Provost Corps. The Australian Provost Corps was not armed and he stressed that under no circumstances would pickets be permitted to carry loaded weapons. The meeting broke up amid promises that the previous night's reprehensible scenes would not be repeated.

In the deathless prose of the police blotter, Commissioner Carroll then set out his summary of the riot for the Queensland Premier's Office:

1. At about 7.10 pm on the 26th instant, two members of the United States Army Provost Corps were checking up on a pass of a member of the US Army personnel in the vicinity of the Australian canteen in Adelaide Street, City.
2. Apparently some members of the Australian Army, obviously with larrikin tendencies, and reinforced by having consumed a

certain amount of drink, resented the action of the US provost men, and interfered, with the result that a fight of a miniature scale ensued.

3. Like the proverbial snowball, the matter developed owing to the fact that about that particular time of the afternoon, a fairly large number of soldiers were in that particular vicinity.

4. Australian soldiers were ringleaders in the disturbance and police reinforcements and military provost men were rushed to the scene as quickly as possible.

5. Unfortunately our own provost men are of little or no assistance in such circumstances, and during the course of the disturbance it was noticed that numerous members of the Australian provost removed their armbands and put them in their pockets; consequently they could not be subsequently identified by the police who might want assistance of a member of the Provost Corps to deal with the soldiers.

6. Australian pickets were rushed to the scene, but such pickets were composed of mainly a conglomeration of units, and some of them were armed with rifles. It was, however, learned subsequently that they were not supplied with ammunition.

7. Soon after the arrival of these pickets, it was noticed that some of the pickets were handing the rifles over to Australian soldiers who were prominent in the disturbance—in fact in one instance I took one such rifle from one of the soldiers making the disturbance as it was handed to him by a picket in my vicinity.

8. Reinforcements of US provost men were also brought to the scene, and one of these had a shotgun, or 'riot' gun with him.

9. It appears fairly clear upon sifting the various pieces of information that this man did not use this gun. He was, however, set upon, brought to the ground, where he was kicked, and it is understood that while he was on the ground being pummelled and kicked three shots were discharged from the gun and it is believed that the shots from this gun were responsible for causing injuries to a number of soldiers, one of whom subsequently died.

10. I now wish to refer to the article written on page 3 of today's *Courier-Mail*, and to point out that this article gives a most misleading picture of the position—in fact portion of the article is untruthful, and to my mind should definitely not have been published, as I take the view that the disturbance was a local disturbance, and undue publication of disturbances involving

military personnel at the present time throughout the length and breadth of Queensland per medium of the press, and outside Queensland, can only tend to have a detrimental effect on morale and the relationship between members of the Australian fighting services and our US Allies.

While Carroll's highly coloured and somewhat contradictory version of events was heading towards the Premier's Office, Major Cummins was organising his picket. Ironically, members of the 2/2nd Anti-Tank Regiment were included among AIF reinforcements who were called up for duty. They went onto the streets of Brisbane with guns loaded, despite Cummins' edict to the contrary.

Gunner Noel Glasgow said: 'We didn't have access to the news, and all I knew was that we were being sent to Brisbane to patrol the streets. About 20 of us drove down from Woodford at four or five in the afternoon. We patrolled the streets, but everyone laid low. We had our tin hats and I had a rifle and ammunition. We had orders to shoot to kill if the Yanks got aggressive with us.'

Glasgow's patrol was under the command of Lieutenant Ron Shea, who said: 'Most of the 2/2nd were on their way to New Guinea and I was with the rearguard party at Woodford. First of all we heard about the riot and then we found out that it was our bloke who had been killed. It came as a shock. We didn't have any other person involved in it, just Webster. The next evening we went past the PX and, if I remember rightly, it was shut up. Our group had to patrol the Anzac Square area, but somehow they managed to melt into the darkness very successfully and I didn't find them again until it was time to go back to camp.'

The aggression that night was all on the Australian side and Australian pickets singularly failed to do much about it. Sergeant Bill Bentson said: 'On the second night I left my barracks and went down Queen Street on my way back to headquarters. I was about a block from Edward Street and I could see all these Aussies in the centre of the intersection. I went down to see what was going on. I saw Americans flying up in the air— you could tell they were Americans because they had light khaki uniforms and the Aussies had olive-drab uniforms. I figured there was something going on down there that I didn't want to get involved in, so I went down on Elizabeth Street and approached the AMP building from the other direction.

'The entrance to GHQ was on Edward Street and all the Aussies in that intersection were looking the other way, so I decided to make a dash for the doorway and just as I started running an Aussie turned around and saw me and shouted, "There's another bloody Yank!" Fortunately, I was a good sprinter and I made it to the entrance and there were two MPs there and they couldn't come in to get me. I went up on the sixth floor where my office was and I looked down at the intersection. There were Aussies all the way up Queen Street and they were militiamen because you could tell by their hatbands that they weren't AIF. It was still dusk and I could see quite well; the sun hadn't really gone down.

'The Aussies would stand back and there'd be a circle and in the circle would be a Yank or two and they were being kicked and hit anyway the Aussies could do it. And there wasn't just one circle, there were three or four circles. Those guys were just being beat. If there was any American walking down the street, they'd grab him and they couldn't get him through the crowd to the intersection so they just pushed him over the top of their heads until they could drop him in the intersection and then another circle would be made and they'd kick them there.

'They were grabbing them by their arms and legs and throwing them up [in the air] to get them in the intersection. This was in retaliation for the night before and it went on for an hour or two. There were no Australian pickets; they took to the bush because the Australians didn't like their pickets very well and there weren't any American MPs either. It was a real schmozzle.

'I wanted to get the fire hose to break it up but the Colonel said, "Don't do that—they'll come up here!" There were reports that Americans had fired tommy guns in the air outside the AMP building, but there were no sub-machine guns. I was there the whole evening and I never heard a shot fired.'

Throughout the night Americans continued to be bashed, some of them badly. Two American MPs were savagely beaten and had their guns stolen; other US soldiers and sailors, including four officers, were also hospitalised. These attacks reinforced in American minds the impression of the previous night that the sympathies of the Australian military law enforcers were with the brawlers. The authorities, inexplicably, did not appear to have considered confining all Australians or all Americans to barracks. They closed both canteens, placed hundreds of pickets on standby to back up the existing forces, and hoped for the best.

There was one major flashpoint when a group of Australians—some waving stolen American MPs batons—confronted about 20 US provost marshals in Queen Street. The Americans lined along the tram tracks with their .45s drawn and shouted: 'Come on if you want it.' An Australian officer prevented a bloodbath by persuading the American commander to get his men into their trucks and move them away.

Colonel Harry Vaughan saw one group of Australians roving at large 'hunting trouble' without any interference from civilian police. As for many Australian MPs, he said: 'I have no idea how many were on duty in the streets. As it happened, I did not encounter any.' Staff Sergeant William J. O'Brien saw an Australian Navy Shore Patrol man standing in front of the dark and silent PX 'waving his arms and pointing to the windows'. He pointed the man out to a policeman as one of the leading agitators in the previous night's affray 'but the policeman refused to take action'.

Most scathing of all in his condemnation of the Australian military and civil police was Captain Hubert J. Scallon, commanding officer of the American 814th MP Battalion, who said: 'I witnessed a group of about 25 to 30 Australian soldiers marching through Queen Street assaulting Americans. They were being followed by the civilian police and, directly behind, the Australian Provost with two cages of the Australian Provost at the rear. This group was allowed to parade through the town for almost two hours.'

The Australian Provost Corps frankly admitted that it did not have the manpower to cope with such widespread demonstrations. Major Cummins said he had been seeking additional MPs for months as the level of violence against Americans had risen.

This explanation did not impress Brigadier-General Stephen Chamberlin, MacArthur's G-3 (Operations), who cabled General Sutherland at Port Moresby that 'further disorder' had broken out between 8 pm and midnight. Groups of four to six Australians were roaming the inner-city streets and attacking individuals, especially singling out MPs and any American escorting a girl. Provosts were not taking preventative measures and were incapable of restoring discipline.

Sutherland was further told that Chamberlin had informed his nominal superior, Major-General Frank Berryman, Deputy Chief of the General Staff, that 'the Australian Army must take decisive steps to terminate this trouble' and that General Blamey should be given the same recommendation.

The situation was actually much worse than many of the senior officers seemed aware. At dinner during Friday evening two members of the Australian Women's Army Service witnessed an attempt by Australian soldiers to storm Christie's restaurant on Adelaide and Edward streets because there were Americans inside. Margaret Scott, a married woman, said she was 'terrified because the men outside were after blood and would never have believed that we were on our own.' Eventually, two provosts escorted them back to their hostel, but another young married woman was not so fortunate. She described her harrowing experiences in a letter to her mother in Sydney:

Brisbane
28 Nov, 42

Dear Mum,

I've got a rather terrible story to tell you. We went to the pictures to see Mrs Miniver at 5 last night and came out about 7.45—and walked into Edward Street to find something to eat. John (and I) were attacked by 400 Australian soldiers—you've no idea what things are like here. We're all right but it's only providence. I'll explain.

On Thursday night two Australians caused a fight in the American Canteen and there was a frightful riot and one of our men was shot and killed and about 20 of each army wounded. So last night all the Australians came to town to kill Americans. The Americans were instructed to keep off the streets and run when they saw bands of Australians—it's worse than war here—you couldn't imagine our men could be like it. Anyway we hadn't heard about all this and we were just walking calmly down a main street, Edward, and suddenly marching down the road came these hordes of militia and they saw John and yelled, 'There's a bloody Yank—kill him!'—and rushed us.

I got knocked over twice and hit in the stomach and back and jaw, but I couldn't see John except for about 10 soldiers punching him. Honestly, mum—I can't explain the terror [of] all these hundreds yelling, 'Kill him— kick him—kick his brains out'—in a civilised world and country you cannot imagine anything like this—onto one man and he couldn't do a thing, didn't stand a ghost of a chance.

I tried to get through to the chemist's shop where we were outside when they set onto him—and was beaten back again and I was screaming and trying to find someone to help me—but no one would—finally I got hold of some soldiers' shirts and made them listen to me. I cried that he was my husband and hadn't done anything—and they said, 'It doesn't matter, kid, we're going to kill him like they murdered our lads—only not with guns, but kick him to death.'—It probably sounds fantastic—but it's all as it happened. Meanwhile I grabbed some more by the shirt and hit out, crying all the time, and finally made so much noise that they let me get through a bit to where I had last seen John being punched.

You can have no conception of what it is like here—I'm simply terrified and it was only that we happened to be in the one place where there was a shop open—the chemists—that I have a husband at all. They killed quite a few Americans last night by kicking them to death—and shot one— it's so horrible that it's unbelievable. The chemist, a very big man, ['Big

Bill' Edwards] *protected John—plus two Australian sailors—they half*
closed the shop with the Australians threatening to wreck it unless John
came out—imagine 400 to one man.

The chemist called them scum and swine—and told them to go—and
they wouldn't and I stood with him crying, trying to make them listen to
me—telling them to leave us alone—and all they'd growl was, 'We're
going to kill him.' Have you ever seen a mob gone mad? Well, it's the
most dreadful thing I've ever come up against.

John bathed himself, luckily he got away with a few punches on his face
and jaw and split hands—but when they let me in, I was afraid to look
at him as I know what they do, they kick them in the face and mouth.
These are our men, I'm so ashamed—it didn't worry them that I, John's
wife, was there—they told me to get the hell out of the way as they were
going to kick his brains out.

Eventually they got tired of waiting and dispersed gradually but it was
a full quarter hour—and then they spied another poor American and went
to 'get' him—poor devil. We sat around and John called a cab after a
while and we considered it lucky to get here as all down Queen Street there
were mobs of men fighting—usually with one American being kicked to
death in the middle. Things are frightful and a high officer (Australian)
told us that they couldn't do anything as they haven't the military police
to deal with them—but we just can't go out after dark now.

There were no American deaths, just a lot of bad maulings and severely
damaged reputations. Bill Benston said: 'The Australians put 21 Americans
in hospital that night and three or four fellows in my headquarters turned
up in the morning with arms in a sling and black eyes.'

The Americans clearly felt indignation and bitterness over the second
wave of attacks. Their testimony to the Board of Inquiry about the Battle
of Brisbane and its violent aftermath was peppered with references to the
incompetence and indifference of the Australian forces who were
supposed to be controlling the mob.

Allied land forces intelligence officers were concerned about the
damage that the outbreaks of anti-Americanism would cause in
propaganda terms. 'There are, unfortunately, in Australia irresponsible—
or worse—elements, whose ill-considered actions play right into the
hands of enemy Fifth Columnists and it is certain that they make full use
of them,' they noted in a classified report at the time. 'An instance of
this occurred on the night of November 26 at Brisbane when a member
of the American military police attempted to arrest an American soldier
who was in the company of an Australian soldier at a canteen. According
to reports, the Australian resented the arrest of his American companion

and struck the MP, which led to a first-class "brawl" between American and Australian soldiers on the one hand, and American Provost personnel and some others, on the other. Shooting took place with the result that one soldier was killed and a number of casualties occurred.

'This incident—serious enough in itself but not apparently premeditated—was seized upon by some ill-disposed persons and feeling was inflamed, so that the following night, 27 November, a much uglier incident occurred. It appears from reports that organised gangs set out to "beat up" any Americans they could find, and had it not been for prompt action by the authorities concerned, a very dangerous situation might have developed. As it was, there were a number of casualties. It must be impressed upon all ranks that this kind of thing is exactly what the enemy wants, and is what his Fifth Columnists are always trying to foster.

'Any indication of such trouble brewing should immediately be reported to Unit Security Officers or Field Security personnel. Assisting or failing to report this activity is equivalent to fighting for the enemy.'

New tactics were adopted the following day, Saturday 28 November, to head off further trouble. Mobile picket and provost groups were assigned to definite routes covering the whole city area with instructions to deal 'immediately and vigorously with any untoward behaviour'. Vehicles entering the city were stopped and searched and some Australian servicemen were arrested, including a jeepload of commandos allegedly armed with grenades and other weapons.

Before going on duty, the patrols were addressed by their officers. In the words of Major Cummins, 'it was pointed out to them that the vicious behaviour of a small section of the Australian forces was bringing the Australian Army as a whole into disrepute, and it was their duty to crush it'. But all was quiet on the Brisbane front-line that night.

After 72 hours of mayhem in the Queensland capital, the spotlight returned to the authorised fighting in New Guinea. General Clovis Byers, having criticised MacArthur for going to New Guinea, suddenly found himself heading in the same direction with General Eichelberger after his 'most urgent' summons from the commander-in-chief.

Byers, Sutherland and Kenney were present when Eichelberger reported to MacArthur on the verandah of Government House at noon on 30 November. MacArthur told Eichelberger: 'The fact that I've sent for you, with your rank, indicates how much importance I attach to the taking of Buna. Never did I think I'd see American troops quit. I can't believe that those troops represent the American fighting man in this war. I would be discouraged if I thought so. I believe they need leadership to galvanise them.

'They are sick, but Bob, a leader can take those same men and capture Buna. If you don't relieve the commanders, I shall. Harding has failed miserably. Send him back to America or I will do it for you. All the battalion commanders must go! Time is of the essence! The Japanese Army may land reinforcements any night. If you don't take Buna I want to hear that you and Byers are buried there. My staff tell me that you should have three or four days to get into the problem, but I can't give them to you. You must go forward in the morning!'

As Eichelberger and Byers discussed the dire implications of MacArthur's orders later that night, the *Pensacola* was fighting for her life off the southern Solomons. The cruiser that had escorted the first American troops to Australia almost exactly a year earlier was in a taskforce of five cruisers and six destroyers commanded by Rear Admiral Carleton Wright. The taskforce intercepted eight Japanese destroyers which were attempting to deliver supplies to Guadalcanal. In the engagement that followed, the brave old warrior was badly damaged by a Japanese torpedo, but she managed to limp to safety.

The following afternoon Eichelberger and Byers flew to Dobodura, where Eichelberger told Harding: 'Forrest, I have been ordered by General MacArthur to bust you, but stick by me and I'll try to keep you here.' After inspecting the front-line on 2 December, Eichelberger confronted Harding at his headquarters and told him bluntly that the reason Buna was taking so long to fall to the 32nd was that his men were cowards and his officers incompetents.

Harding had been Eichelberger's classmate at West Point, but he was an honourable man and he refused to take the easy way out by agreeing with his accuser and blaming the men under his command. Eichelberger fired him the next day and also relieved 20 other officers of their commands. He reorganised his forces, then ordered the 32nd to mount a new attack against Buna, which failed with the same degree of bloodshed as all previous attempts, but with one notable exception: 18 men succeeded in reaching the beach to the east of Buna and thus completed the encirclement of the village.

The official history of the 32nd Division states: 'A particularly controversial aspect of the campaign centres around three related factors: the interference of senior commanders, and sometimes of their staff officers, in the operations of lower units sometimes several command echelons below them; the international quality of the chain of command; and finally, the continued and extensive mixing of combat units. The common factor in these matters seems to have been the constant pressure of, first, the situation as it existed, and, second, of General MacArthur himself. Where there was failure, these pressures resulted in senior officers jumping in directly in an attempt to get results.'

Eichelberger said: 'The 32nd was originally a Wisconsin–Michigan national guard outfit. It went into Buna "high" on itself, full of confidence, but quite unprepared and untrained for the miseries and terrors of jungle so alien to the experience of boys from the clipped green lawns and serene streets of the small-town Middle West. Almost all troops are afraid in battle because all men are afraid. That is where leadership comes in.'

However, the latest failed attack at least convinced Eichelberger, who had seen much of the fighting at first hand, that the Japanese positions were too strong to be overrun by frontal assaults. Only tanks, artillery and bombing were going to dislodge the enemy.

At Gona, however, the Japanese were close to breaking point. Although their fortifications had been effective in keeping the Australians at bay, they had also had the effect of imprisoning their occupants. With the sea forming a natural barrier behind them and the Australians holding the jungle, swamps and kunai grasslands in front, the Japanese defenders were caught in their own death-traps. Hygiene was non-existent and the stench from dead bodies so appalling that many of them had to fight in respirators.

On 4 December, Blamey wrote scathingly to Curtin from advanced headquarters, Allied Land Forces, New Guinea, about MacArthur's command and the performance of American troops at Buna. He said that, in the field, 'American troops cannot be classified as attack troops. They are definitely not equal to the Australian militia, and from the moment they met opposition sat down and have hardly gone forward a yard. The action, too, has revealed a very alarming state of weakness in their staff system and in their war psychology. My faith in the militia is growing, but my faith in the Americans has sunk to zero.'

Meanwhile, Mark Muller's temperature had sunk to normal and he had recovered sufficiently to take note of his surroundings in the 105th Field Hospital at Seven Mile Airdrome. He said: 'After the fever broke, I had a visit from a former classmate at Cornell University, Captain Bob Tabor, who was in the 128th Infantry, 32nd Division. He had been wounded and was being evacuated back to Australia. I asked him about the nurse who saved my life and he called her over.'

Tabor said: 'I'd like you to meet the best nurse in the hospital, Lieutenant Helen Kathryn Hoffman. Meet a college classmate of mine from Cornell—First Lieutenant Mark Twain Muller.'

Helen smiled and said: 'He's my patient, so we've already met.'

Tabor said: 'Do you mind if I give my friend this bottle of Listerine to wash out the taste of fever?'

'Go ahead. Leave it on the field table by his cot.'

Tabor winked at Muller as he put the bottle down; the Listerine was White Horse Scotch whisky. Over the next couple of days, Muller made so many visits to the bathroom with his bottle of 'mouthwash' that Lieutenant Hoffman told him: 'You're the neatest, cleanest patient I've ever met.'

Muller said: 'We got talking and Helen told me she'd trained at Charity Hospital in New Orleans. Her family lived in a farming district around Pittsburg, north-east Texas, she had seven brothers and a sister called Mary Lou ... oh, we talked a lot.'

Before he left the hospital, Muller said to Helen: 'If you ever come to Brisbane, perhaps there would be some way I could repay you for your kindness.'

Helen laughed at the idea of ever getting away from the mangled bodies of the wounded, the fever-ridden patients, the young airmen burned in crashes and the other victims of the New Guinea nightmare.

'This unit go to Brisbane?' she said. 'You've got to be kidding!'

Muller was discharged from hospital on 5 December and flew back to Brisbane the following morning on the same plane as General George Kenney. Four days later on 9 December the news came through from a tiny, blasted village on the north coast of Papua: 'Gona's gone!' The Australians then combined with the Americans to kill virtually every one of the Japanese troops defending Buna.

The final nail was hammered into MacArthur's reputation by none other than General Eichelberger, who said of his commander-in-chief: 'The great hero went home without seeing Buna before, during or after the fight while permitting press articles from his GHQ to say he was leading his troops in battle.'

On 14 December, five days after the fall of Gona, General Blamey found time to turn his attention to the anti-American riots in Brisbane. Security aspects of the disturbances had been investigated by members of the Military Intelligence Branch and their 'MOST SECRET' report had been flown to him at advance headquarters.

The report, presented on 4 December after the investigators had conducted some rapid on-the-spot inquiries, was an odd combination of factual reporting and barbed comment, plus some fairly tame suggestions for tackling the problem. It did, however, have the redeeming merit of assembling in one document most of the key issues that were damaging the morale of Australian troops and causing dissent with their American Allies:

1. When Australia was in immediate danger of invasion some nine months ago, US air corps and army troops began to arrive here in large numbers. Since then, friendly relations based on comradeship and common service against the enemy, which have existed between the two forces in Australia, have been marred by a long series of street brawls, stabbings and actual fights between small groups. The incidents have been widespread, but have occurred principally in Townsville, Brisbane and Melbourne. Disturbances occurred in Brisbane as recently as 24, 26 and 27 November.

   On the first of these occasions a group of from 15 to 20 Australian soldiers attacked two enlisted men of a US submarine crew, apparently for no better reason than that the sailors refused to give the Australians money. When two USN Shore Patrol men appeared on the scene and tried to extricate the victims, they were themselves assaulted and were beaten up by the mob. This incident is all the worse as leave to submarine crews is always short and the men never have more than a few days ashore.

   On Thursday, 26 November, a brawl involving several hundred men altogether started in the Australian canteen when some Australian soldiers objected to the arrest of a US enlisted man by the US Provost. Additional American MPs were summoned, shots were fired, and as a result one Australian soldier was killed and at least 16 wounded, including civilians.

   The following night there were further incidents, though on a much smaller scale, and in addition individual American army and naval officers and isolated American MPs were assaulted in the streets and in some instances badly bashed. Thanks, however, to strong action by the military and civil police, an increase in the size of the provost patrols and to other precautions which were taken, there have been no further serious incidents since. It is plain, however, that feelings on both sides are running high and that only a spark is needed to touch off the explosive material which undoubtedly remains.

2. An analysis of these and other disturbances shows that the brawls and fights fall into two definite classes:
   (a) Brawls between groups of American and Australian troops or, less frequently, between Americans and Australians together against the Military Police, whether American or Australian.
   (b) Assaults by organised gangs on isolated individuals.

Disturbances in the first class are unpremeditated and normally occur only when the troops are under the influence of liquor. Assaults on individuals, however, are quite different. They are apparently carried out either by 'packs' composed of our worst elements who are hunting for a victim or by bands of hooligans in uniform who are bent on giving rein to their lower instincts.

3. There does not seem to be any clear-cut single reason for the disturbances in class (a). Whenever large numbers of high-spirited young men are thrown together for duty or on leave, there is always the risk of incidents. This is especially true when the young men are of different nationality with different national outlooks and backgrounds. It is important, however, to try to find the more immediate causes if future trouble is to be avoided and it has been established that the following are at least contributing factors to the disturbances:

(a) Drunkenness.

(b) The different rates of pay and allowances between the two forces. It is admitted that some American troops have not been discreet in their attitude and have 'flashed' their money about. Further, most American soldiers and sailors are able to afford a far higher standard of living than are their Australian opposite numbers. All this leads to a feeling of resentment on the part of Australians—however irrational that resentment may be. Such things as the better quality of cloth and fitting of American uniforms, their leave facilities, conditions in their camps, and lower prices in American canteens all tend to augment the ill-feeling.

(c) Discrimination in shops, hotels, cafes and by taxi drivers. In all these, it is normal apparently for Australians, whether officers or men, to be passed over in favour of Americans. More attention and service is given to Americans, and Australians are frequently kept waiting for long periods while Americans who have come later are served first. Some lines of goods, both in hotels and in retail shops, are unofficially reserved for American troops who, it is thought, will pay higher prices.

(d) The 'girl' question. Australians of the better sort are resentful of the loose behaviour of many Australian women, whose husbands are serving abroad, with American servicemen, and of the cheap regard in which a large number of American troops appear to hold Australian girls. In particular, they do not like the way Americans 'paw' them and embrace them in public. Australians of other types are annoyed when Australian girls refuse their company, but soon afterwards are seen to accept the advances of the first Americans that offer.

(e) The intentional stirring-up of trouble by interested parties. There are definite indications that in numerous cases disturbances have been instigated by civilians for their own ends. It remains to be seen whether these men are criminals, who wish to take advantage of disorder for robbery and violence for their own gain, or malcontents who are professionally 'against the Government' and are only anxious to embarrass the authorities, or straight-out enemy agents.

(f) A general hostility towards Americans. This is unfortunately widespread among Australian troops and is partly caused by the attitude of superiority frequently affected by US soldiers themselves. Constant boasting of what the American Forces have done and will do in this war is resented and the tendency of some Americans to draw their knives and guns too freely makes them despised by men who are accustomed to settle their disputes without recourse to arms.

(g) The Militia question. It is known that American soldiers have sometimes picked on Australians who are not in the AIF, and have jeered at them for staying at home when better men were fighting their battles. These taunts have led to hot retorts and from these to blows is a short step.

When brawls have once started, feelings on both sides are further roused by the complete failure of the men of each nation to understand the attitude towards violence and the normal police methods of the other. The carrying of arms, especially firearms, is provocative to most Australians and is apt to be regarded as a direct challenge which should be taken up as soon as possible. On the other hand, Americans are quite unable to comprehend the attitude of the Australian Military and Civil Police and consider that their normal methods of handling a difficult situation are 'namby-pamby' and the result of spineless fear or culpable weakness.

4. The causes of the cowardly attacks on individuals are harder to determine. Undoubtedly there is a 'dingo' element among some Australian troops, which finds a natural outlet for its semi-criminal instincts in these outrages and which 'gets a kick' out of organised brutality when the victim has no chance of hitting back. It is probable, however, that there are other factors: in at

least one case, robbery was certainly the motive. In others, irresponsible young men with a taste for violence have given way to their lust for blood under the impression that they would hereby 'get their own back' for real or imagined wrongs. In others again, the intention may have been to create ugly incidents which would lead to fresh quarrels between the two forces. This is known to have been the policy adopted by the enemy in other countries, and there is no reason to suppose that Australia is exempt from his attentions.

5. One of the most serious aspects of the disturbances was that on at least two occasions recently Australian officers were present and did nothing to stop the brawls or to control their men. The duty in this respect of all Australian officers and NCOs is clear. It is of the utmost importance that every step should be taken to combat the spread of ill-feeling between the men of the two armies and to prevent a recurrence of incidents which, if unchecked, may have a serious effect upon our combined war effort. To do this is the responsibility of every officer and man at all times, whether he is on duty or on leave, and whether the men who are engaged in the brawls are members of his own unit or not.

Apart altogether from the natural obligations of courtesy between Allies and of pride in their own service and country, it is plain that Australia owes her continued existence as a free nation today to the presence of American air corps and land troops in Australia and in New Guinea and in the Solomons, and also to the protection of the US Navy. Furthermore, the flow of American munitions and war material of all kinds has enabled the Australian Army itself to complete its equipment and, in particular, to have at its disposal weapons and vehicles which would not otherwise be available. Reports of the brawls between American and Australian troops, of actual attacks upon American officers and men, and of the general feeling of hostility shown by some unthinking Australians are bound eventually to become known in the United States. The disastrous effect on public opinion can be imagined. It is the duty of all Australian officers and NCOs, especially those in close contact with the men, to do everything in their power by lecturettes, by informal talks at odd moments and by their own atittude and example to bring these factors home to our Australian troops and to do whatever they can to promote a spirit of friendliness and comradeship with our Allies. Much can also be done by the influence of the troops themselves. There is no doubt that the vast majority in every unit are common-sense, decent men whose one aim is to get on with winning the war, and who deplore the riotous behaviour of irresponsible elements. Moreover, it is certain that practically all Australians feel nothing but contempt for the cowardly assaults by organised gangs of hooligans or worse. The education of this large majority to take an active part in preventing disturbances and in developing an attitude of friendliness towards American troops will help materially. It is equally important, however, that the causes of the ill-feeling and hostility that exist should be recognised and that the Army should ensure that whatever it can do to remove these causes will be done as quickly and as completely as possible.

6. Lastly, there is no doubt that lack of discipline, especially self-discipline, on the part of some Australian troops themselves is largely to blame. Few of our men stop to think that, when the AIF was in England and in the Middle East, the differences of pay and general living conditions between ourselves and the British troops were much more unfavourable to the latter than they are now to us in respect of the Americans. It is certain that the preferential treatment frequently accorded to Australians in the shops and hotels of Cairo and Jerusalem was just as galling to the 'Tommies' as our present experiences in Australia are to us. The British troops, however, 'took it' and we have to show that in the interests of our nation—if for no other reason—we can do the same. Already it has been noticed that men who have seen service overseas consistently hold aloof from disturbances and brawls in which their more inexperienced comrades so readily take part. Furthermore, it has been found that the nearer one gets to the scene of active operations, the less evidence is there of ill-feeling or friction. In New Guinea, for example, where Australian and American troops are fighting side by side against the enemy, there is complete harmony and mutual respect between the two forces. It seems, in effect, that one has to come back to rear areas, far behind the firing line, to find men sufficiently inexperienced, untrained, or misguided as to indulge in brawls and quarrels with those who are fighting on the same side as themselves.

7. To sum up, our job is to win the war and we must not make the task any harder by playing the enemy's game. We, who are not in the actual fighting zone, must not sabotage the efforts of

those who are. We must permit no dissension to spring up on the home front. Our duty to our country does not begin and end on the battlefield. We must ensure that nothing is allowed to detract from the united strength of the Allies or to impair the friendly relations which should exist between comrades in arms. Most of our men realise this already, but they must also be brought to realise that they themselves have a responsibility in enforcing it and in helping to keep the disturbing elements in check.

Blamey, of cource, already knew most of this from earlier Intelligence reports and when he had digested the new points, he sent copies of the report to both the Minister for Defence and the Minister for the Army in Canberra, with the comment: 'I consider it of such importance that I thought it advisable to bring the matter before your attention.' The Minister for Defence added the report to other dossiers which had been compiled from various official sources on the disturbances and sent the whole file to the Prime Minister.

Curtin subsequently wrote to the Queensland Premier: 'It will be appreciated that large numbers of troops are present in Brisbane as a result of the grant of recreation leave to units in Queensland, and because of the importance of that city as a staging area. Moreover, the location of various headquarters and administrative units in or near the city increases the number of soldiers present. When on leave, these troops, naturally, are not under any immediate disciplinary or other control except when an offence is committed.

'It had been ascertained that some members of the Provost Corps were instructed to remove their armbands and to mingle with the crowd in an attempt to apprehend certain of the ringleaders. An investigation has been made by the Army Department which states that there appears to be no foundation for the belief that some members removed their armbands with a view to avoiding their duties. Further, the allegation with regard to handing over rifles has not been substantiated. It appears that pickets arrived at short notice and were armed with rifles. These pickets were not at first recognised as pickets by the police, who in two cases wrested rifles from a member of the picket, probably because he was wearing a felt hat instead of a steel helmet.

'The preliminary report of the GOC, Queensland Line of Communication Area, indicates, however, that at about 7.50 pm on 26 November two US military policemen, one of who was armed with a riot gun, attempted to force their way through the crowd towards the canteen in which the other US military police were located. They were threatened by a number of Australian soldiers, and one of the US soldiers, after he had retreated against the outside wall of the canteen, warned an Australian soldier to stand back or he would shoot. The Australian soldier attempted to seize the gun and one shot was fired inflicting wounds from which the Australian soldier subsequently died. Two other shots were fired immediately afterwards, and a number of Australian soldiers received gunshot wounds, some of which were serious.'

Curtin agreed that the less publicity given to the disturbance 'the better for everyone concerned', and he said the Defence Committee had consented to a relaxation of brownout restrictions to permit brighter lights in Brisbane streets.

The Australian command ultimately acknowledged that its troops alone were responsible for the Battle of Brisbane. It moved some units prominent in the brawling, placed the city out of bounds to others and tightened controls on the rest—reinforcing MP strength and closing the bar at the Australian canteen. Five Australian soldiers received minor sentences for their parts in the riot, the worst offender getting six months' hard labour on five charges, including assaulting a police constable and striking an officer.

Very little changed, however. Remedies such as 'lecturettes' on a soldier's duty, 'informal talks at odd moments' and appeals to 'take it like the Tommies' had no chance of dealing with the underlying causes of the friction. The Australian soldier remained the poor relation of his American counterpart. He seemed incapable of accepting that the issue was not a question of American privilege, but his own shabby treatment at the hands of his government.

Lieutenant Bill Thomas, who subsequently investigated the conditions of Australian troops when he was promoted to major on Blamey's staff in 1943, said in reference to the Battle of Brisbane: 'The Australians had grievances, and they had very solid reasons to be aggrieved. The Yanks had everything—the girls, the canteens and all the rest of it—and our blokes were completely ostracised in their own city. The damage had been done. The wounds were very deep.

'It's a wonder there wasn't more upset.'

Private Norbert Grant was court-martialled but found not guilty of the manslaughter of Edward Webster on the grounds of justifiable homicide. It was claimed he was 'in fear of his life' at the time the shots had been discharged.

Edward Webster's death notice in the *Courier-Mail* told his story, almost: WEBSTER. *At Brisbane on November 26th, 1942. Gunner Edward Sidney ('Teddy') Webster, Anti-tank, formerly of Millmerran, aged 31 years, beloved Husband of Alice and Father of John.*

Alice Webster said: 'I had just got back to Millmerran from Brisbane and the army advised me that Teddy had been killed in the Battle of Brisbane. I was told the Yanks took fire on the Australian boys and he was the unfortunate one that got killed. It was terrible—I was left with a little boy under three years of age.'

Lieutenant Ron Shea said: 'Webby had a great idea of mateship—he'd back up his mates if any trouble arose. At the funeral, we had our own party from the regiment; there were 10 pallbearers and I suppose a dozen or so more coves were asked to attend. We took a truck down from Woodford. There was his family and a few of his family's friends, but it wasn't a large funeral.

'Webster was out of the army altogether, so the army did not bury him as such, but we gave him the full honours. He had the Africa Star and the Active Service Star, those were campaign medals which were awarded when he got back to Australia from the Middle East. I had to do the Army part at the funeral, escort the coffin, pay him the final respects. I can remember forming the guard of honour, but I can't remember where we buried him.'

Webster (Ed, Teddy or Webby) was buried at Toowong cemetery on a grassy knoll beside a running creek with bunya pines and conifers flanking the grave. Some of the headstones in the cemetery were decorated with cherubs signifying the flight of the soul to Heaven, or with ivy leaves symbolising hope and immortality, and classical urns and statues and rousing inscriptions from the Bible abounded.

There had not been time to get a headstone for Edward Webster, but a few lines from C. J. Dennis about the death of Ginger Mick would have sufficed as his epitaph:

> *A gallant gentleman . . . Well, let it go.*
> *They sez they've put them words above 'is 'ead,*
> *Out there where lonely graves stretch in a row:*
> *But Mick 'e'll never mind it now 'e's dead.*
> *An' where 'e's gone, when they weigh praise an' blame*
> *P'raps gentlemen an' men is much the same.*

Epilogue

MARK Twain Muller was recuperating at Greenslopes hospital in Brisbane in early 1943 when he noticed a familiar figure talking to one of the doctors. Despite her predictions, Helen Hoffman had made it back to Brisbane and was working at the hospital. Muller fulfilled his promise to repay her kindness towards him in New Guinea and invited her out to dinner. The couple started courting and were married after the war. Muller rose to the rank of colonel in the US Army before retiring to Dallas, Texas. He returned to Brisbane in 1991 for a reunion with some of the surviving *Pensacola* veterans.

Sergeant Bill Benston married Joan Staines in July 1943 and they lived in the United States until he retired from the army in 1964. They moved back to Brisbane, where they now live happily in Toowong.

Lieutenant Bob Firehock also married an Australian girl and returned to live on Queensland's Sunshine Coast.

Norbert J. Grant's court martial took place in Brisbane in February 1943. Owing to a reporting or copy-taking error, Grant's name was printed in the *Sunday Mail* as 'Norman Grant', an error that has been perpetuated in subsequent written accounts of the incident.

We discovered Grant's true identity by searching Bill Bentson's archives, which included a listing of all members of the 738th Military Police Battalion on active service in Brisbane at the relevant time. We further discovered from Alton Jensen that the battalion had headed north from Brisbane and taken part in the liberation of Manila.

The Veterans Association in Washington declined to provide us with any details of Grant's present whereabouts, or even whether he was still alive. Through other sources, however, we tracked down two Norbert J. Grants who had served with the US Army in World War II. Both said they had not served in the military police.

Alice Webster moved back to Millmerran, where she proudly raised Ed Webster's son, John. The Battle of Brisbane in which Webster was killed became the most shameful local secret of the war.

To the citizens of Brisbane, it was like it never happened.

Mafeesh!

—◄o►—

Sources

T HE authors are extremely grateful to the people of Brisbane who made the researching and writing of this book a labour of love. Their enthusiasm and good-natured support were invaluable in guiding us through the many difficulties we encountered in investigating the Battle of Brisbane.

Wherever possible, we obtained eye-witness accounts of the events we were describing, whether it was the actual fighting in the streets of Brisbane or, equally important to our story, the build-up of anti-Americanism in the preceding months and the effects on the conduct of the war in New Guinea.

In alphabetical order, we conducted our own interviews with the following Australian and American servicemen and civilians: Ivan Bradshaw, William A. Bentson, Kenneth Blyth, Bruce Eglinton, Pauline Eglinton, Bob Firehock, Joy Foord, Noel Glasgow, Helen Hoffman (later Mrs Helen Muller), Alton C. Jenson, Mark T. Muller, Marjorie Robertson (later Mrs Marjorie Glasgow), Estelle Runcie (later Mrs Estelle Pinney), Ronald Shea, Joan Staines (later Mrs Joan Bentson), Beryl Stevenson (later Mrs Beryl Daley), Bill Thomas, Gloria Valentine (later Mrs Gloria Bradshaw), Basil Veal, and Lance Watts.

Mrs Alice Webster spoke lovingly about her husband, Gunner Edward Webster, but gracefully declined to comment further.

As well as quoting from official documents in Bill Bentson's comprehensive archive, we have also drawn selectively on the letters, wartime diaries and recollections of the following US servicemen: Jack Allured, Henry Bartol, Jesse Bumpass, Cliff Causton, Bill Daly, Frank

Fujita, Bobb Glenn, Willard A. Heath, Lloyd V. Henrichs, Clifford Johnson, Louis H. Kohl, Paul R. Lutjens, Bob McMahon, Mark T. Muller, Kenneth R. Scurr, Howard L. Steffy, Byron Wilhite, and Walter G. Winslow.

Our gratitude goes to the National Archives of Australia and the Queensland Archives, as well as to the staff of the Oxley and Brisbane City Council libraries, who dealt with our many requests with patience, dedication and good humour.

We read every edition of the *Courier-Mail*, the *Sunday Mail* and *Truth* published in 1942, as well as magazines and periodicals from that year. Most of our material on Edward J. Leonski came from the excellent coverage of his court martial published in the *Sun News-Pictorial*, Melbourne.

The books we read included:

Beaumont, Joan, *Australia's War 1939–45*, Allen & Unwin, Sydney, 1996.

Bramall, Field Marshal Lord, *The Imperial War Museum Book of the Desert War 1940–42*, Sidgwick & Jackson, London, 1992.

Brune, Peter, *Those Ragged Bloody Heroes: From the Kokoda Trail to Buna Beach 1942*, Allen & Unwin, Sydney, 1991.

—— *The Spell Broken: Exploding the Myth of Japanese Invincibility*, Allen & Unwin, Sydney, 1997.

Campbell, Rosemary, *Heroes and Lovers: A Question of National Identity*, Allen & Unwin, Sydney, 1989.

Churchill, Winston S., *The Second World War*, Cassell, London, 1959.

Clausen, Henry C. & Lee, Bruce, *Pearl Harbor: Final Judgment*, Crown, New York, 1992.

Cusack, Dymphna & James, Florence, *Come In Spinner*, Heinemann, Sydney, 1951.

Ebury, Sue, *Weary: The Life of Sir Edward Dunlop*, Viking, Sydney, 1994.

Elphick, Peter, *Singapore: The Pregnable Fortress*, Hodder & Stoughton, Sydney, 1995.

Gailey, Harry A., *The War in the Pacific*, Presidio Press, California, 1997.

Gilbert, Martin, *Second World War*, Weidenfeld & Nicolson, London, 1989.

Hasluck, Paul, *The Government and the People 1942–45*, Australian War Memorial, Canberra, 1970.

Horner, D. M., *Crisis of Command: Australian Generalship and the Japanese Threat 1941–43*, Australian National University Press, Canberra, 1978.

Johnston, George, *War Diary 1942*, Collins, Sydney, 1984.

Keneally, Thomas, *Homebush Boy: A Memoir*, Sceptre, Sydney, 1995.

Lack, Clem, *Three Decades of Queensland Political History 1929–60*, Brisbane Government Printer, Brisbane, 1989.

Lauer, E. T., *32nd Infantry Division World War II*, Madison, Wisconsin, 1956.

Long, Gavin, *The Six Years War: Australia in the 1939–45 War*, Australian War Memorial, Canberra, 1973.

MacArthur, General Douglas, *Reminiscences*, Heinemann, New York, 1964.

Mann, Molly and Foott, Bethia, *We Drove the Americans*, Angus & Robertson, Sydney, 1944.

Milner, S., *Victory in Papua*, US Army, Washington, 1957.

Moore, J. H., *Oversexed, Overpaid & Over Here: Americans in Australia 1941–45*, University of Queensland Press, Brisbane, 1981.

Paull, Raymond, *Retreat from Kokoda*, Heinemann, Sydney, 1958.

Perret, Geoffrey, *Old Soldiers Never Die: The Life of Douglas MacArthur*, Andre Deutsch, London, 1996.

Potts, E. Daniel and Potts, Annette, *Yanks Down Under 1941–45: The American Impact on Australia*, Oxford University Press, Melbourne, 1985.

Rivett, Rohan, *Behind Bamboo: An Inside Story of the Japanese Prison Camps*, Angus & Robertson, Sydney, 1947.

Ross, Lloyd, *John Curtin: A Biography*, Macmillan, Sydney, 1977.

Smurthwaite, David, *The Pacific War Atlas 1941–45*, CIS, Melbourne, 1995.

Tsuji, Masanobu, *Japan's Greatest Victory, Britain's Worst Defeat: The Capture of Singapore 1942*, Spellmount, United Kingdom, 1997.

Whitington, Don, *Strive to be Fair*, ANU Press, Canberra, 1977.